The Super Age

The Super Age

Decoding our Demographic Destiny

Bradley Schurman

HARPER
BUSINESS

An Imprint of HarperCollins*Publishers*

The graphs on pages 6 and 7 were created by and are owned by the author.

HarperCollins books may be purchased for educational, business, or sales promotional use. For information, please email the Special Markets Department at SPsales@harpercollins.com.

FIRST EDITION

Library of Congress Cataloging-in-Publication Data:

Names: Schurman, Bradley, author.
Title: The super age : decoding our demographic destiny / Bradley Schurman.
Description: First Edition. | New York, NY : Harper Business, 2022. | Includes bibliographical references and index. Identifiers: LCCN 2021033579 (print) | LCCN 2021033580 (ebook) | ISBN 9780063048751 (hardcover) | ISBN 9780063048775 (ebook)
Subjects: LCSH: Population forecasting. | Age-structured populations. | Aging—Social aspects. | Older people. | Youth.
Classification: LCC HB849.53 S28 2022 (print) | LCC HB849.53 (ebook) | DDC 304.601/12--dc23
LC record available at https://lccn.loc.gov/2021033579
LC ebook record available at https://lccn.loc.gov/2021033580

ISBN 978-0-06-304875-1

22 23 24 25 26   FB   10 9 8 7 6 5 4 3 2 1

*For my family—both blood and chosen—
as well as a special class of incredibly gifted and insightful
colleagues in the United States and around the world.
I am beyond thankful for each and every one of
you who believed in me and my vision.*

Contents

Preface

This is not a book about aging or getting older, nor is it a road map for living a longer life; there are no tricks for "aging better" included within. This is not a book about the science of longevity. And this is decidedly not a book about health care, pensions, or nursing homes—though these are important subjects often associated with the old—nor does it delve into geriatrics and gerontology, even though they are, perhaps, two of the noblest professions in the world.

This is, however, a book that examines the way two megatrends—declining birth rates and the radical extension of human life (longevity)—are intersecting to form a super-megatrend that is creating a sharply different, vastly older, and a more generationally diverse society than the one humanity has lived in before. This super-megatrend, more commonly known as "population aging," is a seismic event that is upending and reshaping most of our social, political, cultural, and economic norms, and it is doing so in the biggest and developed economies, as well as the smallest and emerging ones. It is leading us into a new era that I call the Super Age, a profoundly different period from any other in the history of the world.

For just over two hundred years, population aging has been happening slowly and quietly. Though these changes have sped up and become more dominant in recent decades, this super-megatrend has almost always taken a back seat to other hot topic issues of the day, such

Age Distribution of the World Population—by Sex—from 1950 to 2018 and the UN Population Division's Projection until 2100

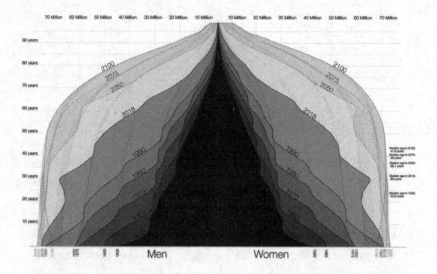

Data source: The United Nations Population Division—World Population Prospects 2017; Medium Variant. The data visualization is available at OurWorldinData.org, where you can find more research on how the world is changing and why. Licensed under CC-BY by the author Max Roser.

as globalization, automation, digitization, urbanization, and climate change, at least in people's imaginations, but that's about to change. The emergence of a global pandemic, coupled with social, racial, and political unrest, and a contraction of life expectancy, shined a light on the experiences of our older population that few could ignore. In nearly every way, the emergence of covid-19 and the scattershot response to the pandemic gave us a greater awareness of the demographic change that is already happening, as well as helped us recognize the wants and needs of our increasingly older population.

Population aging, unlike some other megatrends, cannot be debated. Thanks to centuries of diligent counting through mechanisms such as the census, as well as the individual contributions of enumerators who go door-to-door, countries have a very accurate representation of their people and their demographic profiles, including their age.

Our demographic futures are well mapped, but what is unclear is how these changes will impact our social and economic functions.

Population aging is a reality, and it's happening all around us at an alarmingly fast pace. Whether you realize it or not, your life and the lives of your family and friends, as well as your neighbors and coworkers and all other global citizens, have a role in this great demographic transition. This period of humanity will present great challenges for some and will be particularly difficult for public officials and governments that have to grapple with policy decisions that may be unpopular, including reimagining social welfare programs that would have been considered untouchable a generation ago. However, the opportunities for social enrichment and economic change far outweigh the costs, especially for the private sector, but only if individuals and organizations are willing to accept them as well as meet the realities of this new era head-on.

We all have a role in creating the future of the Super Age. We will all age, we will all care for family members as they grow older, and we will all be confronted by the rapid changes of this coming era. But these seismic shifts will give us the opportunity to remake the world, and the Super Age can be a period that is more just, equitable, and united across generations.

The Super Age

PART ONE

A History of Age

| 1 |

Underfoot and Everywhere

Change is inevitable. This is something that humanity figured out a long time ago, yet somehow it still manages to surprise the casual observer. People who identify, understand, and adapt or harness change are often the biggest winners in society—think Steve Jobs, Jeff Bezos, and Warren Buffett.

Sometimes change arrives slowly and without much fanfare. Other times, it rushes in with great flourish, a disruption event such as the global pandemic. Regardless, it is happening everywhere at every minute and every hour of the day. And you can experience some change in real time, if you know where to look.

The same can be said for the change that is happening to populations around the world. For most of human history, the average age of the population didn't change much. Even in the darkest times—during wars, famines, and natural disasters—and periods of great advancement, societies remained, on average, very young places that were home to very few old people. That was due to the fact that the vast majority of individuals died during birth, infancy, or childhood. Only a select few were spared the challenges of malnutrition, natural and man-made disasters, and diseases to mature into fully formed adults. And even fewer of them made it to old age.

Since the beginning of humanity's rush toward industrialization and progress, societies have been getting older. This shift started out slowly just over two hundred years ago, at least in the industrialized West. However, the demographic transition has sped up in the last hundred years and hit a feverish pace starting around the middle of the twentieth century—life expectancy nearly doubled and birth rates cratered. In some countries, the shift has happened at a quickened pace, occurring in less than a century for those such as Japan and a half century or less in some such as China.

Over the course of this decade, some of the world's largest and most developed economies, as well as some of its smallest and least advanced, will become incredibly old. At least 35 of the 195 nations on this planet will have, at a minimum, one out of five people over the age of 65, the traditional retirement age, by 2030. In the next two years, those aged 65 and over will be equal to those under 18 in the United States. And by 2050, one in six people worldwide will be over 65, one in four in Europe and North America. The most surprising fact is that the number of persons aged 80 years and over is projected to triple, from 143 million in 2019 to 426 million by 2050, making this group the fastest growing demographic in the world.

Visualizing the Demographic Shift

For much of human history, population tables have looked like pyramids, with large numbers of children at the bottom and small numbers of old people at the top. The average human life expectancy, from the classical period up until the middle of the nineteenth century, hovered around 30 years. But this statistic distorts the picture of how the world actually was: a place distinguished by high infant and child mortality rates as well as poor public health and sanitation, and little financial security. Life was hard and relatively short for the vast majority of people, but in contrast, if you were wealthy and privileged, you had a pretty good chance of growing to an age we would consider old today. The best modern example of the former is Niger, the youngest country in the world, where more than half of the population is under the age of 14. In contrast, more than half of Monaco's population is over 53.

Population Pyramid Niger (2022)

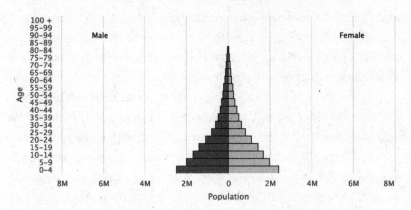

US Census Bureau, International Database

Population Pyramid Monaco (2022)

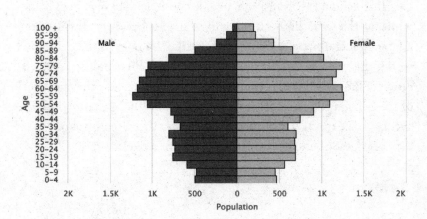

US Census Bureau, International Database

The demographic transition has come in waves and has been roughly tied to periods of great economic and technological development and disruption, such as the industrial revolutions. In his book

The Fourth Industrial Revolution, Klaus Schwab, the founder and executive chairman of the World Economic Forum, explained that there have been four distinct periods of industrial revolution throughout history, including the current one, which began in 2011. He described an industrial revolution as a period of a number of years during which the appearance of "new technologies and novel ways of perceiving the world trigger a profound change in economic and social structures." Advances such as steam power, the age of science and mass production, and the digital revolution all preceded the dramatic technological and social changes that we are experiencing now.

As a rule, primitive society begins with incredibly high birth rates and incredibly high mortality rates, with most deaths happening among infants and youth. The result is low population growth and very few older people. Then, as a society matures and advances, living standards begin to improve. Access to clean water and safe food, housing and sanitation, medical treatment and vaccines becomes more commonplace, which reduces the number of people who die at a young age. Society moves from the fields to the factories—it urbanizes—and people become more dependent on technology to perform tasks they once did themselves.

Throughout this transition, people continue to have a lot of babies while, at the same time, they begin to live longer lives. This leads to a larger general population, as well as an older one. In the developed world, this process started near the end of the First Industrial Revolution (1760–1840) and continued at a quickening pace through most of the Second Industrial Revolution (1860–1920). In that period, the average life expectancy in the United States increased by about fourteen years and the total population more than tripled.

1860   **1920**

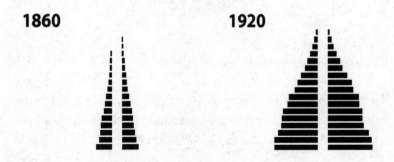

As society continues its march forward and makes advances in areas of science and education, the likelihood of a child living into adulthood improves exponentially, and fewer children are born on average. Societies transition into places marked by low birth rates, low infant and child mortality rates, stable overall mortality rates, and increased longevity. This began during the end of the Second Industrial Revolution (1860–1920) and progressed throughout the Third Industrial Revolution (1960–2010) until today. The most impressive gains happened in the twentieth century.

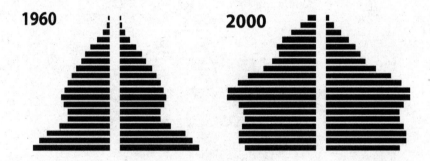

During the twentieth century, global average life expectancy nearly doubled. In richer countries, people started having fewer children, and the ability to reach retirement age went from a privilege reserved for an affluent minority to something that all of us began to expect. The demographic pyramid began to square off and the sides to slope far less steeply. Retirement communities, AARP, and my favorite TV show, *The Golden Girls*, were all products of this period. At the other end of the life span, teens and young adults emerged as separate and distinct groups of people, replete with their own wants and needs (and entire industries that wanted to serve them).

Aging has sped up in recent years, and a growing number of countries have passed or soon will pass the point where at least 20 percent of the population is over the age of 65. This change signals the start of a new era for humanity—the Super Age—the first time in the history of the world in which older populations will outnumber younger ones.

Making Sense of the Super Age

The Super Age world will be sharply different from the one we have lived in before. Germany, Italy, and Japan were the only countries that met the Super Age definition just a few years ago, yet ten countries went over the tipping point in 2020. Over the course of this decade, the percentage of people above what is traditionally defined as retirement age will grow in and meet this designation not only in industrialized countries but also in a growing number of smaller and poorer ones such as Cuba and Georgia.

Population Pyramid Germany (2022)

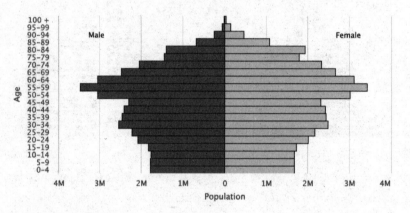

US Census Bureau, International Database

The Super Age has advanced toward us quietly and without much fanfare. In 2018, for the first time ever, there were more people older than 64 than children younger than 5 alive on our planet, and it barely registered in the popular media. In the Super Age, people will live far longer, we will have fewer children, and "post–retirement age seniors"—typically defined as people 65 and older—will become, at a minimum, a third of the population in some societies, as they nearly are in Japan today. This reality has already arrived in some rural counties across the United States.

If we do nothing about these demographic shifts, we will face some serious structural challenges. For example, if the retirement age

Population Pyramid Italy (2022)

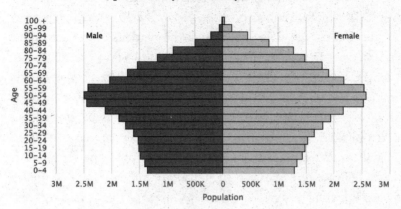

US Census Bureau, International Database

Population Pyramid Japan (2022)

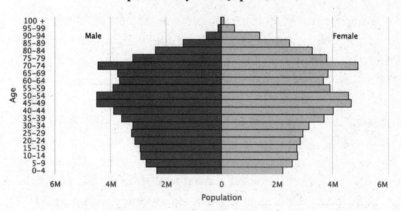

US Census Bureau, International Database

doesn't change and life expectancy continues to increase, there will be relatively more people claiming pension and medical benefits and fewer people working and paying income taxes. The fear is that this will require very high tax rates on the current, shrinking workforce, which will lead to increased generational strife and economic stagnation. A society that continues to time limit working lives to age 65 could also face a shortage of workers, which could push up wages, causing wage inflation and making everything more expensive for everyone—a particularly difficult burden on those that are retired or on fixed incomes.

The Super Age will also change the markets for products and services, creating opportunities as well as problems for some companies. An increase in the numbers of older people will create a bigger market for goods and services developed specifically for older people. In some cases, older people will supplant younger people in some product categories altogether, as in Japan where more diapers are now produced for adults than for children. However, all kinds of companies in nearly every product or service category will have to shift their business models to keep up with the aging consumer landscape. This is already challenging the way companies market to and communicate with their customers, as more and more are forced to consider how to engage either older or generationally diverse audiences—something they have never before had to do.

Americans over 50, for example, are already purchasing two-thirds of all new cars, and the average age of an Apple Watch user is 42 and is going up each year. Older people are also driving up the growth and cost of luxury apartment living in urban areas. Active, wealthier older people may be marketers' new Millennials, meaning that companies may begin to focus their energies away from youth, a demographic they have targeted for nearly a century. If companies want to survive this period, they will need to develop products and services for older consumers or generationally diverse audiences.

In the Super Age, new approaches to education, including lifelong learning, will encourage older individuals to return to universities or enter training programs later in life. Learning should happen throughout life and not just at the beginning. These may be formal degree programs but could also be made up of training in technical or technological skills. Such programs will likely be the provenance of the rich to start with. However, they will be essential for all, if individuals are to remain active in the economy for their entire productive life.

The failure to address the Super Age in a meaningful way could wreak havoc on families, organizations, and countries and their economies. But if we choose to be proactive and confront the shift head-on, we will have an opportunity to make big changes that could have a lasting impact and create a more positive, productive life for everyone. There are also little things that we can do today and throughout this period as individuals, organizations, and governments to smooth the transition.

The covid-19 pandemic illustrated just how poorly prepared societies were for the shift to the Super Age. During the early days, way too much attention was placed on the disease being something that disproportionally affected the old—about 80 percent of all deaths were among people over the age of 65, and about 40 percent of all deaths were among people living in or working at nursing homes. At best, ageism and our general disregard for the oldest members of society—many of whom were highest risk—slowed our collective response. At worst, the lack of a prompt response helped create the perfect environment for the disease to linger, spread, and mutate, which resulted in the unnecessary deaths of millions of people worldwide, as well as stymied economic growth, which led to recession.

The pandemic also shined a very bright light on the inequalities that negatively impact the longevity of historically marginalized groups. In the most extreme cases, one or even two generations—up to around forty years—separate those with the highest longevity from those with the lowest in the United States and around the world. The latter have less time to earn a living, save, and pass wealth to their progeny, which contributes to the growing chasm of social and economic inequality that we're confronted with today. Sadly, these individuals tend to get sicker earlier and more often than their privileged peers, which means they also bore the brunt of infections and deaths due to covid-19.

Societies will need to reimagine home and community to be more inclusive of people of all ages and abilities. Most communities have their roots in the early and middle twentieth century, when populations were a lot younger. These places, including some of the biggest cities in the world, are riddled with barriers that aren't a problem for a younger, able-bodied population. Stairs are everywhere, including at the entrances to many transportation systems, and streets are often poorly lit. Many public spaces also lack areas to rest or use the toilet, two issues of importance for everyone at any age.

Construction of all projects, both new builds and renovations, should consider age in their design process by actively engaging an older or generationally diverse and abled population, and designers should consider the best ways to seamlessly incorporate accessibility into public and private infrastructure projects. Communities should work to make the built environment as barrier free as possible by incorporating the principles of hallmark legislation such as the Americans with Disabilities Act. And all individuals should be encouraged to consider longevity in home design through either tax incentives or public information campaigns, especially in areas such as the bathroom, where a fall is more likely to cause significant harm and hospitalization than a fall anywhere else in the home.

Many people also have to consider what living a longer life will mean for their traditional life course, since the Super Age will force us to reconsider not only the needs of older people but also how increased longevity is impacting the life decisions of younger populations. Many individuals will delay buying a car or a home, which will dramatically reshape those markets. More people will postpone getting married or having kids, too, and some may reject doing either or both altogether. A growing number of individuals will have multiple careers, many will have to work much longer than previous generations did, and most everyone will be a caregiver at some point. Some may even choose to rethink their death or at least their funeral.

All of these shifts will bring incredible opportunities, especially for the individuals and organizations that are willing to meet the Super Age challenges head-on, but they have to be willing to see the change first in order to be part of the solutions that will serve this great demographic transition.

The Road That Got Me Here

I first noticed an early harbinger of the Super Age nearly twenty-five years ago when traveling from Washington, DC, where I was attending American University, to my hometown of Pittsburgh. A key stop on that road journey is the midway point between the two cities, Breezewood, Pennsylvania, where I got off Interstate 70 to take a break before hopping onto the turnpike.

The demographic shift that I witnessed between DC and Breeze- wood was stark. DC was a young, vibrant, affluent city filled with people from around the country and the world. Breezewood, on the other hand, was an older, depressed, poorer town and filled with people from, well, Breezewood. It was not at all uncommon at the time to see older men and women—many well into their seventies and some into their eighties—working in fast-food restaurants or cleaning bath- rooms, jobs that used to be reserved almost exclusively for teenagers.

The image of these older people working these tough jobs after retirement age was jarring. I remember asking myself, "Why are they not retired and enjoying these last years of their lives?" My grandpar- ents, in their eighties at the time, had left the workforce nearly three decades before and were enjoying a comfortable retirement. They had never lived overly privileged lives, and they were arguably middle to lower middle class; my grandmother had been a special-needs pub- lic school teacher, my grandfather an elevator installer. Their comfort had been made possible by a long life of hard work, personal austerity, and robust private and public pensions.

By the time I was nearing graduation, my grandparents were hap- pily ensconced, albeit at the beginning of their health decline, in a continuing care retirement community (CCRC) in Oakmont, Penn- sylvania. CCRCs are built communities where there are typically a minimum age for entry (around 55) and multiple levels of living and care. At the time CCRCs usually included independent living, as- sisted living, and nursing care. I saw that the people in the community were not only more affluent than average, but they were also more age diverse: it was not at all unusual to see residents as young as 60 hob- nobbing with others as old as 90 or even 100.

At that point, I realized that the demographic shift I was witness- ing was seismic and would affect nearly every economy on the planet in my lifetime. From that point on, I dedicated my career to under- standing how the aging of the population was affecting social and economic norms. I focused my endeavors to uncover the best policies and practices being developed by public and private sector organizations to address one of the great questions: What can we as individuals do with all of the extra years, and what should we as a society do with all of these old people? There has to be something better than their serving burgers or scrubbing rest stop toilets during what are supposed to be their years of rest and relaxation.

For more than twenty years, I have traveled around the world observing, reporting, and advocating for a better understanding and embrace of the Super Age. I've worked closely with national governments, as well as major multinational organizations, including the Asian Development Bank, the Organisation for Economic Cooperation and Development, and the World Economic Forum, to develop better policies for our increasingly older world. My advocacy and expertise around extending working lives has touched employers as big as ThyssenKrupp, and my research into harnessing the opportunities presented by the Super Age has moved major companies such as IBM to rethink their approach to product and service delivery, as well as the demographics they serve.

Throughout all of that, I learned that aging remains relatively the same as it was in classical times: it is challenging, fraught with pitfalls, and successful only for a few. What has changed is that on average more people are living longer and healthier lives than ever before, and society needs older people more than ever. Some experts have suggested that we're extending middle life—also known as the middle-plus years—while others insist that a new life stage is emerging altogether, akin to the emergence and then dominance of teenagers and retirees during the last century. Experts universally agree that we're not tacking on extra years of decline at the end of life, but inserting more healthy and productive years into the middle.

No matter what name we give to this life extension, all of the extra years mean that we will have more time than ever before in history to learn, to work and earn, to consume, to contribute, to volunteer or give care, to spend time with friends and family, and to enjoy life. It also means that we will have to fundamentally rethink the way our society is ordered, as well as challenge ourselves to adjust our individual lives and adapt the organizations we serve to the new realities of the Super Age.

One need look no farther than the current president of the United States, Joseph R. Biden, who, at the age of 78, became the oldest person ever to be elected to that office. President Biden, who is known for his physical fitness, works out five days a week with a routine that includes crunches—forty-six for the forty-sixth presidency—and regular rides on his Peloton, a high-tech Wi-Fi-connected stationary bicycle that comes with live streaming and recorded spin classes.

The new reality is all around us already in our everyday lives. Think for a minute, if you can, of the last time you saw a couple out and about with a child. Did you ask yourself, "Are those people the child's parents or grandparents?" I know I have, and I know many older friends who have been confronted with that question about their own children, often to their chagrin.

If you've visited a playground or park, especially in urban areas, you'll find traditional younger parents alongside older parents in their forties, fifties, and even sixties. Parenting is no longer just the provenance of youth, and the data support this observation. Though the overall birth rate in the developed world is down, American women aged 40 to 49 are actually seeing an uptick in the number of pregnancies. When I shared this observation on the *Today* show in 2019, the producer confessed to me that she was one of those older mothers in her fifties.

The Super Age shift isn't just playing out on the playground, it's also happening in the workplace. During a recent visit to an Apple store, I was helped by a man in his seventies, who was one of the most personable and knowledgeable specialists I've ever encountered. When I pressed him on why he was working well past traditional retirement age, his answer was simple yet startling. Earlier that year, his father had passed away at 106 after a battle with Alzheimer's disease. In his estimation, which he based on his father's longevity and his current health condition, he had at least another ten to twenty years to work and needed the income. Plus, as he shared in hushed tones, he really enjoyed the friendships and camaraderie of working in a generationally diverse retail environment with younger people.

The reality of the Super Age is starting to set in for more and more individuals who are nearing retirement or are already retired. During a railway trip across the United States to research this book, I encountered numerous men and women from various economic backgrounds who all expressed apprehension about the prospect of retirement or a desire to return to full-time or part-time work after they had already retired. One woman, who had left her job as an administrative aide in an elementary school at the age of 60, confessed that she had retired from her job too soon. Less than a year into her first retirement, she was planning a return to work.

Now imagine the apprehension that baby boomers must feel when it comes to their physical decline and mortality. Though neither of these issues is new or particularly pleasant to talk about, previous generations have largely dealt with them in silence and for a shorter period of time. But today, the increase in the number of people living longer with chronic conditions, coupled with the proliferation of social media, allows more of us to share our stories and strategies for living longer with more and more people around the world. With more people aware of the realities of longer life, we could see more individuals and organizations attempting to "solve" for aging and its related diseases, whether by extending the lives of human cells, lengthening telomeres, or repairing or replacing entire organs or body parts that have worn out over time.

As we greet the Super Age, we will be forced to change. The way our economy works will have to be profoundly different; culturally, we may face new battles between the old and the young, which could have massive impacts on our politics, technology, and lifestyles. We also face a challenge: a large number of older poor people who are locked out of modern life in fast-vanishing rural communities. However, the growth of a larger gray group presents vast economic opportunities as companies address the needs of these new, empowered consumers and tap their expertise in product design, marketing, and human resources, to name a few.

Countries can't do much to influence the pace of aging in the coming decades, but they can shape what human longevity and old age will look like. By looking across countries and outcomes, we can begin to understand what choices can be made today to shape the future of the Super Age.

In many ways, the promise of the Super Age is impressive, because it offers society one of the rare opportunities to reset and recalibrate for a new reality and to create a world that is more equitable and sustainable. However, its full potential can be realized only if long life is rethought and investments in human development are spread out over a lifetime, not just during the first quarter of life, and include older people as vital participants in all parts of the social and economic fabric of society. Imagine if the social and economic potential of the young was sidelined. That choice would cripple most economies, so why do it to older people, the fastest-growing demographic? Their immense potential will transform industry, reinvigorate economies, and remake society in ways we can only dream of.

I often tell people that it doesn't take a crystal ball to be a demographic futurist. However, it does require a willingness to look back to the past for inspiration for the present and the future, an openness and eagerness to examine patterns and explore data, and a boldness to make predictions. This book is an attempt to do this; it reviews not only our historical attitudes toward older people but also our obsession with youth and the perennial quest for immortality (or at least a longer life). I'll talk about the scientific and social achievements that have led us to this point, and I'll predict what will happen if we do nothing to address the institutional and systemic issues around age, race, and geographic location. And I'll conclude with a vision of the future, as I see it, as well as some short-, medium-, and long-term actionable prospects for opportunity in this new era.

| 2 |

How We Got Here

Demographic upheavals invariably lead to new social and economic conflicts and changes. As the dawn of the Super Age opens, we are witnessing the emergence of a new group of older people who are unwilling to go quietly into old age. They are starting businesses later in life and having great success; a 2018 study out of the Kellogg School of Management at Northwestern University found that the average age of the founders of the very fastest-growing new tech companies is now 45. Other older people, such as my father at 71, are growing or maintaining their businesses well past retirement age. Their influence is growing socially, economically, and politically, yet they are still the target of outdated ageist attitudes and beliefs.

It is imperative for everyone to understand that there are some fundamentals to the human condition—everyone who is born will grow older and eventually die, regardless of their age at the time of death. Living to an advanced age isn't novel, either. However, the ability to achieve a long life has remained elusive for the vast majority of the population for nearly all of humanity, a privilege reserved for a select few. That changed recently, and today a lot more people—a majority, in fact—now have the ability to reach our historical definition of old age. To provide context, nearly 78 million baby boomers were born in the United States from 1946 to 1964. The vast majority of them reached adulthood, and their population, which ranges in age from 58 to 76 today, is over 71 million. By 2050, the US Census predicts, at least 30 million of them—more than a third—will still be alive.

At the same time, a growing number of adults have chosen to have fewer children or no children at all, which is in stark contrast to previous generations. The biological imperative, as well as the expectation for women to produce a large family, has all but disappeared from the modern world. The social and economic conditions that called for more kids no longer exist.

These changes, in terms of both extended longevity and decreased birth rates, represent a fundamental reordering of the demographic order and a shift away from the young world humans called home for millennia. None of it would have been possible without human ingenuity and the steady march of progress during the last two hundred years.

My grandfather Thomas was one of the earlier common people to benefit from the human advancements that translated into longevity gains. The eldest of eight children, he was born in the spring of 1914 to a dirt-poor family in the coalfields of western Pennsylvania. They were people who, quite literally, didn't have a pot to piss in. At the age of 14, more than a year before the advent of the Great Depression, he entered the mines with his father in an effort to help financially support his entire family. He never attained more than a middle school education.

At the time of his birth, nearly one in three children died before their first birthday. The rates were even higher for children like him who were born to impoverished families. Those lower-class kids were almost always at greater risk of developing malnutrition and diseases, much as they are today, but in far greater numbers, since poor living conditions were nearly ubiquitous at the time. They often wouldn't have access to medical care, even if they got sick.

Children at that time encountered deadly or debilitating diseases such as tuberculosis, polio, the Spanish flu, and, in my grandfather's case, coal workers' pneumoconiosis—more commonly known as "black lung"—which he developed while working in the mines as a child. Over the course of his lifetime, the infant mortality rate in the United States declined by over 90 percent. Advances through the years paved the way for him to live to the age of 90, dying just two weeks shy of his ninety-first birthday in 2005.

But all the while researchers were focused on solving infant and youth mortality, which led to more people being able to live a long life, they neglected to address the social and economic injustices that are often lobbed at older people, often collectively referred to as ageism. The world, which had become an increasingly older place with each passing year, remained reliant on old-age stereotypes that had developed well over two thousand years before, often to the detriment of the economy and society at large. The irony is that people aren't just living longer than ever; they are also more physically active and mentally stronger than previous generations were, realities that are often obscured by what we can see—gray hair, wrinkles, and birth dates.

Our new demographic reality won't mean much if we don't understand how we arrived at this point, so there is great value in understanding where humanity came from and how it got here in order to grasp where it is going. Society must constantly recalibrate its attitudes to meet the challenges, as well as opportunities, of today and tomorrow. Longevity gains will be meaningless if they aren't put to good use.

Old Age for Everyone

In 1914, the year of my grandfather's birth, the average life expectancy in the United States was 52 years, and it was likely even lower for poor people like him who were born into abject poverty. Beating the odds by nearly forty years was nothing short of exceptional. What wasn't exceptional was old age itself; old age as a life stage has been around since the beginning.

Even in the ancient world, there were people we would consider today to have reached old age. In classical times, if a child survived the earliest years, the likelihood of making it past 60 was relatively common: it is estimated that between 6 and 8 percent of the population of ancient Rome were over 60. As today, it wasn't unusual for individuals to live longer, with a few lucky outliers even pushing past age 100. In fact, in classical literature, there are multiple references to individuals living to a "ripe old age."

The word *old* isn't new, either. It has been around since the dawn of our Western linguistic history. Researchers from the University of Reading in England believe it is one of the oldest words in the English language (around 15,000 years old) and that it was one of the first ways ancient Europeans used to describe the differences among themselves.

Historically, living to old age was reserved for those who had good financial and social means, much as it is today. This included those who were wealthy and fully engaged, either in work or civic life, for the duration of their lives: the first Roman emperor, Augustus, for example, lived to be 75; Michelangelo was 88 when he expired; and America's own Benjamin Franklin stuck around until he was 84.

Today, when people think about longevity, as well as success in old age, it looks much as it did back then. Some of our greatest corporate leaders, actors, and authors have donned this mantle, remaining active and working well past traditional retirement age: the "Oracle of Omaha," Warren Buffett, is 91; the "Grand Dame of Television," Betty White, is 99; and the Pulitzer Prize–winning author Herman Wouk lived to be 103—he published his final book, *Sailor and Fiddler: Reflections of a 100-Year-Old Author*, at 100 and passed away in 2019. The oldest members of the House of Representatives and Senate are 88, and the average age in the two legislative bodies is 58 and 63, respectively. These are just a few of the many people who have chosen to stay engaged for their entire lives.

The line of demarcation between what society deems as "young" and "old" has historically hovered around sixty-five years, plus or minus five years. According to Karen Cokayne at the University of Reading,

England, in *Experiencing Old Age in Ancient Rome*, "From around the first century B.C. onwards, the age of 60 or 65 was commonly mentioned as the threshold of old age." That was also the age when individuals were released from public obligations, such as jury duty and military service. It's important to note that individuals of every age were expected to work until they physically could not do so, regardless of their exemptions from other duties. This was necessary for their economic survival.

The tradition of exemption continued well into the Middle Ages and the Renaissance. In her 1993 article "Who Were Old in the Middle Ages?" Shulamith Shahar detailed how those who had reached the age of 60 were exempted from military service, town watches, and trial by battle. There are examples of waived military service at this age in England, the Latin Kingdom of Jerusalem, and Paris. Other regions and cities in Europe, such as Castile and León, Modena, and Florence, absolved individuals over the age of 70. The age of exemption from compulsory public service for other areas, such as jury service in England, was generally 70; payment of taxes, 60 or 70; and compulsory labor, 60.

The privileges for older people bubbled over into religious lives, too, especially those in Christendom. In twelfth-century Iceland, individuals over 70 didn't have to fast during Lent, and this tradition continues today; it was practiced in Judaism and Islam, too. If an individual was over the age of 60, he or she was not required to scourge him- or herself during high holy days in Venice but was directed to stay in church and pray.

These exemptions may have been well intentioned at the time and may have been welcomed by a portion of older members of the congregation. However, they may also have had the unintended negative consequence of sidelining or age profiling older members of the Church based on their birthdays and not their physical capabilities. The perception that people over the age of 60 were not able to participate in the same rituals as their younger peers established and then reinforced ageist stereotypes based exclusively on age and not at all on ability.

Establishing Financial Security in Later Life

Old-age pensions have been around since the earliest days of recorded history. However, they were not distributed or administered equally, or for the modern purpose of creating a secure income in later life. One of the first pensions was administered by Roman emperor Augustus Caesar in 13 B.C. in an effort to retain his soldiers' fealty and prevent rebellion, and it was designed for those who had given twenty years of service to the empire. According to Vauhini Vara in a *New Yorker* essay on the origin of pensions, "A soldier would earn, in a lump sum, a pension. . . . Pay the veterans off, the reasoning went, and they'll be less inclined to overthrow you."

There are numerous examples throughout the following centuries of governments providing pensions for military service as well as some professions, almost always with the goal of providing financial security in later life. Some feudal lords, for example, left part of their fortune to the loyal subjects who survived them. Aging members of the clergy could also receive a meager income from the Church, as well as care. And occasionally, public servants received a pension. However, it's important to note that just because some individuals received pensions, that did not mean that they retired, at least in the context of retirement as it is understood today. People generally worked until they were no longer physically able to do so.

In the United States, starting in the mid-1800s, certain municipal employees—firefighters, police, and teachers, mostly in big cities—started receiving public pensions, too. But the benefits were doled out on different bases to different types of people: inconsistency in pension provision was, perhaps, its most consistent trait for most of human history.

In 1875, the American Express Company started offering private corporate pensions, the first of their kind. The stated goal was to reward the company's rail, barge, and horseback delivery service workers who had been "injured or worn out" as a charitable way to ease them out of the workforce. Again, that tied in to the ability of a worker to do a job and was not necessarily tied to chronological age.

As industry grew and mass production expanded, older workers provided a challenge to labor-intensive jobs. Not only was it felt that they were unable to keep pace, but there was also an interest in getting younger, abler, and more affordable workers into these positions. As a result, many companies began offering pensions as incentives to get older workers to step aside. This practice continued well into the twentieth century and is still pervasive today, even though it has been changed to include "buyouts" and "early retirement" offers, which further incentivize older workers to exit the workforce at even earlier ages.

It wasn't until 1881 that pensions assumed their modern form, when Otto von Bismarck, the first chancellor of the German Empire, presented a radical idea to his government: it should provide universal financial support for older members of society. The idea was radical because during most prior human history, pensions had not been universal and people had been expected to continue to work until they were no longer able to do so. According to the Social Security Administration history archives, Bismarck put forward the proposal to revive the German economy and stave off pressure from socialist opponents. His idea ended up in a letter from Kaiser Wilhelm I to the government: "those who are disabled from work by age and invalidity have a well-grounded claim to care from the state."

It would take eight years to pass that legislation, but by the end of the decade, the German government created a first-of-its-kind old-age income system, which provided for all citizens over the age of 70. The invention wasn't just a profound paradigm shift for Germany and the people who lived there; it became the standard for many industrialized and developed nations around the world. In fact, universal public pensions became a hallmark of developed countries in subsequent decades. Workers began to expect that the state would provide some income to them later in life. Today, most economic security experts count the state pension as one of the three pillars of retirement income, the other two being personal savings and corporate pensions. The move by Bismarck paved the way for modern retirement, but it certainly did not create it.

Getting to the age of 70 was a big "if" in the time of Bismarck. The pensionable age was thirty years more than the average life expectancy in Germany at the time. Even if an individual reached pensionable age, it was still likely that he or she would work until he or she was no longer able to. The advent of the Bismarck pension, in many ways, was the starting line for the democratization of old age, meaning that more people, regardless of income or lifetime earnings, would be given an opportunity to live in old age, rather than just scrape by until death. It represented a shift of responsibility from filial piety to social welfare. The family took a back seat to the government as the primary provider of income, and later medical care, in later life.

Just prior to the Bismarck pension, during the late eighteenth and early nineteenth centuries, a groundswell of public health measures and medical innovations—inoculation against smallpox, the use of professional midwives to make childbirth less deadly, the cultivation of citrus fruits that prevented scurvy—significantly extended the human life span. But as Angus Deaton, a Princeton economist and Nobel laureate, has shown, the benefits of those practices went largely to the rich. In the mid- to late nineteenth century, the rich lived twenty years longer than their contemporaries did. For the poor people of the era, life remained short, due in large part to the reality that those "of means" were more likely to have access to and embrace innovation.

Public pensions and, perhaps more important, public health and social innovations didn't fully develop until the twentieth century. The radical, near-universal access to economic and health security that developed during that period drove an extension of human life that would not have been possible otherwise. The result was that governments that invested in those protections saw average life expectancies increase dramatically. The global institutions that were created by these same governments eventually began to establish many of the innovations around the world, which contributed to a precipitous drop in infant and child mortality, further pushing the average life expectancy up worldwide.

The most recent century witnessed the development and implementation of many health care innovations that were made available to the public, rather than being reserved for the rich. In 1928, while studying influenza, Alexander Fleming discovered penicillin, an anti-biotic, which by the 1940s was being mass-produced by the US phar-maceutical industry. In 1914, Marie Curie, who was instrumental in the discovery and understanding of X-rays, put the first mobile X-ray machine onto the battlefield of France. In 1977, Raymond Damadian became the first person to complete a full-body scan of a human being to diagnose cancer, using a method well known today as magnetic resonance imaging, or MRI. All of those advances chipped away at mortality, especially for adults, and increased average life expectancy.

The rapid progress of medical research and health care in this era was reinforced by enormous improvements in communication among doctors and scientists throughout the world. Through publications, conferences, and later computers and electronic media, doctors and scientists freely exchanged ideas and reported on their endeavors. The development and distribution of not one but multiple vaccines for covid-19, some of which employ novel mRNA technology, that occurred in partnership with multiple companies and was funded by multiple countries is the result of the decades of global collaboration that began just after the end of World War II.

Improving Infant and Childhood Mortality

At the end of the war in 1945, some governments created national health and social welfare systems, such as the National Health Service in the United Kingdom and Santé Publique in France. In the countries that were unable to afford national health and social welfare systems, organizations such as the World Health Organization and the World Food Programme, as well as private sector organizations, stepped in and began providing basic food and health security. These interventions drove down infant and child mortality and increased longevity, albeit at different rates globally.

At the same time as governments were helping to extend the lives of the old, the advent of labor and social protections for children in the workforce and at home aided in the lowering of youth mortality.

Child labor laws restricting the employment and abuse of young workers were instituted in the United States under the Fair Labor Standards Act of 1938. These provisions in the United States, as well as similar measures in other developed countries, were designed to educate young minds and keep children out of work that was deemed a threat to their physical safety and wellbeing. As more children survived their youth, they were given the chance to grow old.

According to the World Health Organization, these interventions in health and social policy worked. In the past thirty years alone, the infant mortality rate has more than halved worldwide. The number of annual infant deaths has more than halved, too, declining from 8.7 million in 1990 to 4 million in 2018. From 1990 to 2017, the mortality rate in children declined by 37 percent. Still, almost a million children between ages 5 and 14 died in 2017, so there is room for improvement on top of these gains.

A third element of twentieth-century demographic change has also had powerful results. Over the course of the century, wealthier societies managed to lower the birth rate through a combination of increased sexual education, family planning, and access to birth control. Harsh economic realities and the rise of the double-income household, as well as shifting gender norms and responsibilities, also played major roles in this change. Education, as it turns out, is one of the most powerful forms of birth control.

More economically developed countries, including most of Europe, the United States, Japan, South Korea, and Australia, have witnessed their birth rates decrease precipitously. For nearly all of these countries, birth rates declined shortly after their respective baby booms. In the 2017 *Lancet* Global Burden of Disease (GBD) study, researchers found that worldwide, women in 1950 had an average 4.7 children in their lifetime, twice the replacement level of 2.1 births per woman. But by 2017, the birth rate had all but halved to 2.4 children, just above the replacement level.

But the world averages mask the vast variations among nations. The BBC cited estimates that "The fertility rate in Niger, west Africa, is 7.1, but in the Mediterranean island of Cyprus women are having one child, on average. In the UK, the rate is 1.7, similar to most Western European countries." In some Eastern and Latin American nations, the decline has been faster, and the dubious honor for lowest birth rate in the world belongs to Taiwan at 1.07. The rapid decline presents greater challenges for societies but also greater opportunities for disruption and innovation.

The implications of these shifts are dramatic, since most national social welfare systems are predicated on having a relatively large, young working population that pays taxes to support a relatively small, older retired population. National economies, which are built on the false premise of perennial growth, could begin to contract. Population growth in Africa, coupled with population contraction in the Americas, Asia, and Europe, signal that Africa will likely be the most populous continent by the end of this century, Islam may be the most observed religion, and there will be more older people everywhere. The United Nations has even suggested that the global population will peak at 11 billion this century, based on current demographic projections. The global median age will likely tick up from 31 to 42.

But what happens when national population growth slows, stalls, or reverses? The world is about to find out. The natural and more holistic response is to work to make the economy more inclusive, as Japan is attempting to do by clearing the way for more women and older people to work, relaxing some immigration rules, and employing robotic technologies wherever possible. Some of the more rapidly aging countries, such as China, which reported a population contraction in 2020 for the first time since 1949, may signal how demographic realities and economic policy can better align in order to sustain growth during this transformative period.

The Effects of Rapid Demographic Change

China's population exploded in the middle of the twentieth century with the fertility rate reaching its peak of 6.4 births per woman in 1966. In its attempt to modernize the economy and curb overpopulation, the government changed the country's reproductive pattern with its one-child policy in 1979, likely the largest social experiment in the history of humanity. It's estimated that up to 400 million births were prevented.

The one-child policy not only drastically reduced the number of children the country produced, it also disrupted the natural balance between male and female births and contributed to population aging. An easing of this policy in recent years hasn't yielded the increased birth rate that was anticipated by the Communist Party. Today, China's fertility rate, which is estimated to be between 1.2 and 1.6, is well below the 2.1 replacement rate, so its population will likely shrink by 2.5 percent, or approximately 28 million people, by 2050. For reference, that's roughly equivalent to the population of the entire state of Texas today.

In the same period, the average life expectancy in China was dramatically extended by just over a decade. That extension of longevity, combined with the declining birth rate, doubled the median age of the population from around 21 in 1979 to just over 38 in 2020. For reference, it took the United States over a century, or more than three times as long, to double its median age. Today, the two countries have roughly the same median age, but by 2050, the median age in China is projected to increase to 47, while that in the United States will increase to only 41, a nearly 16 percent difference. This may not seem like much, but the juggernaut speed at which China is aging has left many wondering how the country will adapt.

China's demographic change has left the country's leadership struggling to change retirement norms to meet demands: the normal pension age at present is 60 years for men, 50 years for blue-collar women, and 55 years for white-collar women. This means that although some threats to China's security, such as environmental pollution, will remain, other challenges, such as continued economic growth, will emerge, especially if the country is unable to manage its transition into the Super Age effectively. This is due largely to the seemingly never-ending supply of cheap human labor that is finally beginning to dry up, a workforce dependency ratio that is completely lopsided, a pension system that is not fully matured, and a growing demand for caregivers, both family and professional. All of these could add up to create a major drag on China's economic growth.

During my time at AARP, I met with Vice Premier Ma Kai, the fourth highest ranking official in the Chinese government at the time, at Zhongnanhai, China's White House, to discuss the pressing demographic issues facing China. Ma had been charged with guiding China's response to demographic change. I learned that China's leadership sees demographic change as a clear and present danger to its continued economic ascent and the country's demographic and economic policies need to align if its future is to remain bright. Countries of all sizes and at all stages of development could learn from this intersectional approach, since the two issues are so intimately connected.

China is not alone in witnessing a rapid decline in birth rates, and these developments could have lasting social and economic ramifications in regions throughout the world, potentially stymieing the prospects for economic growth and leaving some nations in a sort of development purgatory—no longer developing but not yet developed. Less economically successful countries in the region without national reproductive policies, such as Thailand and Vietnam, have also experienced birth rate contraction and rapid population aging. Halfway around the world, Mexico and Brazil are still regarded as relatively young nations but are witnessing dramatic decreases in their birth rates, too. Unlike their richer counterparts in the Americas, Asia, and Europe, none of these countries has had the opportunity to create wealth or sustainable national social and economic welfare systems, which portends a challenging future for their younger generations, who may have to expend a great deal of personal time and wealth caring for aging parents and society if nothing is done to adapt to the change and welcome older people as active participants in the future.

The changes that are under way in widely different economies, as well as in societies in varying stages of development, should underscore the fact that the wants and needs of the older population as well as the experience of aging should not be seen as universal. Older populations are not a monolithic hoard of cardigan-wearing pensioners shuffling down the road to a nursing home while gobbling up all of the resources. They are as diverse as the general population, if not more so, so a one-size-fits-all approach toward engaging them is folly. Sadly, our ageist bias toward older populations has been formed, fixed, and reinforced as long as humans have been on this planet; that's a problem and one that needs to be countered.

Understanding Uneven Attitudes and Experiences

Regardless of the increasing size of the older population and the decrease in the number of younger people, prevailing attitudes toward youth and age have remained relatively unchanged. For almost the entirety of human history, people who reach old age have been seen as burdens who neither can nor should play a useful role in society. The exceptions: those who have achieved financial independence, political power, or popular success.

According to University of Manchester professor Tim Parkin, "Classical authors such as Cicero and Plutarch would have us believe that the elderly were revered, active citizens of ancient Rome. But upon closer inspection, it appears that older people may not have enjoyed as respected or as powerful a place in Roman society as has been supposed." Yet the Romans created the Senate, which was made up entirely of *senes*—Latin for "elderly"—suggesting that older people were revered. In fact, they were not.

The reality is that success in old age has almost always been tied to one's economic situation, and this mostly holds true today. Before the advent of the state pension and the development of modern retirement, those who weren't able to work became the wards of their adult children or extended family, if they were lucky enough to have them. Many elders slid into traditional gendered and generational roles. Those who didn't have family or finances were generally thrust into poverty and homelessness.

In the modern day, individuals can receive help from public economic assistance programs, but in practice, it can often be hard for them to navigate the complex bureaucracies in order to gain access to public housing or institutionalized long-term care. Even Cicero, a champion of older people in Roman times, opined, "Old age will only be respected if it fights for itself, maintains its rights, avoids dependence on anyone, and asserts control over its own to the last breath." People who fall on hard times in old age will most likely be ostracized and marginalized and will almost always be sidelined.

It should come as little surprise that fortune in older age, much like fortune in life, was often tied to gender, much as it is today. Men often aged "better," because they were given the license and support to do so, and women were mostly left out of most conversations and opportunities that didn't involve having children or tending a home. It wasn't until the Middle Ages that some of the first, most negative, and most pervasive attitudes toward older women were etched into popular scientific and cultural beliefs. Those beliefs invariably revolved around menstruation and the ability to have children, much as they do today. Menstrual blood was considered to be impure, harmful, and destructive. However, menstrual blood was believed to be far more dangerous to women and society when it stopped flowing due to menopause, causing women to become venomous and erratic. Although not as explicit today, unfounded beliefs about women's physiology and psychological makeup persist, especially about older women, in their personal and professional lives.

The Greeks saw aging as a downward slope of decrepitude. They even worshipped Geras, the god of old age, who was represented as a shriveled-up man holding a cane. This starkly contrasts with the systematic admiration of and respect for the elderly in ancient China. Confucianism and Hinduism, like Christian doctrines, promote filial piety and the care of elders. This, in combination with the interdependent or collectivistic culture that promotes group or community needs over individual needs, leads Eastern cultures to express a greater reverence for older people, but even that comes at a cost.

Older people in Asia are often forced into traditional gender and elder roles (gardening, child care, and so on) and prevented from retaining their employment. The same issues—losing economic power or security, or declines in health—remain when they are removed from the economy, especially at a time when there are fewer younger people to fill their roles. But "Eastern culture" includes a great many countries with a diverse range of cultural beliefs and practices at varying stages of development, and it would be unfair and unwise to assume that the experience of older people is consistent across countries in the region.

The historic attitudes toward aging and the older population are counterintuitive and counterproductive. Society, especially its younger members, is betting against the future, and more important their own future, when it sidelines the potential of older people, or forces them into traditional roles. The fixation on being young and rejecting aging and the older population is getting into the way of progress and may hamper the potential of the Super Age.

Ageism and Generational Conflict

There has always been resistance to accepting old age, and society has always treated older people differently, which is likely due to a general discomfort with the aging process. But it wasn't until 1969 that one of my earliest mentors, Robert Butler, the founder of the International Longevity Center, gave this negative and pervasive bias toward older people a name: *ageism*.

In an interview with the *Washington Post*, he said, "People talk about aging gracefully, which is what they want to do of course. So, naturally, they don't want to look at people who may be palsied, can't eat well . . . who may sit on the curb and clutter up the neighborhood with canes. Until our society builds [a] more balanced perspective about age groups, this lends to embittered withdrawal by old people." But the negative attitudes toward older people extend far past those who are "in need" and often extend down to "younger older" populations, groups of people who may be chronologically older but are physically and mentally healthier than previous generations of the same age cohort.

Ashton Applewhite, the author of *This Chair Rocks: A Manifesto Against Ageism*, suggests that language, whether intended to or not, is often used to diminish older people, and she's right. The words that individuals use when speaking to or about older people often attempt to box this population into an outdated, ageist construct. This disrupts and diminishes their dignity and agency "in condescending generalisations that assume vulnerability and dependence instead of resilience and independence." Societal ageism can negatively impact the mental and physical health of those on the receiving end. Internalized ageism can have similar effects on individuals.

As with other aspects of identity, age is only one piece of the puzzle. Catalyst, a nonprofit that consults with leading companies on inclusive HR practices, highlighted the gendered aspects of ageism in a research brief: "Older women face marginalization based on 'lookism,' or gendered youthful beauty standards in addition to the unfounded societal biases that older employees are less innovative, adaptive, and generally less qualified. In one study, women managers reported feeling pressure to adhere to societal beauty standards and maintain a young look. As an example, women are almost twice as likely as men to feel compelled to dye their hair."

Men generally don't have to deal with these unrealistic standards, and the two genders are not judged consistently as they age. Men have historically had greater license to "age naturally," a freedom that is not extended to women. However, even that liberty goes only so far. A growing number of men are regularly indulging in procedures such as liposuction, tummy tucks, and fillers. A healthy, youthful appearance is seen as a necessary tool to compete in the modern world.

Let me be clear: there is nothing wrong with wanting to look good for as long as possible, even if that includes employing age camouflage such as hair dye and plastic surgery. However, there is a fine line that separates vanity from a break with reality. All too often, ageism spills over into rational decision making and the prejudice felt toward the old, which can result in bad public policy and generational conflict. It can get into the way of individuals' making the right choices about their finances and their health.

Intolerance and misunderstanding of older people have spilled into public policy which was perhaps best captured in 1988 by the late

British journalist Henry Fairlie, who faulted "greedy geezers" for their luxury at the expense of future generations in the *New Republic*. The truth is that most older people, especially the oldest old, are far from wealthy. They are, for the most part, interested in contributing to society through either paid or volunteer work. Yet the "greedy geezer" label stuck and resentment between generations (baby boomers and the Greatest Generation in this period) continued to fester.

Economic attacks on specific groups of people generally flare up in bad economic times and subside in good, due in large part to the growing economic pie and shared prosperity. Wage stagnation since the Great Recession has caused intergenerational resentment to harden, this time between Millennials and baby boomers, largely because the income gap between the richest rich and the poorest poor grew at an astonishing rate.

The relatively recent saying "OK, Boomer" is a perfect example of this. It was popularized on the social media platform TikTok and is regularly used by younger people to politically challenge older people, who are deemed to be out of touch on issues such as income and the environment, or to culturally box in those they no longer deem cool. Younger people see "OK, Boomer" as born of the frustrations they feel about the status quo, whereas older people see it as an unfounded and dismissive ageist attack on an entire generation of people. Platforms such as TikTok enable generational attitudes to be broadcast far and wide and allow generational conflict and attitudes to play out in real time around the world.

Late in 2019, AARP fell face forward into the "OK, Boomer" debate when its publications chief, Myrna Blyth, was quoted in an interview as mocking the lack of financial resources that younger people had acquired. "OK, millennials," Blyth reportedly said, "but we're the people that actually have the money." Unfortunately, Blyth missed the mark with her wry reply, since more than two out of three TikTok users are aged 13 to 24 and therefore solidly Gen Z. Her comment was met with swift condemnation in social and traditional media as one more way that older people were out of touch. AARP has since apologized, but the damage had already been done. Unfortunately, this comment served to widen the generational rift, rather than attempt to heal or at least address it.

We have created two dominant societal narratives over slightly more than forty years: one of a richer, younger, more urban society, the other of a poorer, older, more rural one. These narratives are most prevalent in the United States, but they are also evident across Asia and Europe, especially in recent elections and referendums. Unfortunately, the narratives leave a lot of gray space—no pun intended—between the haves and the have-nots.

In the 1980s, baby boomers began to embrace short-term conservative policies that chipped away at social protections, which set the stage for generational conflict. Workers' protections were undone. Unions were busted. Infrastructure renewal was sidelined. Public pensions and health care were constantly under siege. And serious politicians started to argue that cutting taxes for the rich would benefit everyone, as the cuts would encourage the wealthy to spend more money, which would "trickle down" to the rest of the populace. Boomers in the United States, in many ways, were betting against their future selves by eroding the foundations of some of the most important social welfare programs, including Social Security and Medicare. Ageism got into the way.

There's an adage attributed to various writers throughout history that "any man who is under 30 and is not a liberal has no heart, and any man who is over 30 and not a conservative has no brains," but for the first time in recent years, age began to play an outsized role in elections and referendums. Recent research in the United States and the United Kingdom has illustrated that age—not class—is a better predictor of voting behavior.

This has had significant implications in the United States, where older voters influenced the election of President Donald J. Trump in 2016. According to CNN exit polls, voters aged 45 and over favored Trump over Hillary Clinton by eight points, 52 to 44 percent, whereas voters younger than 45 favored Clinton by fourteen points, 53 to

39 percent. Given the complexity of the US political system, older voters from rural states helped deliver the presidency to Trump, even though he lost the popular vote by almost 3 million votes.

In the 2016 presidential election, 71 percent of Americans over 65 voted, compared with 46 percent of 18- to 29-year-olds, according to US Census Bureau data. This trend in older people voting more continued in the 2020 election, and had it not been for a surge in younger voters in battleground states, Joe Biden would likely have lost the vote in the Electoral College while winning the popular vote by a margin greater than Hillary Clinton did in 2016.

The disproportionate weight of the older vote is not unique to the United States. In 2016, there was a similar experience in a referendum in the United Kingdom, where, *Time* magazine reported, exit polls showed that only about 19 percent of voters between the ages of 18 and 24 supported a British exit—"Brexit"—from the European Union. However, among retirees, who had come of age before the European Union was created, a staggering 59 percent wanted the country to leave. Of 33 million ballots counted, Brexit won by a slim margin of around 1.3 million votes.

Older people have always been more active in democracies, and politicians tend to reward older voters, for example by promising increases to—or at least not to cut—social welfare programs. However, a shift to a Super Age electorate could foreshadow a protectionist period in which those of pension age and above vote to keep or extend social welfare benefits to the detriment of sustainable fiscal policy and the younger population. Areas such as education and the arts could take a back seat to those favored by older voters, including health and economic security.

We do better when we come together, and there is plenty of room for the generations to work in unison. Issues such as the environment, as well as social and economic justice, have wide support among the generations. There's a huge overlap in the issues faced at work, too, and a growing number of both younger and older people are taking on the challenging role of family caregiver. And none of these issues are tied to age.

Moving Forward

Today's older population is confronting the notion of what it means to be relevant, creative, productive, and sexy. Led in large part by women, they are pioneering the empowerment of people later in life and rejecting traditional roles.

I think about these trailblazers often because they are the early architects of the Super Age. What they do to combat ageism will have a direct impact on my own later life, given that I have a greater than 50 percent chance of living past 95 and have no intention of ever fully retiring. Their impact will be even greater for my youngest relatives, since they have a greater than 50 percent chance of living past 105.

There's a saying that "demographics aren't destiny," but demographic change is inevitable, and it is happening at an astonishing rate and in places where most government and business leaders aren't necessarily paying attention. Population changes may have radical effects on our industries, our workforce, our education systems, our health care systems, our public policy, and even our environment. These effects can be catastrophic if ignored. However, they also present incredible opportunities if understood and managed effectively. There's great power that comes from uniting the generations to work together on common goals, but it is essential that both young and old level set their expectations and check their bias at the door.

| 3 |

The Altar of Youth

Societies revere the young and celebrate them at birth, throughout the milestones of childhood, and into adolescence and early adulthood through rites of passage that have deep historical, cultural, and religious foundations.

There's a good reason to celebrate youth, too. For much of history, just surviving childhood was considered a success. Around 25 percent of babies in the first century in Rome died in their first year, and up to half of all children died before the age of 10. It wasn't until the modern era that those numbers started to turn around and living into adulthood became the norm rather than the exception.

Our cultural obsession with youth, like our attitudes toward older people, was likely fixed into the earliest moments of our civilization. Perhaps one of the first recorded discussions of our fascination with youth comes from Herodotus (ca. 484–425 B.C.), known as the "Father of History." Herodotus wrote about a group of people called the Macrobians, who were believed to have lived in modern-day Africa and were known for their longevity and youthfulness. The fact that Herodotus mentioned them suggests that the ancient Greeks were concerned with issues of longevity and youthfulness, much as we are today. In his writings, he also spoke of a mysterious pool of water that the Macrobians used regularly that he speculated may have held some of the power of their youth.

The myth of the fountain of youth has been common throughout history, perhaps because individuals have always chased youth or immortality. I get it—aging and death can be incredibly scary, if only because both are unknown. Larry Minnix, who was my CEO at LeadingAge (formerly the American Association of Homes and Services for the Aging) when I worked there in the early 2000s, often exclaimed, "Americans are the only people on the planet who think death is an option!" Though Larry missed the mark on the idea being exclusive to Americans, he was right that people have always challenged aging and death; but, as I always say, "the Reaper always bats a thousand."

Legends of healing waters originated in diverse cultures in the Canary Islands, Japan, Polynesia, and England and involved historical figures such as Alexander the Great, who was said to have discovered a "river of paradise" in the fourth century B.C. However, there is no one more famous in his quest for the fountain of youth than Juan Ponce de León, the Spanish explorer who traveled with Christopher Columbus on his second voyage to the Americas.

By the nineteenth century, the quest for the fountain of youth had given rise to Central Europe's great *Kurorte* ("cure towns") with lavish spas for the wealthy and rising bourgeois class. According to David Clay Large, the author of *The Grand Spas of Central Europe: A History of Intrigue, Politics, Art, and Healing*, spa towns were "the equivalent of today's major medical centers." Much like the "fountains of youth" of lore, the baths offered no real efficacy.

Today, the idea of fountains of youth seems somewhat foolish. However, this hasn't hindered our quest to remain young and purchase products and services that will help us attain longer life, firmer skin, or greater sexual vigor. We also consume vitamins at an astonishing rate, even though they typically have little or no clinical effect. Men and women nip and tuck their bodies, as well as buff and fill their wrinkles, for the duration of their lives. Their obsession with youth blinds many to the reality that they will eventually get old and die. This decoupling from reality may also have detrimental effects on mental and physical health that, oddly enough, contribute to aging at a faster rate.

In our lifetime, we've witnessed the rise of the beauty and anti-aging industries. We've seen organ transplantation move from science fiction to reality. And we've seen the acceptance of the "little blue pill" as a drug for men who've lost their spark downstairs.

Adults have always had a tendency to chase after youth and all of its trappings: flawless, firm, wrinkle-free skin; great hair; reckless abandon, coupled with not a care in the world and next to zero responsibilities; as well as fully functioning sexual organs and stamina. Many people today do whatever they can to keep themselves committed to looking and feeling younger than they actually are, whether through living a healthy lifestyle, undergoing plastic surgery, buying the newest (read: youngest) fashions, or keeping up on the latest popular culture and social media trends; a 60-year-old friend of mine recently went out of her way to tell me she was on TikTok, as if it were some kind of relevancy badge of honor.

The reasons people chase youth may be varied, but they tend to center around the fact that most people are told every minute of every hour of every day of every year that being young is better than being old. This is reinforced not only in daily messages but also in a barrage of marketing directed at the youth market. According to Statista, in 2018, youth advertising surpassed $4.2 billion worldwide, and this expenditure was expected to reach $4.6 billion by 2021. In 2015, 500 percent more was spent on Millennials than all other groups combined.

It may be hard to believe, but until the late 1940s, the youth market in the United States wasn't even considered to be "a thing." However, years of postwar prosperity and population growth created a large and financially influential enough group to attract the attention of a small group of pioneers who were eager to develop new products and services, as well as marketing and communications channels to reach the young dollar, sometimes at the expense of the older one.

The founders of the youth market capitalized on demographic change, as well as the shifting social and economic norms that emerged after World War II. They were able to tap into generational angst and speak directly to young people through targeted publications and on radio and television programs. They leaned into the narrative that younger people were somehow more special than those who were older, and the idea became dominant. And they commoditized traditions and ceremonies that had once been reserved to celebrate the transition into adulthood and made them seminal moments in a teen's life.

Pioneers in product development and marketing and communications should take note of how the youth market emerged, because it provides a road map to understanding how other generationally distinct markets can come into existence. Today, there is a growing population of older people in middle age and later life who are working and remaining active consumers with larger disposable incomes for longer periods of time. They may not attract the built-in admiration that younger people do thanks to millennia of ageist bias, but they do have more wealth. The Super Age market is arriving, and exploiting the youth market isn't the only way to make money anymore.

Tradition, Tradition!

The roots of our modern birthday traditions are borrowed from different cultures throughout history, but they all add up to create a celebration that is near universal today. The Greeks gave us birthday candles, the Persians gave us birthday dinners, Romans gifted us with drinking to excess, Germans gave us the modern birthday cake, and Americans gave us the birthday song. It's not unusual today for young children to have large birthday parties or to proclaim their age to anyone who will listen. It's also not unusual, on occasion, for the oldest old to do the same.

Birthdays have invariably been used to mark and measure our position in society. Their passage grants access to certain privileges, including the rights to drive, vote, drink alcohol, and serve in the military. Above all, they have been used almost exclusively to mark the transition into adulthood. However, they also provide general guidelines for the youth market to define itself.

Christianity, especially early Catholicism, is well documented as having borrowed from the rites, rituals, and traditions of other cultures. In Catholicism, boys and girls become adults, as well as full members of the Church, around the age of 14, when they take the sacrament of Confirmation. This age was likely borrowed from the Romans. Roman boys changed into adults at the discretion of their father, around the ages of 14 to 17. During the ceremony, boys shed their *bulla*—a type of necklace worn to mark and protect young boys—and traded their childhood toga for an adult one known as the *toga virilis*. At that point, they became men as well as full citizens and eligible for military service. Girls, on the other hand, became women as early as 12, when they were betrothed to their future husband, at which point they gave up their toys to the goddess Artemis.

The shifts from childhood to adulthood in early Eastern and Western cultures were oddly similar and abrupt—one day individuals were children, and the next day they were adults. That typically occurred around the age of puberty. Boys in ancient Greece became men around 17 or 18; girls became women by 15. In Japan's Heian period, court nobles and samurai held a ceremony called *Genpuku* in which boys between the ages of 12 and 14 became men. And, starting sometime in the Middle Ages, Eastern European Jews welcomed boys into adulthood at 13 via a ceremony called Bar Mitzvah; it wasn't until 1922 that the ceremony was extended to girls through the Bat Mitzvah.

Over time, as populations began to age, they also began to move away from religion and from religious traditions. This is likely due to increased levels of educational attainment, and the observation is backed up by data from a 2018 survey by the Pew Research Center that stated, "Overall, adults ages 18 to 39 are less likely than those ages 40 and older to say religion is very important to them in 46 out of 106 countries surveyed." This doesn't necessarily mean that the world is becoming less religious, but there is a strong correlation between the aging of a society and its lack of religiosity. For example, only one out of ten people in Japan, the world's oldest continuously existing country, believe that religion is important, and membership in US churches recently dropped below half of the population for the first time ever.

In some cases, societies began creating new secular traditions to celebrate the shift into adulthood, such as the debutante ball, held at age 16 to 21, for European and American girls, and the *quinceañera*, held at age 15, for Latin American girls. In other cases, society codified tradition into law, such as military conscription, more commonly known as "the draft," at age 18 for boys in the United States, or gaining the right to vote, at age 16 to 21 in most democracies. In other cases, new traditions came into effect with new technology, such as obtaining a driver's license at age 16 to 18.

Teenagers and the Baby Boom

During the Second Industrial Revolution, societies began moving away from the notion that children magically turned into adults overnight, and a new life stage known as adolescence emerged. This new period of life allowed children to transition slowly into full adults, rather than being thrust into the deep end of adulthood while still children, as they had been in previous generations.

Adolescence likely occurred in wealthier households first, followed by the emerging middle class and, eventually, the poor, as more and more children were no longer forced into the fields or factories to support their families. The Fair Labor Standards Act of 1938, which was designed to "protect the educational opportunities of youth and prohibit their employment in jobs that are detrimental to their health and safety," likely had a major impact on normalizing childhood and adolescence by keeping children out of work, especially in mills and mines, and in the classroom.

By 1900, thirty-four US states had compulsory education requirements, and by 1910, 72 percent of Americans attended some school. By 1918, every child in the United States was guaranteed a basic elementary education. Today, according to the Education Commission of the States, "24 states and the District of Columbia require students to attend school until they turn 18 years old, 11 states require students to attend until they turn 17 and 15 states require students to attend until they turn 16." High schools, which were unheard of in most of the United States prior to 1900, became commonplace during the first half of the twentieth century, and by 1940, 50 percent of adolescents held a high school diploma.

In many ways, extra education became the key to breaking the cycle of poverty and helped increase the wealth of nations, but it also created an environment in which children had the freedom to grow into adulthood in ways they had not been able to before. It also gave options, especially to young women, that included more than being a mother and a caregiver. Society began to recognize that adolescents were no longer just children, nor were they fully formed adults. Instead, they were something new, unique, and in between.

Sometime after the Second World War, the term *teenager* began to be used as a blanket term for adolescents. However, instances of "teen" and "teenage" can be found as far back as 1899. In a speech at the Thirty-Seventh Annual Session of the Minnesota Educational Association that year, high school principal John N. Greer from Central High School in Minneapolis, Minnesota, explained:

> Boys and girls in their teens! What a problem in psychology and child study is represented by these words! How little of it is written or yet understood! They are not men and women, nor yet are they children. They typify the period when hope and fancy and ambition grow apace. To them the future is grand and attractive, and to be easily conquered. Self-consciousness is just blossoming. Egotism is in luxuriant bud. The mind discriminates not between the liberty and the license of thought.

Today, we throw around the term *teenager* with ease, but that's largely thanks to the postwar baby boom, as well as the booming postwar economy, in which people had access to good jobs and more disposable income. During that time, the teenage years became not only a stage of life but a market to be reckoned with. The first large generation of teenagers, whom we now call baby boomers, would fundamentally change the world.

Teenagers and the Youth Market

The journalist Derek Thompson noted in a 2018 article for *The Saturday Evening Post*, "The teenager emerged in the middle of the 20th century thanks to the confluence of three trends in education, economics, and technology. High schools gave young people a place to build a separate culture outside the watchful eye of family. Rapid growth gave them income, either earned or taken from their parents. Cars (and, later, another mobile technology) gave them independence." Other technologies, including personal computers, pagers, mobile phones, and smartphones, as well as social media, would eventually play a big role in future generations and their quest for independence and adulthood.

In any new market there are pioneers, and the youth market was no different. Had it not been for Eugene Gilbert, who in 1945 founded Gil-Bert Teen Age Services, the first marketing research firm focused on teenagers, and Helen Valentine, the founder and editor in chief of *Seventeen*, the first magazine for female teenagers, in 1944, the youth market might not exist as it does today. Both Gilbert and Valentine are credited with identifying and treating teenagers as unique and different from children and adults.

According to a two-part profile in the *New Yorker* in 1958, titled "A Caste, a Culture, a Market," Mr. Gilbert was early to the game. In the spring of 1944, he was working as a stock boy selling shoes. Sports shoes weren't selling, so Gilbert proposed a study to his boss to understand why. He discovered that teenage boys were unaware that the store was even selling them. Once the store began advertising to teenagers, sports shoes began flying off the shelves.

Gilbert did two things that were considered radical at the time. The first was that he hired teenagers to engage other teenagers in market research; he rightly believed that they didn't trust adults. The second was that he increased the awareness of teenagers by writing a weekly column called "What Young People Think," which was distributed by the Associated Press. Before long, Marshall Field's, Esso, the US Army, and *Seventeen* magazine were clients.

Seventeen, under the initial stewardship of Helen Valentine, provided unique content to teenage girls and a dedicated channel for advertisers. According to *Advertising Age*, "Its editorial content, fashion pages, and special features, combined with a rapid circulation growth, created a perfect vehicle for advertisers to reach young consumers." *Seventeen*'s readership exploded to 1 million within the first year, and Valentine is largely credited for introducing teenagers to US companies.

This is important, because up until that point in time, businesses knew children, they knew adults, and they knew older people. Yet virtually all marketing and communications were done toward working-age adults, since they were perceived as the ones with the spending power. Gilbert and Valentine created the environment for a seismic paradigm shift that fundamentally changed the way businesses developed, implemented, and sold products and services.

The Role of Pop Culture and the Media

The awareness of teenagers, as well as the youth market and its counterculture, quickly spilled into the national ethos in the United States. Radio, and the newer medium of television, carried the first sounds and sights of youth culture into American homes and automobiles, and advertisers flocked to them. Before long, the world was introduced to the likes of Bill Haley & His Comets, Bo Diddley, Fats Domino, Little Richard, Jerry Lee Lewis, Elvis Presley, and Chuck Berry.

Berry, who died at the age of 90 in 2017, had a particular impact because he understood teenagers better than any other artist of the time. Not only did he sing to them, but some of his earliest hits were about them and their experiences, including "Sweet Little Sixteen." According to *Billboard* magazine, "Berry injected a cocksure 'we know better than the adults' attitude into rock—something his predecessors and peers hadn't yet dared to do. That youth-privileging outlook was essential in transforming rock n' roll from a musical fad into an irresistible attitude and lifestyle that infected teens and spread across America (also, it arguably paved the way for the massive generational divide of the '60s)."

It's worth noting as an aside that so many of the cultural and social touch points that we identify today as belonging to boomers weren't actually created by boomers; they were only consumed by them. This is vitally important today, because we cannot assume that boomers will design products and services or innovate marketing and communication strategies for themselves. There is a wide opportunity for the preceding generation, as well as Gen X, Millennials, and Gen Z, to tap into the immense size and buying power of the boomers, as long as they are willing to tap into the zeitgeist of the generation.

Many of the social change leaders of the period were also not boomers. In a 2019 article for the *New Yorker*, Louis Menand noted, "When the youngest boomer graduated from high school, Ronald Reagan was President and the Vietnam War had been over for seven years."

Boomers would make their mark in due time. However, it wouldn't happen until much later in the twentieth century. Elton John, born in 1947, wouldn't have his first hit, "Our Song," until 1970. Stevie Nicks, born in 1948, wouldn't join Fleetwood Mac until 1975. Tommy Hilfiger, born in 1951, didn't establish his namesake brand until 1985. Bill Gates, the "Father of Microsoft," born in 1955, didn't launch his company until 1975; it went public in 1985. Madonna, born in 1958, didn't become the "Queen of Pop" until the 1980s. Bono, born in 1960, didn't achieve international fame until the 1987 release of *The Joshua Tree*. And Sandra Bullock, born in 1964, didn't have her first breakout role with the action thriller *Speed* until 1994, nearly two years after the first boomer president, Bill Clinton, born in 1946, took office.

Scripted television from the middle century highlighted the social conformity of the time but also youth culture and the emerging movements that challenged the status quo: *I Love Lucy* delved into intercultural marriage, *The Honeymooners* touched on racial and gender inequality, and *Leave It to Beaver* examined the influence of teenagers in the modern American family.

It was no coincidence that none of those shows regularly featured older people and most were focused on youth. Those that did touch on older people, through the occasional guest appearance or recurring role, portrayed them as helpless, bizarre, or even comical—especially if they deviated from the accepted archetype of the time—deteriorating or in decline, demonized, or just outright ignored. That meant that many of the most absurd biases were reinforced and broadcast both in this country and around the world. Our sights became fixed on a monolithic view of older people that wasn't positive. This mass media bias persisted from the onset of the television age until recently, when real and rational depictions of older people in popular culture became more commonplace.

Hollywood and the new media establishment have begun to shift their attitudes away from creating programming exclusively for younger people and adults. They are even beginning to adjust the ways older people and older women, in particular, are portrayed. One of the first shows that focused almost exclusively on the lives of older women was the 1980s hit *The Golden Girls*. Today, shows such as *Grace and Frankie* present a more realistic portrayal of individuals in their sixties, seventies, eighties, and beyond. This means that television executives and producers are starting to wake up and see the value in the older market and the marketable stories of an older population.

Advertisers and Brands Take Notice

It wasn't just media that changed in midcentury. Advertising was changing, too, and the seminal moment occurred in 1963, when Pepsi-Cola launched a nationwide media campaign that showed young people doing the things that young people do, including swimming, cycling, and skiing. For the first time ever, the product or its effectiveness was barely mentioned. Pepsi was selling young people a vision of themselves and called to them, "Come alive! You're in the Pepsi generation!"

The Pepsi campaign was essentially an anti-advertisement and may have been inspired by Volkswagen's 1959 "Think Small" campaign. The message resonated with the emerging counterculture, made youth aspirational, and saw success. Due to its success, other companies would use the Pepsi approach as a blueprint to speak to young people. Recent examples include Patagonia's 2011 "Don't Buy This Jacket" and Doritos' 2019 "Another Level."

The shift to marketing to younger people wasn't just a short-term fad. It was dramatic, and its reverberations have been felt for decades, not only in the way products and services are sold to consumers but also in the way they are developed. In many ways, we have come to believe that young people are the most valuable of all of the demographics and youth should be valued before anything else.

Many of the brands that launched for the youth market in the 1960s are brands that we consider to be iconic today: Nike, Ralph Lauren, Calvin Klein, the North Face, and the Gap. For the most part, the youth market has remained central to their strategy. Their advertisements have consistently projected a portrait of youth, adapting to shifting cultural norms of youth culture, rather than aging with their core customers.

By the end of the 1970s, youth advertising and youth culture had intertwined to such an extent that they were a normal feature of life in many developed nations. Recognizing that the most rebellious of the youth cultures of the 1960s had been commodified by entrepreneurs and later by mundane retail outlets, some young people searched for identities that could not be quickly co-opted or that embraced consumers for their own ends; the punk culture of the late 1970s and early 1980s and grunge in the early 1990s are perfect examples of this.

On August 1, 1981, MTV launched. Its target audience was 12-

to 34-year-olds, with a particular emphasis on teens and young adults. It was the first television channel specifically dedicated to this audience, and its goal was to do something unprecedented at the time: to broadcast music videos twenty-four hours a day. Music was not the only thing that was emphasized in this youth culture. TV and film soon found their footing as important to America's youth and society. The famed 1980s teen movie director John Hughes presented his characters as witty and trying to find meaning in their world, in which they were ignored or misunderstood.

My own youth in the 1980s and 1990s was dominated by brands such as United Colors of Benetton, Guess, and Abercrombie & Fitch that actively went after me and my peers by pushing against social and cultural norms and commodifying change. My generation, Generation X, named after the book of the same title by Douglas Coupland, spent our free time in roller rinks and shopping malls. We were the first full generation engrossed by MTV and the first to socially surf the web.

Even though United Colors of Benetton was founded in 1965 by the siblings Luciano, Giuliana, Carlo, and Gilberto Benetton, it wasn't until the 1980s that the company's innovation and marketing prowess grabbed the attention of the youth market in the crowded global marketplace. Much of Benetton's success is due to Oliviero Toscani, the controversial Italian photographer and art director who joined the company in 1982 and was responsible for campaigns that tackled issues such as inequality, racism, and corporate hypocrisy. Those campaigns tapped into the zeitgeist of the time and captivated the youth market; and advertisers of the future will have to tap into an older market with the same vigor.

Teenagers began doing more than challenging the norms of popular and consumer culture; they began to organize and flex their political muscle. They went after the status quos of gender, race, and sexuality. Above all, they challenged the authority of adults.

The idea of pushing back against the establishment isn't necessarily new. It seems to happen with every generation. However, there was something about this period of the middle century that led to greater, and almost universal, distrust of older people. In essence, old was bad and society should value youth above all. The problem with this attitude is that we all get old at some point. Young people were betting against themselves and the coming Super Age.

In 1964, an "us-versus-them" attitude began to emerge. In November of that year, Jack Weinberg, a 24-year-old environmental activist who was involved in the New Left and Free Speech Movement at the University of California, Berkeley, coined the saying "Don't trust anyone over thirty," which became a rallying cry for the boomers as they reached for the reins of social, cultural, political, and economic dominance.

Pro-youth and anti-aging messages bled into popular music, too. The British band the Who sang in 1965, "I hope I die before I get old," and the Beatles asked in 1967, "Will you still need me, will you still feed me, when I'm sixty-four?" The embrace of youthfulness and the rejection of maturity—both the state of being and the state of mind—became central to our belief structure, and it's been damn near impossible to shake.

Over the course of early recorded history, many traditions were based on living a short life. And up until the emergence of the youth culture and even into its formative years, there was a stark line drawn between childhood and adulthood.

No place was this more evident than in the workplace, where men mostly subscribed to the same sartorial style. Visually, adulthood, at least for the first half to three-quarters of the twentieth century, meant being suited in gray, black, or blue with a tie and hair combed back perfectly with the help of some variant of Brylcreem. Adults dressed in a relatively uniform style, regardless of their age. That started to change when the counterculture of the 1960s entered the workplace and older people were systematically displaced.

Youth at Work

The injection of youth culture into the workplace began when boomers entered the workforce en masse in the 1960s. However, it wasn't until the 1990s that Gen Xers inserted "Casual Friday" into the corporate culture and the lexicon. And it wasn't until the 2000s that Millennials made ubiquitous a hoodie and jeans as the de rigueur uniform for the young, innovative, tech-driven, transformative class. The only people who still wear suits in the office are square, part of the establishment, outdated, or old.

We can lay some blame on boomers for the development of our ageist corporate culture and the changes to our approach to work that favored the young. It's even possible to trace boomers' direct influence on the creation and amplification of ageist culture. However, subsequent generations have also been culpable in perpetrating and magnifying negative misperceptions of older people and deifying youth.

Modern-day CEOs, regardless of their ages, have also subscribed to youth before all. The Millennial Facebook founder Mark Zuckerberg famously said that "young people are just smarter." Even Alibaba's cofounder and former executive chairman, Jack Ma, got into the act when he gave this advice to older people at the 2018 World Economic Forum: "When you are 50 to 60 years old, spend time training and developing young people, the next generation. When you are over 60 years old, you better stay with your grandchildren."

The attitude that in the workplace, being young is good and being old is bad stems from unfounded attitudes that all older people are slow, inflexible, and tech illiterate. This overarching negative bias toward older people has prompted a growing number of young men and women in their thirties to have plastic surgery to maintain their youthful look. The Joie de Vivre hotel founder and former Airbnb executive Chip Conley recently began charging individuals as young as 37 $5,000 for a week and $10,000 for two weeks to learn how to be a "modern elder"—"A time when individuals have a lot to offer, but also a lot to learn"—at his Modern Elder Academy in Baja California Sur, Mexico. In the course, participants learn how to see their midlife and beyond as a productive period of life.

From the classical era to the Industrial Revolution, youth and vitality were desired qualities. However, it wasn't until the early twentieth century that we, as a society, began to focus a large amount of our energies on individuals staying, or at least appearing to be, forever young. Today, the US beauty and cosmetic industry alone generates nearly $600 billion per year, projected to grow to $800 billion by 2025. The growth in gyms and plastic surgery is expected to continue, too. More and more of us are obsessing over our physical appearance and want to remain youthful looking. We are rejecting aging. We are rejecting getting old.

The Ugly Side of Beauty

In no other industry are the celebration of youth and the war on aging waged more regularly or with the same level of vigor as in the beauty, fashion, and wellness industries. As with most things, there is a historical background. It's understood that Cleopatra, the queen of Egypt, took a daily bath in sour donkey milk, thought at the time to keep skin youthful in appearance. The Chinese Tang Dynasty empress regnant Wu Zetian maintained her youthful appearance by washing her face with cold water and "fairy powder," carefully harvested and prepared Chinese motherwort. Women in Elizabethan England, on the other hand, placed thin slices of raw meat on their face. And women in eighteenth-century France took baths in aged wine.

It wasn't until the twentieth century that pro-youth and anti-aging messages were amplified. Women, in particular, were bombarded with images of nearly impossible beauty standards that challenged them to fight against the natural aging process, and the earliest advertisements were typically driven by the urges of men. The soap company Palmolive created what is perhaps the earliest and most noted example of anti-aging advertising by inventing the problem of "middle-aged" skin. Beauty companies embraced age shaming as core to their success and preyed upon the anxieties brought about by the unrealistic beauty standards that have plagued women for generations.

It's not just anti-aging messages that are problematic; it is the lack of representation of older people in the media. According to AARP, more than a third of the US population is older than 50, but this group shows up in only 15 percent of media images.

As a culture, we began to internalize the message that aging was somehow bad—something to hide or reduce the effects of. Advertisers didn't just try to capitalize on the youth market, they also tapped into our insecurities about mortality and living longer.

Today, more than one-third of women over 60 say they've used anti-aging products in the last three months. According to Statista, "In 2020, the global anti-aging market was estimated to be worth about 585 billion US dollars. The anti-aging market is estimated to see a compound annual growth rate (CAGR) of seven percent between 2021 and 2026."

For decades, feminists have argued that companies with household names such as Noxzema, Elizabeth Arden, and Max Factor have contributed to an unattainable beauty standard that reinforced a patriarchal, heterosexual, anti-aging society. However, it wasn't until 2017 that *Allure* magazine took the first step to reject the idea of anti-aging. In a statement, it proclaimed, "We are making a resolution to stop using the term 'anti-aging.' Whether we know it or not, we're subtly reinforcing the message that aging is a condition we need to battle— think antianxiety meds, antivirus software, or antifungal spray." This stance was radical because *Allure* is a magazine dedicated to beauty and one that relies on the advertising dollars of the beauty industry to support its publication.

In bombarding the public with messages and images that celebrated youth and sidelined older people, mass media and their intertwined consumerism essentially urged individuals to fight old age, as if it were a battle we could win. Today, mantras such as "70 is the new 50" emphasize the need to be vigorous and vital for as long as possible; however, they provide no alternative scenarios for those with degenerative diseases or loss of cognition or those who are suffering from loneliness. They do nothing more than make people fear the future and getting older.

It's no wonder we eschew celebrating birthdays the older we get. It's no wonder we fight aging at every turn. We would do well to look back to Roman times and celebrate living to a ripe old age, not just being born and being young.

As any parent will tell you, it takes a huge amount of time, energy, and financial resources to prepare infants for childhood, children for adolescence, and teenagers for adulthood. In fact, experts from across society, including but not limited to scientists, sociologists, physicians, educators, and policy makers, develop road maps and development standards to keep young people on track by measuring their health, social, and educational progress. Oddly enough, though, we do nothing to prepare for a long life. There is no road map. There are no standards.

The fictional line of demarcation between old and young, our blanket embrace—dare I say worship—of youth, and our negative attitudes and stereotypes toward older people, are problems. Though the youth culture that developed in the mid-twentieth century may have hardened our historical views that younger people are superior to older people in every way, it is possible and essential for us to turn around and become anti-anti-aging.

We need to be able to celebrate success past the early years. We must normalize the idea of finding love for the first time and getting married in our forties. We should be excited for individuals who choose to have children in their fifties. And we should applaud the brave souls who chase their dreams and become entrepreneurs in their sixties or beyond. Life doesn't stop at age 25; it never has. Being pro-longevity and embracing life past youth is the only way to accurately reflect our new age-diverse society and take advantage of the vast social and economic promise of the Super Age. If we don't, the best-case scenario is that we will lose out on the promise of the future. The worst-case scenario is that the economy will falter and longevity gains will begin to be erased.

| 4 |

Building on Longevity Gains

In 1835, Charles Darwin, the "Father of Evolution," reached the Galápagos Islands aboard the Royal Navy ship HMS *Beagle*. While there, either he or a member of his expedition team captured a tortoise named Harriet, who lived for 176 years and died in 2006 at the Australia Zoo in Queensland.

Harriet wasn't alive only during Darwin's visit; she was alive during the California Gold Rush, the US Civil War, and the invention of the light bulb—all before her fiftieth birthday. Harriet was also alive during other major global events, including the dedication of the Statue of Liberty, the birth of modern aviation, two world wars, the Bolshevik Revolution, the Spanish flu, the Great Depression, the moon landing, the fall of the Berlin Wall, and the September 11, 2001, attacks on the United States, to name a few. But Harriet isn't the only long-lived animal around.

In a 2016 study by the American Association for the Advancement of Science, researchers found that, on average, another animal lived one hundred years longer than Harriet: the Greenland shark, which has an average life span of about 272 years. It is believed that the Greenland shark, which is native to the North Atlantic, can live more than four hundred years.

This means that the average Greenland shark nearing the end of its life today would have been alive for the first Spanish missions to California. The oldest Greenland shark could have been alive when the Pilgrims from England arrived at Plymouth Rock, Massachusetts, or for the debuts of Shakespeare's *The Tempest* and *Henry VIII*.

Other organisms in nature are known to live considerably longer than the Galápagos tortoise and Greenland shark. They include the Methuselah tree, a bristlecone pine in California that is nearly 4,800 years old and considered to be the oldest known complex organism on Earth. Other creatures that age very slowly can live up to hundreds of years, showing little signs of senescence—also known as cellular aging—and include rockfish, clams, lobsters, and jellyfish.

Extended longevity such as that of the Galápagos tortoise and the Greenland shark does not come to humans naturally or easily. In fact, it has remained elusive and constrained, perhaps due to the confines of our imagination; the upper limit today is around 120, and the only verified person to surpass the current upper limit is Jeanne Calment of France, who died in 1997 at the age of 122 years and 164 days.

For the vast majority of history, medical research has focused on improving health on the front end of life. That led to an improved survival rate for infants and children to transition into adolescents and adults, which pushed up the average life expectancy. Today, a growing number of individuals are working to cure age-related diseases. Focusing on the middle and end of life has the potential to push the boundaries of human longevity even further.

Some of the most promising studies already suggest that the first person to live to 150 may have already been born. There is a new class of individuals who are challenging the notion that there is an upper limit to human life expectancy. As noted expert Aubrey de Grey, the chief science officer at the SENS Research Foundation, recently pointed out to me, "We're approaching longevity escape velocity," meaning that once we pass the known upper limit of human life expectancy, there will be little stopping us from extending life even further. It's akin to humanity reaching for the heavens; at one point, manned orbital travel seemed impossible, but we made it into space, landed on the moon, and established a space station, and witnessed the first "space tourists" rocketing to the stars.

No matter how long we extend healthy life, it will mean nothing to society if we don't adjust our collective attitudes toward longevity and toward older people. Currently, most people see them only as a social and economic burden. Extending healthy longevity and closing the longevity gap—the difference between life spans of different peoples from different genders, races, regions, and economic groups—will help turn that narrative around so that we can tap into the incredible economic and social potential of older people. We can empower people to remain part of society for the duration of their lives.

Malleable Mortality

Even though humans have lived very short lives during most of history, they've nearly always been consumed with their mortality. Our ancestors were so obsessed with it that they thought themselves to be the only animals that understood death. In fact, as late as the early 1970s, the anthropologist Ernest Becker wrote in his Pulitzer Prize–winning book *The Denial of Death*, "The knowledge of death is reflective and conceptual, and animals are spared it." Our behaviors, on the other hand, are ensconced in religious traditions and the relentless chase for the fountain of youth, as well as the erection of monuments that stand to our memory long after we have departed this earth.

It wasn't until recently that we began to learn that other creatures understand death, too, including dolphins, whales, elephants, and chimpanzees. Though the idea that humans are the only species to understand death has begun to fade, it seems very likely that humans remain the only species that is fixated on the end and, in many cases, on how to slow the rate of aging, extend life, or cheat death.

The late nineteenth and early twentieth centuries were when society first started to measurably improve the human condition and extend the human life span by employing advances in nutrition, sanitation, social welfare, and scientific ingenuity. These innovations were almost always made with the intent of improving infant and child mortality. With a pinch of luck and a dash of circumstance, we quickly became aware that those advances could also be used to prolong our longevity. But it wasn't until very recently—in the last thirty years—that a select few scientific pioneers and large-dollar investors began to believe in and invest in ways to extend human life past the realm of our wildest dreams.

Up until that time, researchers had focused nearly all of their energy and resources on improving the survival rate and living conditions of infants and children in both the developed and the developing worlds, which resulted in a longer average life span. The shift in focus to extending life for adults by improving healthy adult years is a radical departure from the past and will be a hallmark of the Super Age. It will also be where big-money investors will place their bets, since the potential return on investment is very good.

Although the likelihood is very high that longevity will be extended, there is no guarantee. We would be wise to heed the words of my colleague Andrew Scott, one of the inspirations for this book and a coauthor of *The 100-Year Life: Living and Working in an Age of Longevity* and *The New Long Life: A Framework for Flourishing in a Changing World*, and his now regularly expressed opinion, "Human life and longevity are inherently malleable."

Andrew's point is as aspirational as it is ominous and reminds us that life expectancy can expand as well as contract. There have been notable cases in history, especially recent history, when life expectancy gains have been erased, due in large part to individual behaviors or bad public policy. This means that if people want to continue to extend life, they will have to continue making the right decisions and investments to support this goal. Governments, in particular, will need to encourage people to eat better, exercise more, and engage in preventive care.

Obviously, there will be hiccups, and some of them will be out of our control, including major health events such as the covid-19 pandemic. Preliminary 2020 data from the Centers for Disease Control and Prevention (CDC) recorded a significant drop in life expectancy because of the pandemic, which brought US life expectancy down to 2006 levels. And early in 2021, the US government reported that life expectancy had dropped by nearly two years—the largest drop since the end of World War II.

The big challenge is improving in areas in which the government has control. In the United States more than seventy thousand people died in 2019 of drug overdoses, making them the leading cause of injury-related death, according to the CDC. Suicides and the drug epidemic, driven largely by the worsening economy, combined with prescription and illicit opioid addiction, pulled down the US life expectancy for three years starting in 2014. Alcoholism, smoking, and poor diet, which led to a slew of noncommunicable diseases such as cancer and diabetes, also played a big role in holding US longevity down.

In another example, austerity, which came into effect in the United Kingdom in 2010 in response to the Great Recession, had a negative impact on that country's longevity gains. In the groundbreaking study *Fair Society, Healthy Lives: The Marmot Review*, Sir Michael Marmot and his team found that the draconian government cutbacks to social welfare and health care programs increased and, in many cases, exacerbated the gaps between the rich and the poor, including life span.

The Marmot Review further noted that austerity had led to an expectation that more people will live in poor health for a longer period of time, which, ironically, ends up costing the government more money. Austerity stalled national life expectancy gains that had been increasing for more than a hundred years, reversed them for lower-income people, and perhaps delayed the United Kingdom's entry into the Super Age. The report was explicit in its assessment that improvements to life expectancy have stalled in the UK's poorest areas, and women in the poorest 10 percent of all areas have experienced longevity declines.

We must be ready for setbacks as we reach twenty or even thirty more years of healthy life. We must be ready for disappointments, even as scientists make new breakthroughs in understanding the mechanics of aging and we push past the current upper limits of longevity. We will eventually push past them, but our progress may be interrupted or held back at times by poor personal decision making, bad public policy, and yes, even pandemics.

Disease Management

The awareness of science during the First (1760–1840) and Second (1860–1920) Industrial Revolutions paved the way for germ theory, which led to the cleaner water and improved sanitation standards that revolutionized the way we produce and consume food and water, dispose of waste, and live. It also led to the discovery of the positive effects of handwashing by the Hungarian physician Ignaz Semmelweis in 1847. Semmelweis was mocked for his discovery and ironically died of sepsis in 1865 at the age of 47 due to an infected cut on his hand. All of those scientific breakthroughs started us on the way toward longer life spans.

Government also began to take a larger role in the protection of human life and social welfare. Protections for laborers, especially child laborers, became normal. Governments started to provide clean water, treat sewage, and dispose of refuse. It was a period in which governments began to set standards for food supply production and protection. Arguably, those interventions came in response to major events or seminal exposés such as Upton Sinclair's novel *The Jungle*. Regardless, they have had the effect of improving human life and longevity.

It was in that period that scientists began to improve upon Edward Jenner's smallpox vaccine and Louis Pasteur developed the first rabies vaccine. It was the dawn of bacteriology, when developments such as pasteurization, the process by which water and certain packaged and nonpackaged foods are treated with mild heat to eliminate pathogens and extend shelf life, became widely used. Scientists began developing antitoxins and vaccines to combat diseases such as anthrax, cholera, diphtheria, plague, tetanus, tuberculosis, and typhoid, all of which rapidly improved the likelihood that an infant would live through childhood and make it to adulthood.

The end of the First World War, which occurred between the first two industrial revolutions, brought with it one of the greatest pandemics the world has ever seen. The "Spanish flu," caused by an H1N1 virus, likely originated in the United States and, according to the CDC, caused the deaths of an estimated 50 million people worldwide, including 675,000 in the United States.

By all accounts, the Spanish flu was a disruptive event on a scale far greater than the current covid-19 pandemic, which has raced around the world at breakneck speed. The primary difference between the two is that the latter most afflicted the old, while the former most afflicted the young. In fact, 99 percent of all Spanish flu deaths were among people under the age of 65. Compare that to the 80 percent of all covid-19 deaths that are among people over the age of 65.

Both outbreaks forced the world to rethink its attitude toward disease and how best to respond. As today, during the Spanish flu pandemic there was no coordinated national response in the United States, outside of general guidelines. In the current pandemic, there has been more of an international response, thanks in part to institutions such as the European Union and the World Health Organization, but for the most part, nations have been on their own in deciding how to deal with the disease. The most effective advice that individuals have been given today, outside of getting vaccinated, all but matches the advice given by C. E. Waters, a chemist who worked for the US Bureau of Standards as chief of organic chemistry, in his 1918 poem "Rules for Influenza": in essence, wash your hands, wear a mask, and avoid crowds.

According to Lloyd Alter, a professor at the Ryerson School of Interior Design in Toronto, our response to disease and our ideas about sanitation are the story of modern architecture, too. In 2020, he told me that "The modern style of the house is based around germ theory; light, air, and openness are central tenets." These ideas of germ theory contributed to the development of the bathroom and sewage systems that we are accustomed to today.

Elizabeth Yuko explained in a 2020 Bloomberg CityLab article, "How Infectious Disease Defined the American Bathroom," "The modern bathroom developed alongside outbreaks of tuberculosis, cholera and influenza; its standard fixtures, wallcoverings, floorings, and finishes were implemented, in part, to promote health and hygiene in the home at a time of widespread public health concerns." These "at-home" innovations were key to cutting the mortality rate and extending longevity, too.

Coming out of the covid-19 pandemic, I expect that we will see several modifications in the places where we live, work, and play. Hand-sanitizing stations, whether a sink with soap and running water or a hand sanitizer container, will become standard at the entryway of most homes and businesses. People and builders will finally embrace Japanese bidet-style toilets, which sanitize themselves and close automatically before flushing. Businesses will likely require temperature checks upon entry, to create a more disease-free environment. The fourth modification, and perhaps the most costly and long term, is that businesses will install machines to create negative air pressure, which regularly brings in fresh air from the outside, thus lowering the risk of airborne disease transmission. All of these interventions will lead to lower levels of infection from communicable diseases, which will lead to a decrease in deaths and an increase in overall longevity, in a way similar to the decades after the Spanish flu.

The years following the Spanish flu, especially the middle of the twentieth century, saw vast improvements in vaccine research and development. Advanced methods of growing viruses in laboratories led to many discoveries and innovations, including the creation of a polio vaccine in 1955. That discovery, by Jonas Salk at the University of Pittsburgh, was a national success that has, over time, all but eradicated the disease; polio can still be found in some of the poorest and most disadvantaged communities around the world, including places like Pakisan, Afghanistan, and Nigeria. Scientists went after other common childhood diseases, too, such as measles, for which they developed a vaccine by the late 1960s. There was a vaccine for mumps by 1967, rubella by 1969, and MMR (measles, mumps, rubella), a single vaccine that covered all three, by 1971. All of them enabled more children to live into adolescence and adulthood, which increased overall life expectancy.

That period also saw the development and rapid expansion of organ transplantation, which also contributed to extending life. The first human-to-human kidney transplant occurred in 1954 between identical twins in Peter Bent Brigham Hospital (now Brigham and Women's Hospital) in Boston, Massachusetts. It was followed in 1966 by the first pancreas transplant at the University of Minnesota by William Kelly and Richard Lillehei. In 1967, the first liver transplant occurred at the University of Pittsburgh, done by Thomas Starzl. The first successful heart transplant also took place in 1967, at Groote Schuur Hospital in Cape Town, South Africa, by Christiaan Barnard. The US Department of Health and Human Services reported that an amazing 39,718 transplants were performed in the United States in 2019. On the surface, these might not sound like longevity extenders, but every life saved in the short term and the long term contributes to the overall extension in average life expectancy.

Clean Water, Full Stomachs

In the late 1960s, the United States passed a large amount of legislation aimed at improving the environment by reducing toxic air pollution, cleaning up hundreds of streams and rivers, and creating a permanent, federally empowered Environmental Protection Agency, which came into effect in 1970. Similar undertakings occurred across OECD (Organization for Economic Cooperation and Development) countries in Europe and Asia, too. These, of course, all led to improved global health standards and increased average longevity.

In the United States, only 4.1 percent of the population, or just over 3 million people, were aged 65 and over in 1900, the first year data for the 65-and-over population were collected. In 1950, the figure was 8 percent; in 2000, it was 12.4 percent. In 2020, the US population aged 65 and over was 16.9 percent, or about 56 million people, and it will climb to 22 percent, or just over 96 million people, by 2050. That means that by around 2040, just after the United States enters the Super Age, the population of people over 65 will be greater than the entire population just over a hundred years ago.

In 1900, 30 percent of all deaths in the United States occurred in children less than 5 years of age compared to just 1.4 percent by the end of the twentieth century. The same general downward trend has been happening globally, too, ever since the UN Inter-agency Group for Child Mortality Estimation began collecting data in the 1950s. In fact, since 1990, according to the World Food Programme, the global under-5 mortality rate has dropped by nearly two-thirds, from 93 deaths per 1,000 live births in 1990 to 39 in 2018. This is equivalent to one in eleven children dying before reaching age 5 in 1990, compared to one in twenty-six in 2018.

The Future Is Here

Once scientists solved for youth mortality, a select group of them began looking at the other end of life, studying the intricacies of DNA and other molecular biodynamics that may be poised to offer even more dramatic boosts to longevity. This comes not from setting out explicitly to conquer aging per se, which remains somewhat controversial in mainstream science, but from researchers developing new drugs and therapies for maladies of growing old, such as heart disease and diabetes. They are being funded by billionaires and venture capital firms that believe that they will receive a good return on their investment.

It's generally believed that aging influences our risk of developing many diseases, particularly chronic, noncommunicable diseases. According to the National Council on Aging, roughly 80 percent of older Americans have at least one chronic disease, and nearly 70 percent have at least two—the most common being hypertension, arthritis, and diabetes. According to a 2017 RAND study, a shocking "60 percent of [all] American adults now live with at least one chronic condition; 42 percent have more than one."

As sanitation and science improve, which invariably leads to the conquest of infectious diseases, such as smallpox in 1980, and our societies become older, the prevalence of infectious diseases will decrease, while noncommunicable diseases will become more of a threat and take up more resources. A 2018 report by the Milken Institute suggested that the cost of treatment for the top seven noncommunicable diseases plus the loss of productivity among all age groups costs the United States alone nearly $1 trillion annually. The greatest and most recent exception to this rule was the outbreak of covid-19 in the United States in 2020, which cost trillions of dollars and threw the economy into recession.

There are plenty of things that we as individuals can do to live a longer and healthier life. Dan Buettner, for example, in his groundbreaking 2008 book, *The Blue Zones: Lessons for Living Longer from the People Who've Lived the Longest*, attempted to identify why individuals living in certain communities around the world—from Okinawa, Japan, to Sardinia, Italy, to Nicoya, Costa Rica—live exceptionally long lives with relatively compressed morbidity. He found the general thread to be that Blue Zones occur where individuals live in tight-knit communities, remain physically and mentally active, and eat a healthy, locally sourced diet. Older people in these locales also manage to stay closely connected and intertwined with the social and economic fabric of their communities.

Doctors and public health officials today nearly universally advise individuals to eat well and stay active throughout their lives. They also warn against the dangers of drinking and smoking too much. However, there is a growing body of evidence to suggest that our social connections play an outsized role in our longevity, too. In fact, according to a 2015 study from Brigham Young University, social isolation heightens health risks as much as smoking fifteen cigarettes a day or having alcohol use disorder. Just staying connected to family and friends and being integrated into one's community could very well extend human life, and more importantly, healthy human life, by years.

How many years might be added to a life if healthy behaviors, social connectedness, and scientific breakthroughs are combined? A few longevity enthusiasts suggest a possible increase of decades. Most others believe in more modest gains. And when will they come? Are we a decade away? Twenty years? Fifty years? What happens if the paradigm shifts toward treating aging as a disease? Even without radical scientific change, the United Nations estimates that life expectancy over the next century could reach nearly one hundred years in the developed world and nearly ninety years in the developing world.

Tackling Aging as a Disease

There are basically two accepted biological theories as to why senescence or cellular aging occurs. The first, known as "programmed theory," suggests that there is an "aging clock" that shuts off certain biological processes at certain times. The other, known as "damage theory" or "error theory," suggests that there is damage to cells and tissue over time. Both theories suggest that the older we get, the less likely we are to be able to fight off disease, decline, and decay. Senescence also contributes to our physical changes, including the graying of our hair and the wrinkling of our skin.

Creating a healthy hundred-year life is not only a noble goal but one that could free up resources that could be used to solve other more pressing issues. If we don't, as Jim Mellon, a coauthor of *Juvenescence: Investing in the Age of Longevity* and an investor in dozens of pro-longevity health companies, told me in 2020, "We may drown under the costs of a longer life with slow decline." But creating a hundred-year life means that we need to shift our thinking about old age.

Jim's opinion is that, up until now and in the near term, much of the research around longevity will bear fruit, but most of it will fail before it gets to human trials. In his words, "There are a lot of things that we can cure at the cellular level or in animals, like mice. However, our models don't consider aging. We'll need to test more of these hypotheses in real-life situations."

The first substantial lab discovery regarding longevity occurred in 1993 at the University of California, San Francisco, where a molecular biologist and biogerontologist, Cynthia Kenyon, made the pioneering discovery that a single gene mutation could double the life span of healthy, fertile roundworms. Her findings demonstrated, for the first time, that aging can be controlled to some degree. That discovery, of course, introduced ethical gray areas if it were to be applied to human longevity, the biggest issues being who would get access to a dramatic extension of life and whether such an innovation would be reserved for the rich.

Kenyon's discovery ushered in what historians in the future may see as the beginning of the longevity gold rush, a period in which large financial investments will fund longevity science, push innovation forward, and presumably extend human life and change the way humans live. She inspired and continues to inspire droves of scientists, including David Sinclair, the author of *Lifespan: Why We Age— and Why We Don't Have To*. Sinclair made his initial discoveries while doing postdoctoral work at Massachusetts Institute of Technology, where he discovered the mechanism that leads to aging in yeast. His work suggests that the "malfunction" of a group of proteins in the human body called sirtuins causes aging. Though his research is promising, this theory has yet to be proved.

Laura Deming, a partner in the Longevity Fund, a seed and Series A venture capital firm that has invested $37 million in longevity science research, was also inspired by Kenyon's work and the "fundamental unfairness" of aging, meaning that so much of it is currently spent in decline. Deming believes that much like our first foray into outer space, the science of longevity needs a single clinical success story to inspire humanity. It will be a momentous and possibly seminal event for humankind, because it will cause the average person to realize the potential of extending human life in real and measurable ways.

In the medium term, which I believe will happen in our lifetime, we will likely witness essential research and experience interventions that will begin to transform human longevity in small but real and meaningful ways. However, they could force some ethically challenging decisions, including whether DNA should be sequenced in utero.

Most longevity experts believe that the first serious leap forward will happen within the next few years. In 2019, one of the pioneers in this line of research, Nir Barzilai, began the first clinical trial with the express goal of targeting aging. Dr. Barzilai is also noted for having discovered the first "longevity gene" in humans. His research has established that the gene variant that leads to high HDL, or "good," cholesterol levels is linked to healthy aging and extreme longevity.

Barzilai's latest project, Targeting Aging with Metformin (TAME), has the potential to fundamentally change the way we age. Unlike the fountain of youth, there is no promise of remaining young forever or turning back the clock. Rather, this drug therapy could change the way individuals age by postponing or preventing the onset of debilitating diseases that are inherently connected with old age. People won't gain youth per se, but they will have the potential to lead longer and healthier lives, which could have huge implications for society.

Another promising and wildly futuristic-sounding project relating to organ regeneration entered clinical trials in 2020. This project, by LyGenesis, a biotechnology company with an organ regeneration program that is affiliated with the University of Pittsburgh Innovation Institute, aims to exploit the function of the lymph nodes. The lymph nodes are essentially the human body's bioreactors, and they are extremely efficient at fighting off disease and replicating tissues. There are about five hundred to six hundred lymph nodes throughout the human body.

LyGenesis uses regenerative biology for a therapeutic life therapy to rebuild tissue and ectopic organs. LyGenesis scientists have already shown success in mice and pigs. Their first clinical trial will attempt to grow healthy liver cells in human lymph nodes. LyGenesis's goal is to create a human liver with low to zero risk of transplant rejection or a bridge therapy that will keep patients alive while they wait for a human-to-human transplant.

When I asked LyGenesis cofounder and CEO Michael Hufford about the future beyond the first clinical trial, he responded, "We [human beings] are here because we have some innate ability to fight infection. The lymph nodes are these little factories all around the body, and we can use them to regrow other organs that can fight off disease, like the thymus, which produces T cells." Growing a new thymus could very well help older people fight off novel diseases, such as covid-19, as well as older, more common maladies, such as the flu and pneumonia, in which around 78 percent of all mortality occurs in the 65-and-over age group.

Living a longer, healthier life implies people will spend less time and money on being sick and will have more time in which they will be physically able and economically productive. This shift will inevitably lower national health care expenditures and give a bump to the GDP. Decreased productivity due to illness and caregiving responsibilities has become a drag on virtually every nation, and although health care spending creates economic activity, it also diminishes national productivity, especially in countries with a higher percentage of older people, resulting in a net loss.

The goal is no longer just to extend life expectancy but also to close the gap between the years that are lived in good health and those that are not. Life expectancy is only an estimate of how many years people might live, whereas healthy life expectancy is an estimate of how many years they might live in a healthy state. Globally, the gap between the two measures has been growing and currently stands at eight years. The gap is even wider when socioeconomic conditions are considered, and poor people always come out worst.

A lingering concern, at least among patient advocacy groups, is that novel therapies and medical interventions can be very expensive and may be available only to the wealthiest members of society. There is an expectation that there will not be equitable distribution to those less fortunate. This could mean that wealthier people, who are already living dramatically longer lives than the poor, could have their lives extended even further.

Investors such as Mellon insist that they wouldn't be in this if its purpose were only to extend the lives of a few billionaires, and none of them are interested in contributing to inequality. They argue that if we are able to cure aging, all of the associated diseases—cancer, heart disease, and others—could be cured, thus saving society trillions of dollars in health care costs. In essence, everyone will win.

Laura Deming went further, offering a frank assessment of older people, our long-life future, and the Longevity Fund's goals: "We want to increase the fraction of your life that is maximum functionality. We want to increase the amount of time individuals can contribute." This attitude is essential for the Super Age. Deming believes that the science of longevity is one of the best ways to combat ageism: "We're seeing both physical and cosmetic drugs and therapies that improve the way people feel and the way they look." Perhaps the only things holding us back at this moment are a lack of good start-up founders who are both pragmatic and efficient and a society that is willing to embrace a population that is older, on average, than ever before.

PART TWO

Demographic Dystopia

| 5 |

Perception Versus Reality

The challenge of actualizing the Super Age comes out of two per-vasive yet contrary narratives about aging and retirement: one is of a well-heeled, well-dressed, physically fit couple hitting a few rounds of golf at the club before meeting their equally affluent friends for drinks on the patio; the other is of a bent-over bag lady sifting through the garbage looking for bottles or cans to recycle or perhaps part of a sal-vageable discarded sandwich. Both are true and undeniable realities, but they are also extreme dominant narratives that get into the way of understanding the tremendous diversity of older populations and often into the way of our ability to envision the Super Age.

Looking past preconceived notions and unrealistic narratives will be an important ability for anyone who is looking to engage older populations. The misperceptions that have been reinforced by popu-lar television shows such as *The Golden Girls* and *The Cosby Show*, as well as blockbuster movies such as *Sixteen Candles*, *National Lampoon's Christmas Vacation*, and *Cocoon*, simply do not jive with the realities of a long life. Historically, a comfortable retirement was elusive for large swaths of the population and rejected by others. Life, especially later life, wasn't experienced equally in years past, and it certainly isn't today, making the bias that we hold toward older people fundamentally flawed. Our attitudes toward older people—specifically that they are retired from work and financially comfortable—tend to be fostered early on and reinforced over time in the home, the media, and the workplace, often without our knowledge or awareness.

This trope is so dominant and pervasive that if you google "retirement," dozens of well-to-do, mostly White couples smile back at you from the screen, presumably from the Florida or Mediterranean coast. This is by design, an ideal cooked up in some midcentury Madison Avenue boardroom, à la Don Draper in *Mad Men*, and reheated and resold dozens of times over the decades until it became central to our perception of the old. However, if we rely on this paradigm, we miss the real opportunities that come with a longer life and the Super Age.

Like all things, the concept of a comfortable and active retirement was created well before the "Mad men" got their hands on the idea. The earliest incarnations of retirement living in the United States date back to the 1920s. During that period, a handful of communities were built across the country by fraternal lodges, labor unions, and religious groups with the intent of providing their older members with a supportive living environment. It was a shift from the previous model of almshouses, convalescent homes, and nursing homes, which had their roots in the seventeenth century and had been designed to deliver care to individuals in an institutional setting.

It wasn't until the middle of the last century that a small group of innovators realized that a whole new group—retirees—was coming of age alongside teenagers, and they sold our predecessors on the idea of an easily accessible, comfortable retirement. In fact, a near-record high 57 percent of nonretired Americans still believe that they will have enough money to live comfortably in retirement. Yet this idea of retirement was due almost exclusively to older people at the time having more disposable wealth than previous generations had had, thanks to generous national pension schemes and corporate pensions. They also had an incredible amount of free time since, in many cases, they had either been removed from the workforce due to mandatory retirement measures endorsed by the government or made redundant due to cost-saving measures.

Much like the development of the youth market, a group of visionaries saw the opportunity to tap into this newly found wealth and free time. They constructed an idealized vision of retirement in which older individuals could stop working without fear of losing their economic security or health care coverage and live in leisure, spending their days on vocational pursuits. They created the modern retiree.

The Architects

Three retirement industry architects had the greatest influence on our foundational idea of what retirement and older age should look like: Ethel Percy Andrus, the founder and executive director of the National Retired Teachers Association (NRTA) and cofounder and executive director of the American Association of Retired Persons, known today as AARP; Leonard Davis, also a cofounder of AARP and the founder and CEO of Colonial Penn Group, a pioneering insurance company designed to provide coverage for people over the age of 65; and Delbert "Del" Eugene Webb, the developer of Sun City, Arizona, the first planned retirement community in the world.

In 1947, the retired educator and high school principal Ethel Percy Andrus launched the National Retired Teachers Association. According to legend, she got the inspiration to start an interest group for retired teachers after visiting her mentor, whom she found living in abject poverty in a chicken coop. As the story goes, the former educator had been forced to choose among the basics—lifesaving medicines, food, and shelter—so she chose to forgo adequate housing. Ethel would not stand for that and created an organization to advocate for the rights of older people, as well as promote massive government spending programs, like Social Security and Medicare.

In 1955, while working to find an insurance company to underwrite age-specific insurance policies for NRTA members, Dr. Andrus met Leonard Davis, who was working as an insurance broker in

Poughkeepsie, New York. Davis not only helped Dr. Andrus secure a Chicago-based insurance company to underwrite her members, but he also helped her launch AARP by providing $50,000 in initial seed capital in 1958.

Davis later went on to launch Colonial Penn Group, which provided insurance coverage to people over 65. The company grew to be one of the nation's largest insurance underwriters, mainly due to its early, intimate, and exclusive relationship with AARP—a relationship that was later broken up by an agreement, also known as a private letter ruling, with the Internal Revenue Service.

AARP began selling a large number of tailored products and services to its members that went well beyond Colonial Penn insurance. Today, it offers travel discounts—air, cruise, rail, car rental, and hotel—as well as discounts on mail-order pharmaceuticals, credit cards, hearing aids, cell phones, restaurants, movies, and WW (formerly Weight Watchers) memberships, to name a few—essentially all the things a retiree needs.

AARP also tapped into the zeitgeist by providing older people with information through its marketing and media channels, including a magazine, newsletters, and a newspaper, which reach nearly 36 million people in the United States today. Those media channels, in turn, sell ads to partner companies and others to drive more revenue for AARP.

Davis's belief that he could make a profit off of retirees proved to be prophetic. And it helped propel AARP to becoming the powerhouse that it is today. AARP's juggernaut success and outsized influence would be unsustainable if the selling of products and services weren't central to its business model. Today, AARP's membership is approximately 38 million, and its operating revenue is close to $1.8 billion per year. It has been called an 800-pound gorilla or overgrown orangutan for its incredible power and influence. Davis, who started his career as an insurance salesman, was once estimated by *Forbes* magazine to have amassed a personal fortune of $230 million before 1980—roughly three-quarters of a billion dollars in today's value. He later bequeathed part of his fortune to create and fund the USC Leonard Davis School of Gerontology, the number one school of gerontology in the United States, as well as the Ethel Percy Andrus Gerontology Center, which is housed within the school.

A few years after the launch of AARP, Del Webb, a real estate developer and co-owner of the New York Yankees baseball club, had a radical vision to design, construct, and open a new community dedicated to the leisure and recreation activities of the retired adult. In January 1960, the Del Webb Development Corporation (DEVCO) opened Sun City, Arizona, the first planned retirement community in the world. DEVCO had hoped to sell 1,700 homes in its first three years but ended up selling a miraculous 2,000 homes in the first year alone.

Webb's Sun City success, which was driven mostly by selling the idea of a comfortable and active retirement, led to copycat innovators who built and operated look-alike communities across the Sunbelt, including the Villages in Florida. Soon, his retirement community model would spread around the world. Webb became so well known for his work that he was featured on the cover of *Time* magazine in 1962, cementing his legacy as a visionary and transformative leader in retirement.

The problem with normalizing the idea of comfortable retirement and older age, a vision perpetrated mostly by large organizations that have profited from it, is that it is patently false. A comfortable retirement is reserved only for a shrinking proportion of the population, an issue due largely to vanishing corporate pensions, shrinking state pensions, and declining private savings. Yet all too often, organizations such as AARP go out of their way to promote the positive side of advanced age, as though these stories are the norm. Their proclamations paint an overly rosy picture of mostly well-to-do people who have the luxury to choose how they will age.

These organizations have failed to recognize that there are parts of this world in which getting older isn't that great and never was. They also fail to realize that aging is physically, emotionally, and mentally challenging for just about everyone, including the well-to-do. And they fail to acknowledge the facts that age-related decline and death are part of life, perhaps because they don't sell particularly well.

Today, access to a comfortable retirement is not a guarantee as governments move to curtail retirement benefits and corporations switch out generous defined-benefit pension plans in favor of cheaper defined-contribution ones. Workers are looking past retirement to a new reality of living in their later years that looks a lot like it did before social welfare programs took off in the twentieth century; this new way of living almost always includes continuing to work for as long as possible.

The shifting of retirement income responsibility and risk away from governments and corporations and back onto individuals is a hallmark of the Super Age. Millennials and younger generations understand this reality, perhaps more than anyone over the age of 40 does, and are working to achieve a stable and secure retirement income, despite near-constant financial headwinds. Nearly three-quarters of Millennials are saving for later life, and they started doing so nearly a full decade before their boomer parents did. More than a third of Millennials believe they will work past 70.

Placing greater responsibility on the individual means that addressing social and economic inequalities earlier in life becomes increasingly important. Savings programs that address inequality up front are one way to help alleviate a degree of income disparity. Understanding the diverse life experiences of historically marginalized populations is essential to creating a more equitable world, especially later in life.

Unequal Paths Toward Longevity

The station that most individuals achieve in later life tends not to be too dissimilar from the one that they were born into. Yes, there is still a chance for upward mobility and the "American Dream." However, it is much harder to attain upward mobility in an unequal society and even harder for people who belong to a historically marginalized group, such as BIPOC (Black, Indigenous, people of color), female, and/or LGBTQ+ (lesbian, gay, bisexual, transgender, queer, and other noncisgender and nonheterosexual identities). The reality is that a comfortable retirement is far harder to achieve when one's life is marked by cycles of poverty and shortened lives that are driven, in large part, by systemic and institutionalized racial, gender, and sexuality biases.

Yet the dominant narrative about older people's wealth and success remains, and the message we cannot seem to escape is that older people, and especially older White people, control the nation's wealth and are living in comfort. The reality is that 29 percent of people over 55 have nothing at all saved for retirement, and most have very little.

"Over 15 million Americans aged 65+ are economically insecure—living at or below 200% of the federal poverty level (FPL) ($25,760 per year for a single person in 2021)." They struggle with rising housing and health care bills, inadequate nutrition, lack of access to transportation, diminished savings, rolled-back social support, and job loss. It has become increasingly difficult, and sometimes impossible, for them to save for and enjoy a comfortable retirement. For older adults who are just above the poverty level, it takes only one major adverse life event to change a positive economic outlook into despair.

A perfect example of this is the fallout from the covid-19 pandemic. Poorer people, especially poor people of color, are more likely to work in frontline and service sector jobs, deemed "essential," and it was these workers who suffered higher infection and mortality rates from the disease. These professions involve high-contact work in close quarters in workplaces from meatpacking to grocery and retail establishments to restaurants and bars. Those who were not employed in high-risk jobs were almost assuredly displaced by industries that severely contracted or collapsed during the pandemic. Lower-income workers either had to risk their lives to survive by working for minimum wage or taking on gig work, or were involuntarily let go from their jobs and left behind in what has been called a "K-shaped" recovery.

The term *K-shaped* is used to describe the uneven economic recovery across different sectors, industries, and groups of people in the economy. People engaged in certain industries, such as technology, rebounded with great effect, and some are in a better financial position than they were before the downturn, while others, such as people working in travel and tourism, have lagged behind or struggled to regain their economic footing. The 630 billionaires in the United States, for example, actually saw their wealth grow by nearly half a trillion dollars, while 40 million people were out of work. As of May 2020, the richest four hundred people in the United States had as much combined wealth as the poorest two-thirds of American households.

To put a point on this, at the time of writing, White people in Washington, DC, my adopted hometown, hold the majority of professional positions, make up roughly half of the population, yet account for only about 20 percent of positive cases of covid-19. Black people, on the other hand, who also make up about half of the population, are more likely to engage in frontline work, were more than twice as likely to contract the virus, and accounted for more than 74 percent of all deaths from the disease.

Individuals who had spent their lives playing by the rules while scrimping and saving at every turn found their lives upended as they or their family members became sick or they were displaced from their jobs by the economic downturn. Wildly costly hospital bills, coupled with loss of income, created a perfect storm that threw many of those rule followers off track. Covid-19 was a disruption like no other, and it took and is taking an especially damaging toll on BIPOC.

The current tragedy is due largely to historic and systemic disparities that have piled up on Black Americans since 1619, the year the first slaves were brought to Jamestown, Virginia. The resulting legacies of segregation and disenfranchisement mean that, as a percentage, Black people are more likely to work in "essential jobs" that pay no more than a state-mandated minimum wage and to live in substandard and sometimes state-supported mass housing that is often located in what are known as food deserts, areas that have limited access to affordable and nutritious food. Black men, in particular, are more likely to be incarcerated than their White peers, which shaves two years off their life expectancy for every year served. All of this has contributed to higher death rates at younger ages than among their White peers and a widening longevity gap, the difference of average expected life spans between groups of people.

The inequalities faced by Black people are so dramatic that they not only contribute to this inequality of life span but are also creating a drag on overall US longevity gains and could have an outsized negative impact on the country's economic growth. The challenges faced by their poor White and Latino peers are having a similar effect. Stanford University's Raj Chetty, who leverages "big data" to understand inequalities, pegged the United States' current longevity gap at twenty years, the highest it has been since the 1870s, with 11.5 percent of US counties having experienced an increase in the risk of death for residents aged 25 to 45 over the period studied (1980–2014), and predicted that it will grow wider in the future.

No previous study had put the disparity at even close to twenty years, and the results of this could range from economic instability to political instability. This research illustrates an average for all people of all races. The extremes are far worse, which further erodes the idea that retirement, much less a comfortable retirement, is a likelihood for most of us, apart from a select few. The shortened life spans of individuals, especially people of color, could also have a calamitous effect on US growth, especially since all demographic signs point to the country becoming a majority minority nation by 2045, approximately fifteen years after the United States enters the Super Age. The exponential growth of inequality may hypercharge these challenges, putting a comfortable later life out of reach for even more people.

This isn't just a phenomenon in the United States, and the longevity gap is even more dramatic when examined from nation to nation and municipality to municipality. For example, the country with the lowest life expectancy in the world is Chad, at 50.6 years, while that with the highest life expectancy is Monaco at 89.4 years—a 38.8-year difference. In the United States, the lowest life expectancy is in Stilwell, Oklahoma, at 56.3 years, while the highest life expectancy is in Fearrington Village, North Carolina, at 97.5 years—a 41.2-year difference. In both cases, a staggering two generations separate those with the lowest longevity from those with the highest longevity, which should illustrate how problematic inequality is for our societies and especially our economies.

The implication of the life expectancy gap is that the people of

Fearrington Village have far more time on this planet, which means they have greater opportunity to generate wealth, especially during their prime earning years (women from 34 to 54, men from 45 to 64), which they can pass on to their progeny. These extra years also mean that more of them are able to contribute nonmonetary support to their family and community, such as child care and volunteering. The people of Fearrington Village will grow richer and older, while the people of Stilwell will remain poor and die young.

Researchers at the Department of Population Health at New York University School of Medicine, using data from the City Health Dashboard, found that dramatic inequalities in longevity could also be found within American cities. According to their 2019 analysis, Chicago had the largest gap in life expectancy between richer, whiter neighborhoods and poorer, blacker ones at 30.1 years. The cities of Washington, DC, and New York City didn't fare much better at 27.5 and 27.4 years, respectively. Those cities also had some of the highest levels of racial segregation in the country.

Much of the disparity can be attributed to a spike in noncommunicable diseases, such as diabetes, and substance abuse, which affects all races and all genders. However, a growing body of evidence suggests that life expectancy is also driven by economic position and access to opportunity, also known as the social determinants of health. Social determinants of health are the conditions in which people are born, grow, live, work, and age, and they are often systemic. They include factors such as socioeconomic status, education, neighborhood and physical environment, employment, and social support networks, as well as access to health care.

The lack of access to opportunity due to race has been compounded over time and can create a dire situation for people later in life in both their physical health and their economic condition.

The consistent thread is that longevity is intimately connected to wealth, which is intimately connected to access to health care and healthy behaviors, which are both intimately connected to race. The areas with the lowest life expectancy in the world and in the United States are made up almost entirely of historically marginalized people;

Chad is nearly all African, Stilwell is nearly all Native American, and both are incredibly poor. Monaco and Fearrington Village, on the other hand, are nearly all White and very rich.

This kind of disparity puts poor people, especially poor BIPOC, at a distinct comparative and competitive disadvantage. Not only are their lives being cut short at an early age, they are also losing vitally important earning years, which limits the amount of generational wealth that they can create. This inability to build family wealth over generations contributes to the growing chasm between those who have the luxury of living longer in the active and comfortable retirement that was conceived by Andrus, Davis, and Webb in midcentury, and those who do not.

Sex and Sexuality

Gender plays a significant role in longevity, too, and cisgender (cis) women almost everywhere, regardless of geographic location or nation of origin, live about six to eight years longer than their cis male counterparts. In the US, Asian cis women live the longest. However, in some countries, such as Russia, cis women can live as much as ten years longer than cis men. The gap started widening about a hundred years ago and continues to widen today, even though studies predict that it may narrow in the future for some countries, due in part to shifting personal behaviors, such as men's curtailing their smoking and alcohol consumption, improving their diet, and increasing the amount of exercise they do.

On the surface, these longer lives may sound positive for cisgender women, but they're not, thanks in large part to lingering systemic sexist and patriarchal issues that our societies have yet to fully resolve. Specifically, if they are employed, women almost always earn less than men, have uneven working lives, and they bear nearly all of the caregiving responsibility for both children and parents as well as homemaking responsibilities (cooking, cleaning, and so on). Whereas many developed nations have worked to close the gender wage gap, it still exists and can make a significant dent in the long-term economic health of many women.

In countries such as the United States, cisgender straight women who serve their families as homemakers and caregivers, rather than in income-generating work, are doubly penalized: not only do they not attain financial freedom during their lifetimes, but their financial security in older age is intimately tied to their marital status and the financial success of their husband. The system was designed this way. Husbands, as it turns out, are a terrible retirement policy.

Even the safety net of the US retirement system, Social Security, is riddled with sexist policies. It can be debated whether or not they were intended. However, the program was designed by mostly White cis male legislators in the 1930s, and the original 1935 act provided only for workers, who were almost always cis male. But the 1939 amendments added benefits for cis women. They were based on what was seen at the time as the "traditional" American family, in which cis straight men were the "breadwinners," or primary earners, and cis straight women were homemakers. Cis women, for example, were required to be married for at least ten years before they were eligible for spousal benefit, and the myriad of rules related to divorce and death would confuse the most seasoned actuary.

Today, even without women relying on men for retirement security, they receive Social Security benefits that are, on average, 80 percent of those men receive. This is due to the fact that women still earn less than men—about 82 cents on the dollar—and the system's rules, as a result, remain fundamentally sexist despite their purported gender neutrality.

In sum, women, whether they be cisgender straight or lesbian, are living longer and with fewer financial resources, which puts them at a significant risk of financial insecurity later in life. In a country like the United States, this translates to women accounting for nearly two out of three older people living in poverty, or roughly 16 percent of all women over the age of 65. BIPOC women are more than twice as likely than their White counterparts to live in poverty. Nearly half of all older bisexual and transgender women in the United States live below 200 percent of the federal poverty line, a statistic that is truly disturbing, meaning that they are the hardest-hit demographic as far as income security is concerned. These disparities can be compounded when geographic location (rural or urban) is factored into the equation. The only group that financially outperforms them all, including cis straight White men, are cis White gay men.

To further punctuate the racial and gender disparity over the life course, according to the National Women's Law Center, Black women earned 62 cents for every dollar their White male counterparts earned in the United States before the outbreak of covid-19. This means that the average Black woman would have to work an extra eight months each year to keep up, which is impossible, and Black women were hit especially hard during the 2020 economic downturn. All of this translates to a forty-year working-life income disparity with a value of up to $941,600, and this was all before the pandemic, which disrupted work for many low-income individuals.

Harsh Realities for Retirement Prospects

Today, 4,618,400 older American women are living at or below the poverty line, which is just shy of the entire population of Ireland. If the United States continues on its current growth trajectory, there will be approximately 73,100,000 older people by 2030, the year the country is expected to become a Super Age nation. Assuming that Americans do nothing to address the systemic issues that foster income insecurity in later life and all other things remain equal, the population of older women living at or below the poverty line will nearly triple to approximately 11,696,000 by 2030, while there will be approximately 8,722,000 men at or below the poverty line.

The existence of large numbers of people who are unemployed or underemployed and living at or below the poverty line is never a good sign for an economy, especially when their numbers are only predicted to grow. At the very least, this trend suggests that the economy is operating below capacity and is inefficient. At the very worst, a greater number of people living at or below the poverty line means that they are unable to purchase as many goods, which leads to lower spending, lower output, and lower growth of the overall economy. As with all things, there is a multiplier effect, which will magnify the economic challenges over time if action isn't taken to create a more inclusive economy.

Only 29 percent, or 73 million, Americans consider themselves to be financially healthy, according to the Financial Health Network, and a disconcerting number of them are not well provided for retirement. A shockingly high 22 percent of all Americans, according to Northwestern Mutual, have less than $5,000 in retirement savings, 5 percent have between $5,000 and $24,999, and only 16 percent have $200,000 or more. Forty-six percent have no idea how much they have put away. According to the Transamerica Center for Retirement Studies in 2019, American boomers have put away only $152,000 apiece, on average, and only 40 percent of boomers have saved more than $250,000.

Yet retirement experts suggest that most people in the United States will require around $1 million to $1.5 million in retirement savings to retire comfortably. There are a number of different ways to calculate this number. However, a generally accepted rule is to assume spending at least 70 to 80 percent of one's normal annual income during the first ten years of retirement, even though that may be too little.

According to the Social Security Administration, the average 65-year-old man today will live until he's 83 and the average woman until she's 86. But at least half will live longer—a lot longer. If humanity continues to add years to life after we exit this dark pandemic period, as I expect it will, children born today will live well past the century mark.

This all leads to a world in which planning for retirement will become a fool's errand. The midcentury concept of retirement, even if a shred of it exists by the time today's children are ready to stop working—and I don't believe it will, due to social and economic trends—might not begin until well past the current average life expectancy at birth, which was 78.7 years in the United States before the pandemic began (it dropped to 77.3 in 2020).

Individuals who maintain an interest in planning for and securing a comfortable retirement often underestimate their life expectancy potential and struggle to forecast the costs associated with a long life without income-generating work. This happens despite a plethora of retirement calculators offered for free by leading financial institutions, major nonprofits, and governments. Oftentimes, these calculators obscure the reality that those who are fortunate enough to be able to plan for retirement are also more likely to live past the average life expectancy. They also fail to illustrate the malleability of longevity when healthy behaviors are adjusted positively or negatively. The mortality rate actually begins to decrease after age 80 and begins to plateau after 105. And making it to 80 is not out of reach for the well-to-do anymore; it's become the norm.

Take me, for example. I am a relatively healthy middle-aged White male living in the United States, so I have a statistical probability of making it to my early eighties, based on my current behaviors, and I have a greater than 50 percent chance of being alive to see the next pass of Halley's Comet in 2061. For the record, that is over thirteen years more than my life expectancy was at birth in 1977.

If I make and maintain positive modifications to my current diet and exercise regime and all social and scientific progress stays exactly the same as it is today, I can extend my longevity by as much as a decade. However, this prediction doesn't consider what could happen if the scientific advancements that are already under way that I discussed in the previous chapter come to pass. Like so many of my generation, I could find myself in the position of living longer, living healthier, but also living worse off financially—because financial forecasts don't account for these scientific strides. I could catch a longevity tsunami—one that would carry me to long life, but could also destroy me financially.

Americans are not alone. Life expectancies everywhere are ticking up. Countries with more robust national pension schemes have warned that those benefits are not sustainable and retirement ages will need to be increased or benefits will need to be decreased. In any event, the Super Age will require more of us to work longer than previous generations did.

The Anti-retirement Reality

Most working-age people of my age and younger are well aware that the comfortable retirement promised to our parents, grandparents, and great-grandparents will not exist by the time we turn 65. Older adults are waking up to that reality, too. Not only do the data scream that many of us cannot afford retirement, but many working-age adults in the United States have suffered from two gruesome economic downturns (in 2008 and 2020). Both of them resulted in the loss of retirement savings, jobs, and earning years, which led to more and more people needing to work past retirement age just to make ends meet.

Even individuals who were well saved and not dealt life-changing economic blows are choosing to work longer, in large part because it helps them remain socially active, relevant, and economically productive, not to mention the added economic advantages of a longer work life, which includes earning more spending money and deferring drawing down their retirement savings. And some people really enjoy working. These two realities collide to give new meaning to the dilemma "Live to work or work to live."

There are already millions of people around the world who are working well past the traditional retirement age, and they offer us a glimpse of a future in which we will work longer. In pre-covid-19 America, the numbers of workers over the ages 65, 75, and even 85 had doubled from their pre–Great Recession levels. According to the Bureau of Labor Statistics, in 2018, that bracket of the workforce was on track to grow by at least 50 percent by 2030. Though it may be hard to believe, in the United States, over 255,000 Americans 85 years old and up were working in the formal labor market before the pandemic. Though workers over the age of 85 are still relatively rare, they aren't necessarily hidden or tied to one particular race or region, but they are generally engaged in less physically demanding work.

Of this group, there are a growing number of older people who are leaving their workplaces either by choice or because they were made redundant and striking out on their own as entrepreneurs, small-business owners, and gig workers. They can be found working in just about every pursuit, but some of them might surprise you.

In 2018, the Kellogg School of Management at Northwestern University released a report called "Age and High-Growth Entrepreneurship." This study found that the average age of the founders of the fastest-growing tech start-ups was 45. More to the point, 50-year-old entrepreneurs were about twice as likely to achieve significant success as their 30-year-old counterparts were.

This holds true for the success rate of small businesses launched by older people, according to a 2019 report by JPMorgan Chase Institute. In the first year, a 60-year-old entrepreneur's company has an 8.2 percent probability of going out of business, compared with an 11.1 percent chance for that of a 30-year-old founder and a 9.6 percent risk for that of a 45-year-old. Older people make up the biggest share of owners of small companies in the metal and machinery sector (47 percent), high-tech manufacturing (43 percent), real estate (41 percent), and health care services (40 percent).

The gig economy is also proving to be fertile ground for older workers. According to a 2019 survey by industry expert Harry Campbell, better known as "the Rideshare Guy," 54 percent of Uber drivers in the United States are over the age of 50, and about a quarter are 61 or older. In Japan, the average age of taxi drivers in 2018 was 59.9 years, and in South Korea, 37 percent of taxi drivers were over the age of 65, the oldest being 93.

Then there are countless more people around the globe who are engaged in a longer work life, working quietly, diligently, and without fanfare as vendors in hawker centers and night markets, stewards and janitors, grocery store clerks and baggers, groundskeepers and maids, receptionists and customer service agents. Though some people may see these jobs as low skilled or unremarkable, they are the ones that keep society humming along, and they are being held by a growing number of older people each year.

These examples offer a preview of the new normal in the Super Age—a time when individuals such as you and me will be able to live, learn, and earn a lot longer than previous generations did. We will remain active consumers for a longer period of time, not the passive recipients of corporate and state pensions of today. Remaining employed later in life does more than keep food on the table and a roof overhead; it can also keep us healthier, both mentally and physically, for an extended period of time, so there is a triple bottom line for extended economically productive years: increased tax revenue, an expanded consumer base, and fewer negative health episodes and costs. These individuals who are working past traditional retirement are pioneers by choice or by circumstance of the new reality—anti-retirement—and the Super Age.

6

The Drag of Ageism

Periods of great change need an all-hands-on-deck approach to problem solving, and the Super Age will be no different. Uniting the generations behind a future that is more generationally diverse than ever before, as well as making sure that every single person has a role, will be necessary at the onset and throughout the transition. An alliance between young and old may seem futile or at least folly, but that's only because generational strife has been so central to the social and economic narrative of the past century. It's time to change that, not only because ageism negatively impacts the potential of both young and old but also because the issues of aging and longevity often intersect with other social and economic justice issues facing the United States and the world.

Younger people are often seen as the tip of the spear, the frontline soldiers, in the social, economic, and racial justice movements, pushing against the status quo and demanding change for their generation. They wear their "wokeness"—a term borrowed from the African American vernacular expression "Stay woke," which refers to a continuing awareness of these issues—like a badge of honor, often bringing their grievances or ideas for change forward via public protest to the perceived gerontocracy, meaning a state governed by old people. For reference, the average age of members of the 116th Congress during Black Lives Matter protests was nearly 58 years for representatives and nearly 63 years for senators, and President Trump was 74. It's no wonder that young people don't believe their voices are being heard, especially since the national median age in 2020 was 38.2.

People aged 18 to 34 accounted for approximately two out of three protestors during the 2020 Black Lives Matter protests in Atlanta, Los Angeles, Minneapolis, and New York, according to a mobile data analysis by Mobilewalla. However, protestors over the age of 55 ranked second, ranging from 20 percent in Los Angeles to 23 percent in Atlanta and Minneapolis to 24 percent in New York City, despite the health risks posed by the pandemic. Protesters in the 35-to-54 age group made up less than 10 percent overall. That made the younger and older populations in those cities the most prolific voices on the streets.

The somewhat unusual alliance of the young and old during that period illustrates that the traditional notion of these groups not having compatible values is outdated. The idea that generations cannot find common ground and achieve some degree of solidarity, especially when dealing with some of the most challenging issues facing our societies, is simply a false narrative. The strength of the multigenerational coalition was important not only for the Black Lives Matter movement but also in the 2020 US presidential election, and it is one of the more compelling reasons Joe Biden won: young people showed up at the polls in large numbers, and some older voters turned away from Donald Trump. A majority of the country's citizens showed that they believe in a more united and equitable vision of the future, rather than one that stokes division and fear.

Identity, Bias, and Youth

Age is an important component of identity. Our description of who we are, in addition to our sex, race, occupation, nationality, and geographical origin, often includes our age or our generation. It is also a component that some ascribe to the human rights movement, as well as a component of the social, economic, and racial justice movements. In fact, the United Nations has been discussing the issue of age as it relates to the rights of older people since as early as 1948 (spoiler alert—it still hasn't passed a Convention on the Rights of Older Persons, UN-speak for a binding treaty). Age discrimination involves treating persons in an unequal fashion due to only their age in a way that is contrary to human rights laws. Though it is often not taken as seriously as other forms of discrimination, it can have the same economic, social, and psychological impacts.

All too often, age is seen as an afterthought in rights conversations, perhaps because it is seen as a barrier only for some—the old—and it is generally assumed that ageism, the stereotyping and/or discrimination against individuals or groups on the basis of their age, is directed only toward the most senior members of our societies. Ageism often manifests itself in offhand comments suggesting that forgetfulness is a sign of being old, products that are marketed as anti-aging, patronizing or infantilizing language, the assumption that older people lack relevance or skills, or simply a preference for the young. However, it can lead to job loss, being refused credit, lower-quality service in a retail or restaurant setting, being left out of clinical trials, or even poor care by health care professionals. In recent years, the term has become more malleable and may be slowly expanding to cover other age groups, including the young. This is not something that organizations that represent older people readily accept.

It is possible for younger people to experience ageism. Young people's experience with this bias should not be dismissed simply because many of the worst examples of ageism occur later in life. It should also not be assumed that ageism toward the young doesn't have negative outcomes, as it does toward the old. The experience of ageism for both groups overlaps remarkably strongly in the workplace. A 2006 study published in *Human Resource Management Journal* found that discrimination on the basis of being "too young" is at least as common as discrimination on the basis of being "too old." Such bias can not only negatively impact the mental and physical well-being of workers but also adversely affect the quality of their work product.

It is not at all unusual for younger people, especially younger employees, to be subjected to denigrating or demeaning language in the workplace. This often manifests as a manager singling out a younger person or blaming his or her inexperience on age; or it could involve calling a young person "kid" or "kiddo" or referring to him or her as the "new boy" or "new girl." Ageist employers may also be reluctant to hire people under 30 because they're unpredictable or "don't know how to work," or they may simply not be willing to help younger people gain the experience and skills they need to grow. Employers are also guilty of taking advantage of free or low-cost labor by young people in the form of internship programs, a requirement for many jobs in the professional class.

For me, ageism as a young professional presented at the most bizarre times—an experience that is not unusual for most workers. At AARP, sometime in my early thirties, I worked on strategies to get the organization to produce more readily available, accessible, and digestible digital content. I proposed creating weekly video shorts on global innovations in aging that could be distributed via YouTube or other social media channels for a domestic and international audience.

The lead internal producer wasn't dismissive of the proposal. In fact, he loved it. But it was what he said at the conclusion of the meeting that still sticks with me today—"Man, you'd be a great presenter for this if you weren't so young," meaning that no matter how good the quality of my idea or my execution of the strategy, I couldn't be on-screen. Someone older and more "AARP-like" who looked the part of a retiree would have to fill the role, regardless of his or her skills or talent. It was then that I had my first taste of ageism and realized that shaming anyone, regardless of his or her age or generation, is real and harmful.

Ageism Toward the Old

According to the 2020 study "Overlooked and Underestimated: Experiences of Ageism in Young, Middle-Aged, and Older Adults," published in *Journals of Gerontology*, when young adults reported experiencing ageism in the workplace, they identified their coworkers as the main perpetrators. Middle-aged and older adults also reported ageism in the workplace. However, they also frequently reported experiencing ageism while seeking products or services in a retail environment. Perpetrators of ageism varied more widely for middle-aged and older adults. Regardless of one's age, age discrimination was almost always experienced in the form of "lack of respect" or "incorrect assumptions." This could manifest itself as being dismissed as outdated or out of vogue or the assumption that an older worker lacks skills, especially technical skills.

There was no greater indignity accorded to older people or a more significant example of modern ageism than during the emergence of the covid-19 pandemic. Whether we like to admit it or not, our societies see older people, especially those who are most vulnerable, as expendable or disposable. Some politicians, including Lieutenant Governor Dan Patrick of Texas, suggested that older people should "volunteer to die" in order to get the economy up and running again. What that did was to promote not only ageism but a horrific form of age-based eugenics while blinding many people to the reality of the disease—namely, that underlying health conditions were a greater driver of mortality than age. The country is now reaping what it has sown with increasing numbers of infections, hospitalizations, and deaths among younger populations.

There is simply no valid moral argument that sacrificing older people is acceptable, regardless of the fact that they are statistically more likely to die of the disease. The attitude of leaders in the United States and around the world—get the economy running no matter if Grandma and Grandpa die—slowed the response to the disease. The highest price was paid with the lives of hundreds of thousands of people who died—both young and old—as well as the thousands of "long haulers," people who suffer from the effects of the disease for weeks, if not months or longer (at the time of writing, the global count of lives lost to the pandemic is over four million).

Unlike the Spanish flu in 1918, which affected mostly younger people, covid-19 was originally thought to affect only the old; initially, 80 percent of all covid-19 deaths in the United States were among people over 65. That statistic lulled many into a false sense of security by taking attention away from better predictors of infection and death, including a host of underlying conditions, such as obesity, diabetes, and heart disease, to name a few.

The Kaiser Family Foundation found that although a disproportionate number of deaths had occurred among people over the age of 65, an even greater number of deaths was happening in nursing homes: 40 percent of all deaths were connected to those facilities. This statistic is particularly macabre because nursing home residents are already discounted by society. Most ended up in those facilities because they could no longer care for themselves and could not afford to have care services in their home.

Though just about all reporting on covid-19 mortality used the 65-and-over statistics, about 60 percent of all covid-19 deaths were among people over the age of 75, and a full third were among people over the age of 85. People aged 65 to 74 accounted for 21 percent of all deaths, while people under 64 accounted for 20 percent. Much of the science discussed earlier in this manuscript that is being employed to extend life expectancy is also working to close the gap between total life expectancy and healthy life expectancy. The hope for the future is that this will narrow the mortality disparity not only for covid-19 but also for other diseases, such as the flu, that kill older people at a similar disproportionate rate.

Apart from experiencing age discrimination with covid-19 and other diseases, the indignities of ageism are also suffered in the workplace. According to a 2018 AARP report, one in every five workers in the United States was over the age of 55, and that number is expected to grow substantially in the Super Age. Nearly 65 percent of these workers said that they had experienced age-based discrimination at work. A majority—58 percent—believed that ageism started around the age of 50. The report excluded younger workers.

Older adults also struggle to retain their employment, due in large part to ageism. Ageism in the workforce is one of the main reasons that individuals lose a job and then can't find an equally good one—or any at all. A 2016 study by ProPublica and the Urban Institute found that "56 percent [of older workers] are laid off at least once or leave jobs under such financially damaging circumstances that it's likely they were pushed out rather than choosing to go voluntarily." Only one in ten workers who found a new job earned as much as they had before their job loss. The remaining 90 percent suffered a significant salary reduction.

Boomers are often treated as "deadwood," and corporations have dropped them by the thousands. Even the members of Gen X are now old enough to be at risk of having their résumés discarded or their positions placed on the proverbial chopping block, and older Millennials, some of whom are now 40 or over, could be next. All too often, this is reinforced by employee engagement and benefits strategies that were conceived with a younger workforce in mind and a focus on "How can we keep you for the next five to ten years?" without much thought being given to "How can we make the most out of your final five to ten years here?"

In an article I wrote for the Society for Human Resource Management (SHRM), I noted that older workers, particularly older public sector workers, tend to stay in their jobs longer than their younger counterparts do. This means that they have the potential to be great assets, but they may also need continuing education. My good friend and colleague Brian Elms, a public sector innovation expert and co-author of the bestselling book *Peak Performance: How Denver's Peak Academy Is Saving Money, Boosting Morale and Just Maybe Changing the World*, put it best: "Employees, just like infrastructure assets, require ongoing care and investments. When we reengage our strongest assets in our organizations, our employees, we spark creativity and innovation throughout our workforce."

Nowhere is our bias against the old, especially older women, more pronounced and on display than in the entertainment industry, where older talent often struggles to get time on-screen. According to the 2019 report "Inequality in 1,200 Popular Films: Examining Portrayals of Gender, Race/Ethnicity, LGBTQ & Disability from 2007 to 2018," researchers at the USC Annenberg School for Communication and Journalism found that only 11 of the 100 top movies of 2018 featured a female in a leading or coleading role who was 45 years of age or older at the time of theatrical release. Though that was over twice as many as in 2017 (5 movies), it was less than half of the movies that featured a male lead or colead 45 years of age or older in 2018 (24 movies). Out of the 100 top films of 2018, only 4 featured a woman of color 45 years of age or older in a lead or colead role. A bright note came in 2021 when three out of four Oscar categories were won by older actors who portrayed characters that illustrated older people—Frances Mc-Dormand (*Nomadland*), Sir Anthony Hopkins (*The Father*), and Youn Yuh-jung (*Minari*). Regardless, the lack of older characters in movies and on television subconsciously cements the feeling that people just disappear after a certain age.

It is true that older people suffer the most apparent bias based on age and that the vast majority of people won't experience the most negative effects of ageism until later in life. This is largely because, unlike with other defining characteristics, none of us is born old. Old age, unlike sexuality, gender, or race, sneaks up on individuals over time, and it is particularly biting because many of us experience a disconnect between our chronological age—the number of times we've been around the sun—and our perceived age; oftentimes this is a difference of ten to fifteen years. This is compounded by the age others perceive us to be.

We're all guilty of ageism toward the old, and the general progression of our bias toward them almost invariably starts with a "harmless" joke. Younger people start by disparaging older people for exhibiting perceived antiquated behaviors or dress, then around middle age we make fun of ourselves for having "senior moments," and we finish life often being the brunt of ridicule or, worse, being dismissed altogether. In almost every way, our younger selves bet against our future older selves, and our oldest selves pay the highest price.

Older individuals regularly have to endure commonplace, widespread, and accepted negative humor and bias. Younger people almost always revel in mocking those of advanced age, and I challenge anyone reading this book to get through a single day without dealing a self-inflicted ageist blow, laughing at an ageist joke, or delivering an ageist critique to someone older (or younger) than yourself.

Costs, Plain and Simple

Ageism shows up everywhere in everyday microaggressions by friends and family, acquaintances, coworkers, and the popular and news media and also manifests itself in product and service design, public policy, the workforce and workplace, marketing and communications, and health care policy. In the era of #MeToo, #LoveWins, and #Black LivesMatter, individuals have become finely attuned, if not sympathetic, to the challenges and prejudices faced by others, yet ageism persists as an accepted bias. We don't care about those older than ourselves.

This bias may be personal and internalized, socialized, or systemic and institutionalized. It exacerbates inequalities as well as magnifies the negative health effects of aging on the human body. It can also lead to unemployment and decreased longevity. In turn, these all drag on the overall social and economic success of virtually every country in the world. Continuing our current, destructive bias based on age has the potential to wreak havoc on our once thriving social and economic systems.

According to a 2007 study published in *Journals of Gerontology*, older people who don't feel useful are more than three times as likely to become disabled and more than four times as likely to die early, as those who have a purpose. If companies make employees redundant, there is a greater chance that they will fall into poor health, which will have a direct impact on their longevity prospects. And thanks to the efforts of Yale epidemiologist Becca Levy and her colleagues, there are data to illustrate the substantial social and economic costs.

In a 2018 study (followed up in 2020), Dr. Levy and her team found that ageism toward the old led to excess costs of $63 billion for a broad range of health conditions during one year in the United States alone. There was evidence that ageism led to poorer outcomes in mental health, including depression, as well as physical health conditions, including shortened longevity. Older adults were also less likely to receive necessary medical treatment, and if they did receive treatment, the duration, frequency, and treatment were negatively impacted. Her review indicated that ageism affected older persons regardless of their age, sex, or race.

The $63 billion cost of ageism amounts to one of every seven dollars spent on the eight most expensive health conditions for all Americans over the age of 60 during a single year. Among the health conditions examined were cardiovascular disease, mental disorders, and chronic respiratory disease. Think for a moment about the irony here: ageism has been proved to make people sick by the millions worldwide, but it also prevents doctors and other health professionals from properly caring for older individuals who are suffering from the negative effects of ageism. The result is a vicious cycle, an expensive, nonsustainable one at that, of which the costs are borne by the same society that perpetrates this incredibly damaging bias.

Following Dr. Levy's landmark study, the World Health Organization asked her to lead a global analysis as part of its Global Campaign to Combat Ageism, which is supported by 194 countries. The study, which was released in 2020, was the largest examination to date of the health consequences of ageism. It found evidence that age discrimination harms the health of older people in forty-five countries across five continents. The study included more than 7 million participants, and the analysis was based on a systematic review of 422 studies from around the world. There was evidence of the adverse effects of ageism on older persons in 96 percent of those studies.

The World Health Organization further concluded that ageism causes cardiovascular stress, lowered levels of self-efficacy, and decreased productivity. Ageism also has mental and physical health consequences, including a decreased will to live, less desire to live a healthy lifestyle, impaired recovery from illness, increased stress, and a shortened life span. Adults with negative attitudes about aging could end up reducing their life spans by as much as 7.5 years. The good news is that if society combats ageism, the opposite will likely occur and there will be positive health outcomes or at least fewer negative ones. Society will have healthier older populations, rather than the sicker ones there are now.

The American Psychological Association concurs, suggesting that ageism is a serious issue that should be treated the same as gender-, race-, and disability-based discrimination, but these should never be equated. It indicates that raising public awareness about the issues that ageism creates can help alleviate some of the negative effects, but that's really only a start. And as the population of older adults continues to increase during the Super Age, finding ways to minimize or eliminate ageism toward both young and old will become more and more important.

Ageism in the workplace is costing us even more than growing health care expenditures. A 2018 report by PwC, "PwC Golden Age Index: Unlocking a Potential $3.5 Trillion Prize from Longer Working Lives," found that OECD nations could see a $3.5 trillion boost to their economies if they pursued more age-inclusive policies rather than continuing along the current path of making older people redundant simply because they are old. These policies could be as simple as incorporating language into recruitment materials that encourages workers of all ages to apply, shying away from utilizing accepted terms such as "digital native," and eliminating requests for date of birth and college graduation in the application process. It could also involve encouraging employers and employees to build age-inclusive teams or create flexible work options such as telecommuting, job sharing, phased onboarding or retirement, and part-time work as part of a talent management strategy.

Nearly every individual is culpable in the proliferation and propagation of ageism in the workforce and throughout society. We must do more in both the public and private sectors to combat its pervasiveness. A lot of times that needs to start with tackling internalized ageism. However, the biggest barrier age discrimination creates is that, like other forms of discrimination and regardless of its costs, it was and in some cases still is sanctioned by the state, so a natural front on the war to combat this bias must be the halls of power of legislative bodies in capital cities around the world.

Public Policy

The cultural acceptance of marginalized groups almost always lags behind public policy, which almost invariably lags behind corporate innovation. Though this may have seemed a perfectly fine approach during an analog period with historic population expansion and during which public policy encouraged the sidelining of the oldest members of the workforce, today, such policies stand in the way of future growth.

Most jurisdictions have removed a legislated age at which people must retire from paid work. However, in some places, such as Japan and South Korea, employers are allowed to force retirement based on age alone—in some cases as low as 55. One of the consequences of systems like this has been the creation of a two-tiered labor market. There is also a significant loss of human capital when people retire and then reengage in potentially less skilled and almost always lower-paid work.

These policies were originally put in place to open up the labor market to younger workers. However, we now understand that for the most part, policies enforcing mandatory retirement ages do not help create jobs for youths, as was originally thought, but do undercut older workers' ability to remain assets in the workforce, as well as productive members of society.

Japan and South Korea are not alone. Organizations including the Asian Development Bank, the Organisation for Economic Co-operation and Development, the United Nations, and the World Bank force retirement before the age of 65—the exceptions, of course, being senior-level executive leaders with the power to negotiate extra years on the job. Many other countries, including the United States, still have age limits on certain professions, such as pilots and police, even though age has nothing to do with people's ability to do their job.

Some countries, including the United States, have moved to outlaw age discrimination in most professions. The Age Discrimination in Employment Act (ADEA) of 1967, the first anti–age discrimination law in the world, protects employees over the age of 40 with respect to any term, condition, or privilege of employment, including hiring, firing, promotion and transfers, layoff, compensation, benefits, job assignments, and training. In practice, this means that employers cannot say that a certain age is preferred in job ads and recruiting materials, set age limits for training programs, retaliate against individuals if they file charges of age discrimination or help the government investigate charges, or force employees to retire at a certain age, except for a few exceptions, as noted above.

Examples of age discrimination have included showing a hiring preference for younger workers or retaining younger workers over older ones during layoffs or organizational restructuring; this can be innocuous and based exclusively on the cost of older, more experienced employees versus younger, less experienced ones. Regardless, organizations should always contemplate the loss of expertise (and institutional knowledge) in their redundancy calculations. They should also consider offering older, more expensive workers the ability to job share or shift into phased retirement, an arrangement that allows an older worker to continue working with a reduced workload and transition from full-time employment to full-time retirement over time. This option may be valuable to both employer and employees, as evidenced by the growth in such programs over the past decade. For many employers, these programs will become a necessity as the traditional working-age population begins to dwindle in the Super Age. Flexible work arrangements will rule the day.

Organizations may also discriminate by offering better terms and conditions of employment to younger workers, providing choice job assignments only to young workers, or not including older workers in new training initiatives or considering them in the development of such programs at all. Workplaces tend to emphasize skills training that is germane to their occupation, such as classes on workplace culture or organizational procedures. Older workers may already have those skills but could benefit greatly from upskilling in other areas, such as technology or communications, which are not always offered or promoted to them, leaving older workers lagging behind their younger peers and at a comparative disadvantage in the workplace.

Regardless of the law, a 2018 survey by AARP found that two-thirds of workers between the ages of 45 and 74 said they had seen or experienced ageism in the workplace. It is worse in certain parts of the country and the economy. Take Silicon Valley, for example, the home of the "tech bro," a subculture of mostly young, mostly White men who spend their free time partying with others like themselves, and the tech industry, where the 150 biggest tech companies have actually faced more accusations of old-age bias over the past decade than racial or gender bias, which is odd, since a North Carolina State University study of Stack Overflow members found that programmers in their fifties exhibited expertise in more areas than younger ones did.

The largest formal accusation of systemic age discrimination in the United States came in the summer of 2020, when the Equal Employment Opportunity Commission (EEOC) decided that the global technology powerhouse IBM, which employs 383,000 people worldwide (IBM stopped providing breakouts of the number of US employees in 2010) and is the world's twenty-eighth largest employer, had been engaged in systematic age discrimination between 2013 and 2018, when it had shed thousands of older workers in the United States.

The EEOC investigation uncovered top-down messaging from IBM's highest ranks directing managers to engage in an aggressive approach to significantly reduce the head count of older workers to "make room for" younger ones. The result could affect around six thousand former employees and cost IBM millions of dollars in settlement payments due to a federal lawsuit. According to EEOC acting chair Victoria Lipnic, "As we've studied the current state of age discrimination this past year in commemorating the ADEA, we've seen many similarities between age discrimination and harassment. Like harassment, everyone knows it happens every day to workers in all kinds of jobs, but few speak up. It's an open secret."

European countries passed age discrimination legislation significantly later than their American counterparts. However, their approach is much more holistic and considers age discrimination as a bias that affects both young and old.

In 2006, for example, Germany introduced the General Equal Treatment Act. The law allows those who feel they have faced age discrimination, regardless of their age, to bring a civil suit against their employer or have their case heard by employment law courts. This unique approach allows for a more universal opportunity to counteracting ageism. The first big test of the law came when the Federal Labour Court disallowed a sliding scale for the number of vacation days based on the age of civil servants. Until the court ruling, employees under 30 were allowed twenty-six days annually, those aged 30 to 40 were granted twenty-nine days, and those over 40 enjoyed thirty days, but public employers must now offer thirty days to everyone. For older employees, the court has also ruled against mandatory retirement ages based on age alone for professions such as pilots.

The UK government also outlawed all age discrimination in the Equality Act 2010, abolished the mandatory retirement age, and prohibited employers from making retirement compulsory starting in 2011. The Equality Act specifically calls out discrimination against the young, who are often underpaid or belittled at work, as well as older people, who are excluded from opportunities to join or remain in the workplace.

Journalistic reporting, lawsuits, and legislative action have all had profound effects in encouraging society to be more age inclusive, but it is not enough. Other marginalized groups have spent decades, if not centuries, fighting for their rightful place in society. The rights of older people are no different. It is important to remember that rights include much more than the law specifies and bias will subside with constant advocacy and awareness in the hope that someday permanent cultural changes will be secured.

Inclusion Champions

Executives of US companies often get a bad rap for their lack of integration of their companies with people of color, women, and LGBTQ+, and sometimes it is well-deserved. However, in the 1940s and 1950s, some visionaries saw the value of racial integration, albeit from two very different perspectives: good business and good morals.

The first perspective, which considers only the bottom line, is the path that organizations today must consider as they begin to compete in the Super Age, highlighting the idea that fair employment is good for business and discrimination is bad for the bottom line. The deliberate exclusion of workers or consumers based on the color of their skin was irrational because it left potential profits on the table. The same holds true for discrimination based on age.

In her 2009 book, *Racial Integration in Corporate America, 1940–1990*, Jennifer Delton of Skidmore College waded into the thorny issue of racial integration in the American workforce. She noted an advertising executive who defended his decision to hire a Black man in 1952, saying "I'm not a crusader. This is a cold calculated move on my part for the dollar sign only. I was not pushed. I was not shoved. I was only moved by the dollar sign." Though there is some question as to whether inclusive hiring practices were profitable at that point in time—largely because they cost a lot to implement—the United States' biggest companies got behind the idea. Corporate America gave the green light to integration.

The premonition of the growing importance of the African American market and the need to hire Black men and women to help meet the needs of these consumers early in US workplace integration is backed up by statistics today. According to Boston Consulting Group, companies with above-average diversity on their management teams report revenue 19 percent higher and profit margins 9 percent higher than companies with below-average diversity. What's wild is that a whopping 83 percent of global executives realize that an age-diverse workforce is key to business growth and success, yet only 6 percent have implemented nonbiased recruiting policies.

Smart companies are beginning to embrace generational differences as an asset and no longer see them as a liability. They are living in the reality of the Super Age, a time in which there will need to be more generational parity in the workforce, because it already exists in society and the marketplace. Airbnb went so far as to recruit the hotel entrepreneur and "modern elder" Chip Conley out of retirement to lead the strategy that would transform it into a hospitality company. Older workers are also the secret ingredient in product and service design and development as companies begin to scramble for insights into older consumers.

Integrating and leveraging diverse ages aren't happening in the United States at the same rate they are overseas. Perhaps this is because there isn't a clear-cut mandate, or perhaps many corporate executives perceive the US workforce and economy as being relatively young and don't see the coming skills shortages. Change is coming to the United States and other nations as the proportion of older people in the workforce continues to grow.

While at AARP, I had the opportunity to work with some of the world's most innovative organizations and economies on their strategies to recruit, retain, and sustain older workers. My hallmark project, AARP Best Employers International, uncovered and rewarded the best practices of organizations as small as Brammertz Schreinerei & Fensterbau, a specialist carpentry company with twenty-five employees located in Aachen, Germany, to the National Environment Agency, a government organization in Singapore, and BT, the leading telecom provider in the United Kingdom. These organizations, as well as others, are varied in size and scope, but they all agree that age-exclusive policies are bad for business and age-inclusive ones are good for the bottom line.

In some cases, such as that of the German automaker BMW in 2009, the leadership realized that the company was going to face a labor shortage within a decade, due in large part to the country's aging workforce. Rather than bury their heads in the sand, they sought their employees' counsel on how to build a more age-friendly plant in Dingolfing. They made a modest investment that made work easier and more ergonomic. The result was improved working conditions, extended working lives, and improved production quality. BMW's inclusive factory design is now a global standard being rolled out at the company's plants around the world.

The leaders of the Japanese retail giant AEON, the largest retail group in Asia and one of the largest in the world, recognized that the company's attitudes toward older people as customers were outdated. To combat this, it transformed three stores into "Grand Generation" shopping centers. The stores moved products for older people from the back of the store to the front, introduced social and health programming during the day, and made single-serve food packaging common in the grocery section, which benefited all single people, regardless of age. These changes, combined with an employee culture that welcomes older customers, have increased profits at the shopping centers by 10 percent and show that investing in marketing to older people can be very profitable.

Sometimes the case studies are intensely personal, like that of Franz Haurenherm. Franz was born in Germany in 1934 and worked at Brammertz Schreinerei & Fensterbau from 1994 until shortly before his death in 2016 at the age of 82. He began at Brammertz at the age of 60 after losing his job at another company that had gone out of business. Alice Brammertz, a member of the management team, recalled to me recently that Franz knocked on the company's door one day and asked if it needed an "old carpenter," and the company had hired him on the spot.

Franz was wildly popular with the Brammertz staff and was seen as the "go-to guy" for all projects, not only because he possessed highly technical skills and had a great demeanor but also because he had a passion for the craft he had spent his whole life perfecting. Brammertz leveraged Franz's experience to its advantage, addressed ageism in the workforce, and maximized intergenerational power by pairing him with its apprentices, some as young as 17, with whom he regularly exchanged his understanding of old-world techniques for their expertise in new-world technology.

Sometimes the case stories are incredibly timely, such as the one of Chicago's "Old Dolls." This group of women nurses based at Northwestern Memorial Hospital has brought their average working experience of forty years to tackling the covid-19 pandemic. Though they know that they are statistically more likely to contract the disease and die of it than non-medical workers are, they are risking their lives for the greater good. They have inspired and mentored younger nurses, working at their side in naturally occurring intergenerational teams.

We need to stop thinking about aging as bad when in reality it has the potential to be one of the greatest social and business opportunities that will arrive in our lifetimes. Today, there are 100 million people aged 50 or older in the United States and more than 440 million in China. According to a Brookings study, "they are projected to spend just under $15 trillion (in 2011/PPP), up from $8.7 trillion in 2020." The over-65 population is expected to nearly achieve this figure by the end of this decade. The economic success of our societies can continue only if our economies become more inclusive of older people. The failure to attack ageism, build intergenerational teams, and develop age-inclusive products and services may cause economic slowdown or recession. For example, the OECD countries, which can expect an average growth rate of nearly 3 percent over the next thirty years, could see that shaved down to nearly 2 percent. This is due to the fact that there will be fewer working-age people to pay for a growing number of individuals in need of financial support and health care. These are individuals who have been made redundant or have retired too soon and with too few resources. This will be a reality if we maintain our current course.

7

Canaries in the Coal Mine

We've entered a period of time when rural areas are perceived as tethered to the past, while urban ones believe they are reaching for the future; this is playing out in just about all facets of society and economy. Yet rural areas can act as canaries in the coal mine, heralding the positive and negative outcomes of a Super Age that is well managed or not. They can act as laboratories for age-inclusive innovation, drive economic opportunity for all generations, and give us a glimpse into the future, when older people will far outnumber the young.

The United States is not alone in this urban and rural divide, even though it may often seem more pronounced to the casual observer. As of 2007, the United Nations reported that for the first time in human history, there were more people living in urban areas than in rural ones worldwide. The challenges that have been born of the growing friction between rural and urban residents have manifested themselves everywhere from the United Kingdom, through the contentious Brexit vote, to France, through the tumultuous *gilets jaunes* (yellow vests) protests. It is also playing out in the electoral trends in countries such as Argentina, Malaysia, and Japan, where older and rural voters have an outsized say in national elections, and in places such as Australia, where far-right nationalist anti-urban politicians have captured the attention of the "gray vote" in the countryside. The apparent social discord between rural and urban areas only tells part of the story, often ignoring other trends—such as globalization, urbanization, digitization—and how they interplay, including demographics and population aging.

In a place such as China, for example, where urbanization and population aging are happening at breakneck speed, entire villages have emptied out as the working-age population departs the fields for the factories, leaving an older population behind to care for school-age children. The shift has been so swift and so dramatic that the Chinese government enacted a law on Protection of the Rights and Interests of the Elderly in 2013, mandating that adult children bear the responsibility for the physical and emotional care of their elderly parents—a Band-Aid solution to a gunshot problem.

The reaction by the state underscores how quickly the shift toward an older, more urban society has been for the Chinese. The confluence of these two trends has in many ways eroded traditional familial structures and support networks. The migration of young people to the cities, which has largely been encouraged by the government, has left a generational imbalance behind in the villages and countryside, so there is an odd irony to the passage of this law.

All across the world, rural communities have been exposed to some of the harshest realities of modernity—automation, consolidation, globalization, climate change, and lower birth rates—which have made it more difficult to maintain a family-owned farm or live a traditional country lifestyle. In the United States, for example, 96 percent of the more than 2.2 million farms are family owned. An astonishing 70 percent of that farmland is expected to change hands over the next twenty years, yet many family operations "do not have a next generation skilled in or willing to continue farming," according to the National Institute of Food and Agriculture of the USDA, meaning that the land will likely be sold to larger corporate interests, such as Cargill and Monsanto.

Rural communities must also grapple with the reality that they are slipping behind in the race to modernize, to become diverse in both age and race, and to build tax revenue to support infrastructure and public institutions. In rural areas that are experiencing positive population growth, it is often driven by retirees seeking a pastoral life. They do not contribute to the public coffers the same way a working-age population does, leaving many rural communities teetering on the brink of survival.

As the Super Age comes into being over the next few years, it will be essential to address the unique demographic challenges faced by rural areas, including extreme population aging and depopulation. The social inequalities and economic disparities faced by rural populations, especially when measured against urban ones, simply cannot be ignored anymore. Rural communities will need more direct support, at least in the short term. However, some of the communities could end up being ideal proving grounds for innovations that will benefit all of us in the Super Age. Rural lands are the new frontier of these challenges.

Contraction

Rural communities around the world are facing the most dramatic challenges of the Super Age. The transition is coming faster there, and they must often contend with having fewer resources, whether health care, education, or financial institutions, all of which were already resource depleted and financially challenged due to the out-migration of the working-age population. To be clear: these tensions are not unique to rural communities; they are just being felt there first. How successful we are at addressing them will determine how we will eventually meet the challenge in suburban and urban communities.

More than a third of all counties in the United States already fulfill the Super Age designation: 20 percent of the population older than 65. However, nearly nine in ten of those counties are rural. This means that rural counties, many of which are already economically

Youngest and Oldest Counties: Median Age of US Counties in 2018

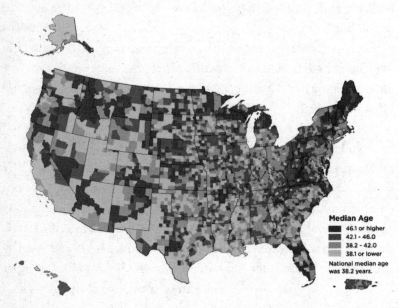

US Department of Commerce, Economics and Statistics Administration, US Census Bureau, census.gov. Source: Vintage 2018 Population Estimate; www.census.gov /programs-survey/popest.html

disadvantaged, are being buffeted by significant demographic head-winds, which could have a compounding effect. Dozens of those rural counties have a 65-and-older population greater than 25 percent of the total population, and a growing number of rural areas have a median age of greater than 50.

Two trends are driving the aging of rural communities: younger, working-age people are leaving for manufacturing and service jobs in cities, a trend that has been driven by consolidation and shifts in consumption, and the older people who are left behind are staying, growing older, and eventually dying off. Over a third of US rural counties are experiencing significant and constant population loss, with some of the most significant happening across the heartland. A whopping two-thirds of the 99 counties of the state of Iowa, for example, are losing population. These trends portend a potential future of older, poorer, and vanishing towns and communities.

Percentage of the Population 65 Years and Over in Rural and Urban Areas by State: 2012–2016

(In percent)

	Rural	Urban	Rural, all ages
Vermont	65.3	34.7	61.3
Maine	62.7	37.3	61.5
Mississippi	54.7	45.3	50.3
West Virginia	52.5	47.5	50.9
Arkansas	50.5	49.5	43.3
Montana	49.6	50.4	43.7
South Dakota	49.4	50.6	42.8
North Dakota	46.5	53.5	39.5
Alabama	45.0	55.0	40.7
Kentucky	44.4	55.6	40.9
New Hampshire	43.3	56.7	39.8
Iowa	41.1	58.9	35.6
Wyoming	40.6	59.4	35.3
Oklahoma	39.8	60.2	33.3
Tennessee	39.2	60.8	33.2
North Carolina	39.2	60.8	33.2
Alaska	37.1	62.9	34.1
South Carolina	36.1	63.9	32.8
Idaho	35.7	64.3	28.7
Wisconsin	35.1	64.9	29.8
Nebraska	35.0	65.0	26.3
Missouri	34.2	65.8	29.3
Virginia	32.7	67.3	24.1
Minnesota	32.4	67.6	26.3
Kansas	32.3	67.7	25.5
Georgia	32.3	67.7	24.3
Indiana	31.0	69.0	27.2
Michigan	29.9	70.1	25.4
Louisiana	28.9	71.1	26.6
Oregon	26.8	73.2	18.5
New Mexico	25.6	74.4	22.1
Ohio	23.5	76.5	21.9
Pennsylvania	23.5	76.5	21.1
UNITED STATES	22.9	77.1	18.9
Texas	21.5	78.5	15.2
Washington	20.6	79.4	15.5
Delaware	20.6	79.4	17.3
Colorado	18.6	81.4	13.7
Maryland	15.8	84.2	12.6
Illinois	14.7	85.3	11.3
New York	14.2	85.8	11.9
Arizona	13.1	86.9	10.2
Utah	13.1	86.9	9.5
Connecticut	13.0	87.0	11.9
Rhode Island	9.9	90.1	9.2
Florida	9.3	90.7	8.7
Massachusetts	9.1	90.9	8.0
Hawaii	8.8	91.2	7.5
Nevada	8.2	91.8	5.7
California	7.1	92.9	4.9
New Jersey	5.8	94.2	5.3
District of Columbia		100.0	0.0

Note: Data based on sample. For information on confidentiality protection, sampling error, nonsampling error, and definitions, see www.census.gov/acs. Source: US Census Bureau, 2012–2016 American Community Survey, 5-Year Estimates

Many people who live in rural areas are also concentrated in US states that have more than half of their older populations in rural areas. From 2012 through 2016, on average, 17.5 percent of the rural population was over 65 compared to 13.8 percent in urban areas, and the gap is widening. Three-quarters of the older adults of the South and Midwest live in rural areas; two-thirds of older adults in Maine and Vermont live in rural areas. The preponderance of older people living in these areas—often retired or working in low-wage jobs—generally leads to an erosion of services and infrastructure, due largely to the diminishing of tax revenues that are generated by an employed population. Serving older people's complex health care needs becomes particularly difficult and expensive when population density diminishes and access to plentiful labor dries up.

The United States isn't alone in this change. The population of rural Germany will drop by 7.3 percent during the same twelve-year period, 2018–2030, while Italy's will fall by 15 percent. By the 2040s, the depopulation of rural Japan will outpace that of nearly every other country in the world. Some predict that hundreds of small cities and towns around the planet will be completely deserted over time. Many more will become unlivable by today's standards.

The rural challenge in Japan may paint a realistic, albeit other-worldly and somewhat dystopic, picture of the future where population aging goes unchecked. The town of Nagoro, for example, on the island of Shikoku about 350 miles from Tokyo, has been experiencing popu-lation aging and decline for decades, with the last child in the village being born about twenty years ago. The youngest person there today is nearly 60, and only about twenty-five people still call Nagoro home.

To compensate for Nagoro's lack of population, the remaining townspeople have placed lifelike dolls of children and adults in the abandoned structures, including the town school, to simulate what life used to be like. They wanted the place to feel normal again, but instead, it now feels surreal. Nagoro is now known as the "Valley of Dolls," a place where scarecrows outnumber humans more than ten to one, and it has received much media attention and reportage.

Nagoro's demographic downward spiral is both cautionary and problematic, because many who have reported on it have treated it as an oddity rather than as an omen and potential reality of the fu-ture. Rarely have the reports mentioned the crippling loss of jobs and essential services, including schools, hospitals, and financial and retail services, that brought Nagoro to this point. Population losses, in many cases, can also lead to an increase in substance abuse and suicide.

The rural challenge boils down to younger people leaving countryside communities due to lack of opportunity and the older people who are left behind not being able to afford to leave. Many older people across rural America own their homes, and as the populations of those areas have dwindled, real estate prices have tanked. If those older people were able to sell their homes, the proceeds likely wouldn't cover a move to a more prosperous urban area or the basic costs of long-term care. They therefore end up losing most, if not all, of the financial assets they built over a lifetime.

Overall, rural seniors in both the United States and Europe are more likely to be whiter and less educated than those living in cities. In the United States, four out of five people living in rural areas are Caucasian. They are more likely to be male and more likely to be living alone or in nursing homes. Studies have found that older adults in rural communities are more likely to suffer from chronic disease—a typical pattern for people with less education, lower income, and less access to medical care. More than one-fourth of rural men and nearly one-fifth of rural women reported that they socialized with others less than once a month, putting them at higher risk of isolation, a social determinant of poor health.

Birth rates are falling in rural areas, too, albeit more slowly than in urban areas. In the period 2007–2017, total fertility rates in the United States fell in rural and metropolitan counties: 12 percent in rural counties, 16 percent in small or medium metro counties, and 18 percent in large metro counties, a gap that is widening. Regardless of these data points, the primary differences between the two populations remain: rural populations have greater outward migration and lower foreign immigration than urban areas do, which is making them older faster. In total, rural areas experienced a net loss of 380,000 people over the past twenty years. The loss would have been much larger—nearly 1 million—if it had not been partially offset by nearly 600,000 immigrants.

Immigrants account for approximately 4.8 percent of the rural population compared to 16.6 percent of the urban one, and the percentage is growing. Yet the future of immigration in the United States remains in question due to the confluence of dwindling rural prosperity, draconian immigration policies, and borders being closed due to the covid-19 pandemic. The loss of this influx could be disastrous, since immigration from abroad is one of the most effective tools to combat population decline in areas experiencing outward migration.

Depopulation is far more prevalent in remote rural counties that are not adjacent to metropolitan areas, whether small, medium, or large cities. There are simply different realities for places such as the Hudson Valley, New York, a weekend retreat for wealthy urbanites from New York City, and Mineral County, Colorado, which is over four hours by car from Pueblo, Colorado, the closest midsized city with a population greater than 100,000. This difference suggests that a one-size-fits-all approach to the challenges facing rural Super Age counties is folly.

Addressing Epidemics of Loss

Rural challenges, especially those associated with population aging and decline, are often neglected in nations dominated by urban interests. However, a vibrant, healthy rural population is essential to a nation's intellectual and cultural diversity. Rural traditions, which may be seen as outdated by urbanites, have made rich contributions to the development of nations. These areas cannot be seen only as the places where food and energy come from, and this is where many countries, especially the United States, have gone wrong.

As rural jobs became automated, fewer people were required to run farms, cut trees, and process food. Individuals who would never have considered a move to the city relocated because there were more opportunities for better pay in urban areas. The trends after the Great Recession of 2008 illustrated that prosperity did not come evenly to rural and urban areas. What followed in rural communities was chronic out-migration by young adults of reproductive age, leaving behind a greater population of aging adults and increased mortality as a result of drug addiction and suicide.

These so-called deaths of despair have killed tens of thousands of people each year for nearly a decade and contributed to a downward trend in life expectancy, not only in rural communities but in the United States as a whole. The term was first coined by the husband-and-wife team of Anne Case and Angus Deaton, the latter of whom won the Nobel Prize in Economic Sciences in 2015. These trends began in the early 2000's, ran almost parallel to the Great Recession, and continued up until 2016.

According to a 2017 report by the American Farm Bureau Federation and National Farmers Union, nearly three-quarters of people directly working in farming "have been directly impacted by opioid abuse, either by knowing someone, having a family member addicted, having taken an illegal opioid or having dealt with addiction themselves." Yet only one in three rural adults (34 percent) said that addiction treatment would be easy to find. Just over a third (38 percent) were confident that they could find care that is effective, covered by insurance, convenient, or affordable.

Rural areas led urban areas in drug overdose deaths from 2007 through 2015, according to the CDC. In 2016 to 2017, urban areas edged out their rural counterparts, even though the female mortality rate for overdose remained higher in the countryside.

Mortality data from the National Vital Statistics System (NVSS) revealed annual county-level trends in suicide rates during 2001–2015 for rural counties, small and medium metropolitan counties, and large metropolitan counties, as well as demographics and mechanisms of death. Overall, suicide death rates in rural counties (17.32 per 100,000 inhabitants) were higher than in medium/small metropolitan counties (14.86 per 100,000) and large metropolitan counties (11.92 per 100,000) during that period.

In 2018, suicide rates were higher among adults aged 45 to 54 years (20.04 per 100,000) and 55 to 64 years (20.20 per 100,000), with the rate highest among adults aged 52 to 59 years (21.56 per 100,000). Younger groups have consistently had lower suicide rates than middle-aged and older adults. The suicide rate rose by more than a third for Americans aged 25 to 64, according to research reported in *JAMA Network Open*. Rural suicide rates were 25 percent higher than those in major metropolitan areas.

These challenges hollowed out the working-age population and supercharged the aging of rural communities. The demographic changes put great strain on the essential services that make them work. Altogether, these shifts began a domino effect that has yet to slow down, creating what feels like a demographic dystopia in many rural communities. Towns that were once vibrant seemingly have little chance of becoming great again.

The Gutting of Education and Health Care

When populations begin to decline, especially among younger income-generating families, public infrastructure comes under a huge strain, and schools are often the first casualty. This is one of the earlier signs of the demographic downward spiral, a period in which essential services, both public and private, begin to shutter with no promise of return. In the past few decades, rural school districts have been merging small-town schools into larger regional ones or closing altogether. This is particularly prevalent in the Midwest, Southwest, and Deep South, where children now have to travel long distances, sometimes for hours, to receive a basic education.

Rural community schools typically close their doors due to shrinking public funding, low attendance, or, in some cases, a desire to lower costs through consolidation. The irony is that time after time, studies have shown that students in small community-based schools often have higher test scores and graduation rates, as well as greater participation in extracurricular activities. These schools are also more attractive to the young families that support the tax base.

When its schools close, a town also loses one of its main hubs of activity and community interaction; it loses its identity. In many cases, this speeds up the demographic change and leads to the loss of other essential services, such as hospitals and health care centers. The loss of hospitals and health care centers has an outsized impact on older people, who often utilize them at higher rates than their younger peers do. Older people are doubly affected by their loss if they are forced to travel a long distance for medical care, since the ability to drive (and specifically to drive long distances) is one of the hurdles of old age.

Over the past decade, more than 120 rural hospitals across the United States closed, according to a study by the Chicago-based Chartis Center for Rural Health. As of January 2020, there were 1,844 rural hospitals in this country, so the closures represent about 7 percent of the previous total. The study also found that the shuttering of these facilities has sped up in recent years, with 19 hospitals closing in 2019 alone—the worst year of the past decade. The closure of these hospitals presents yet another challenge for rural communities that are already grappling with poor access to health care.

It should come as no surprise that these hospital closures are located primarily in states without proper levels of public funding (Medicare and Medicaid) for the most at-risk populations (old, poor, or both), and the trend doesn't show any signs of changing course. This coincides with the decrease in private-pay patients and elective procedures that were the primary revenue drivers of the hospitals that were already on a downward slope. The covid-19 pandemic, which blocked elective procedures in many hospitals, may exacerbate closure rates at hospitals nationwide, prompting the American Hospital Association to request $100 billion in federal emergency funding in 2020, citing rural hospitals' inability to survive big losses for a long period. These closures will force older people to travel for hours, often by car, for basic care.

Before the covid-19 pandemic, according to Chartis, 453 rural hospitals (Critical Access Hospitals and Rural and Community Hospitals) were vulnerable to closure based on their performance levels. Critical Access Hospitals, for reference, are a designation by the Department of Health and Human Services; these hospitals are eligible for greater levels of federal funding. Their shuttering would represent roughly 20 percent of all rural hospitals in the United States—a devastating prospect.

	RURAL PERCENTAGE	URBAN PERCENTAGE
Underlying health conditions (ages 20 to 84)	23.7	3.0
Older adult population scale	15.9	4.0
Lacking health insurance (ages 25 to 64)	20.2	10.5
Distance to county with an intensive care hospital	11.3	0.3

Source: Economic Research Service, United States Department of Agriculture, https://www.ers.usda.gov/amber-waves/2021/february/rural-residents-appear-to-be-more-vulnerable-to-serious-infection-or-death-from-coronavirus-covid-19.

The loss of vital health infrastructure has also played out dramatically during the pandemic. Urban centers bore the overwhelming majority of the first 100,000 covid-19 deaths in the United States, with rural communities making up about 5 percent of the total. However, the second 100,000 deaths were a much different story, with rural communities making up nearly 15 percent of the total. People living in rural areas, it turns out, are more vulnerable to severe illness or death from covid-19 because of underlying health conditions, older age, and lack of medical insurance.

In the most recent surge, which began in late September 2020, the highest case rates were in rural counties, particularly those with no town larger than 2,499 residents. Rural communities in the South and Midwest were hit the hardest, with some losing, per 100,000, the same or a greater number of people than New York City, the global epicenter of the disease during the first half of 2020. Due to a lag in vaccination rates, many of the Midwest and southern states have remained hot spots throughout 2021 with some experiencing a third wave of infections that rival the worst days of the pandemic, even as coastal states have begun to return to some sense of normalcy.

It is not just the health care infrastructure that is faltering; it is also

Cumulative Confirmed COVID-19 Cases per 100,000 Residents by County on February 2, 2021

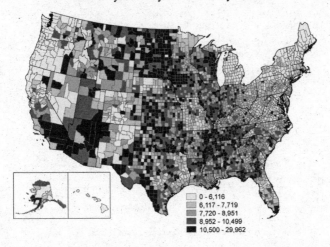

0 - 6,116
6,117 - 7,719
7,720 - 8,951
8,952 - 10,499
10,500 - 29,962

Note: The ranges of COVID-19 case rates shown in the map are quintiles of the distribution, rounded to the nearest integer. For 22 Utah counties, cases are reported for multi-county health districts rather than county-specific rates.

Source: USDA, Economic Research Service using data from Johns Hopkins University Center for System Science and Engineering (accessed February 3, 2021).

Cumulative Confirmed COVID-19 Cases per 100,000 Residents in Metro and Nonmetro Areas, March 1, 2020 to February 2, 2021

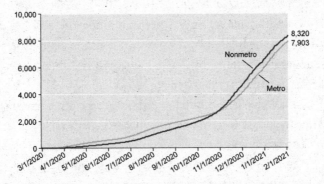

Note: Data for metro and nonmetro areas are based on the 2013 definition of metropolitan and nonmetropolitan counties, as determined by the Office of Management and Budget.

Source: USDA, Economic Research Service using data from Johns Hopkins University Center for System Science and Engineering (accessed February 3, 2021)

COVID-19 case rates in rural (nonmetro) areas surged during summer 2020, eventually surpassing urban (metro) rates.

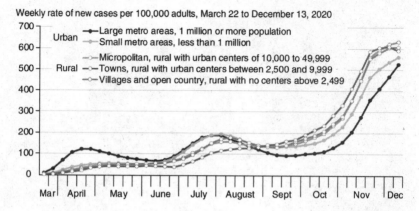

Weekly rate of new cases per 100,000 adults, March 22 to December 13, 2020

Urban
- Large metro areas, 1 million or more population
- Small metro areas, less than 1 million

Rural
- Micropolitan, rural with urban centers of 10,000 to 49,999
- Towns, rural with urban centers between 2,500 and 9,999
- Villages and open country, rural with no centers above 2,499

Note: Chart shows a three-week moving average of new COVID-19 cases per 100,000 adults ages 20 and older, with weekly rates averaged over the previous 3-week period. Micropolitan includes adjacent rural counties when inter-county commuting is substantial.

Source: USDA, Economic Research Service using data from Johns Hopkins University, replacing missing information with data from the New York Times, "Coronavirus in the U.S." dataset.

the health care workforce. The rural health care workforce has aged at a fast and dramatic pace, reflecting a broader pattern of younger physicians rejecting rural practice, according to a 2019 report in the *New England Journal of Medicine*. From 2000 to 2017, the number of country doctors grew by only 3 percent, while the number of physicians under 50 decreased by 25 percent. This means that, everything else remaining constant, by 2030, there will be, on average, only 9.4 physicians per 10,000 people in rural locales.

This challenge isn't limited to physician recruitment and retention. Rural health and long-term care providers regularly raise concerns about the ability to recruit and retain nurses and aides, and this will affect the overall quality of the care provided by that system. This is often due to the ability to find individuals who are qualified, can pass a drug test, and are willing and able to work for the pay offered. These shortages could contribute to increased survey citations in nursing care (as part of the oversight process, the government surveys nursing homes, and when there are problems with the survey, nursing homes are cited for infractions). The situation also increases job turnover across the board and costs for health care providers, and decreases satisfaction for patients, residents, and family caregivers.

The outbreak of covid-19 in the United States in 2020 may have moved up the retirement deadline for many doctors and health care workers, who typically enjoy longer-than-average careers. In the summer of 2020, the Physicians Foundation, a nonprofit group, published a report on a survey of 3,513 physicians stating that 4 percent said they wouldn't return to work due to covid-19 health risks, while 28 percent said that they would "continue to practice but with serious concerns about their health due to COVID-19." Given the age of the rural health care workforce, the projected changes could happen in rural areas even faster.

The Demise of Main Street

Main Street "mom-and-pop" businesses have been under siege for decades, starting with the encroachment of big-box retailers in the 1990s. The retail landscape was further traumatized by an onslaught of retail closures over the past decade, including household names such as JCPenney and Macy's, which disproportionately affected rural America. Even Walmart, the original disrupter and the biggest employer in many states, has closed nearly two hundred locations in the past decade, many of which were located in the smallest country towns.

Since the start of the Great Recession, the growth of small businesses has been concentrated in urban and urban adjacent areas, according to "Economic Recovery and Business Dynamism in Rural America," a report by the Center for American Progress (CAP). During the same period of time, nearly all rural areas have lost thousands of jobs and witnessed a contraction in business creation. Public polices intended to encourage rural start-ups have not always worked as intended, and small businesses that weathered the initial pandemic-related closures early in 2020 may not survive a second lockdown if cases spike without some type of federal or state financial support.

One of the most devasted areas is retail banking. Nearly eight hundred rural counties lost 1,533 bank branches, representing 14 percent of their total branches, according to the 2019 report "Perspectives from Main Street: Bank Branch Access in Rural Communities" by the Federal Reserve. Though urban counties also lost branches, they lost just 9 percent of the branches, according to the report. The findings highlight a broader trend of the widening gap between rural areas and better-served and more prosperous urban centers. Some people may shrug this off, especially given the rise of online banking, but rural communities often suffer from poor broadband access as well as a lack of digital literacy, both of which are needed to access financial services online.

Aging populations, including those in rural areas, have the potential to be contributors, but we must realign our resources to support the development of small enterprises and entrepreneurs that can spur growth. This will require a recalibration of our attitudes toward the economic potential of our older citizens, as well as our collective attitudes toward rural populations.

If we don't make the investments that are needed to bring back Main Street businesses to rural communities, the collapse of those communities is all but certain. Services will be lost, businesses will continue to close, and the remaining healthy populace will move to seek out opportunities closer to urban centers. Only the sick and helpless will be left behind.

Paths Forward

Sadly, there is no clear blueprint for managing the aging and potential emptying out of rural communities. However, if we believe that there is value in the culture and traditions of our rural societies, we must invest in them through public infrastructure projects, as well as utilize technology and innovation through the private sector wherever possible.

If rural communities are to regain their footing, we must look to the best practices currently being used to reinvigorate and serve them. Fortunately, many of the best projects build upon existing infrastructure. We must also take the realities of the current rural predicament into account while addressing urban bias against these areas.

We can also draw inspiration and lessons from previous times when great public sector leaders did great things that affected populations positively. In 1933, a few years after the onset of the Great Depression, President Franklin Delano Roosevelt moved forward with legislation that created the New Deal and the Tennessee Valley Authority (TVA). The TVA was a massive government-supported private sector corporation that built dams to deliver electricity to more than 10 million rural Americans. It is still in operation today and still profitable.

The kind of bold action that was needed to pull the United States out of the Great Depression was not dissimilar from what's being attempted in the American Rescue Plan, one of the largest and most consequential spending plans in US history. Coming in at $1.9 trillion, the hallmark legislation signed into law by President Joe Biden in March 2021 provides significant investments in rural communities by expanding internet connectivity and establishing a homeowner assistance fund to assist struggling homeowners with mortgage payments, property taxes, property insurance, utilities, and other housing-related costs. The plan also attempts to address the needs of families who have lost their homes, students whose schools have moved online, food insecurity, and access to covid-19 testing and vaccinations. The plan implements funding that invests in the people of rural America:

- $500 million to help rural hospitals and local communities increase access to covid-19 vaccines and food assistance
- $100 million through September 2022 in rental assistance for low-income and elderly borrowers
- $39 million through September 2023 to help refinance direct loans under the Single Family Housing Guaranteed Loan Program and Single Family Housing Repair Loans & Grants

Future investments and innovations in the infrastructure of rural communities can take inspiration from other parts of the world. Japan, the country with the fastest rate of rural population aging, is utilizing its postal workers, through Japan Post's Watch Over Service, to deliver much-needed products and services to rural seniors who are at risk of isolation. La Poste, the French postal service, launched a similar service called Veiller Sur Mes Parents (Watch over My Parents) in 2017. Other postal services are looking at similar options. There is even a growing demand for the US Postal Service to add banking to its list of services. It's all part of a movement to leverage existing resources and infrastructure to solve Super Age challenges in rural communities.

England's Newcastle Building Society is already filling the void left by the big banks' leaving communities by serving rural areas through community centers. This approach of serving the countryside is a key part of Newcastle's strategy, and oftentimes, its banks sit alongside other essential community services, such as the post office, and are normally a fraction of the size of a traditional retail bank.

Other existing infrastructure that is no longer being used, such as schools, is being transformed into senior day care centers—a term that is fitting, although I loathe its use because of its connotations with children and the infantilization of older people that it implies. Some communities around the world are also showing that it is possible to merge the functions of schools and senior care under one roof to lower costs and benefit both the young and the old. One of the pioneering sites, Kotoen, which is located on the outskirts of Tokyo, married the needs of the young and the old in 1976. Every day, preschool-age children arrive at Kotoen and are greeted by the full-time residents, some of whom are centenarians. The children interact with their elders throughout the day, including during exercise and at mealtimes, and learn many life lessons from them, including about mortality. Today, it is a model that is being replicated around the world, including in the United States and across Europe.

The German government is focused on ensuring that older adults in underserviced rural areas have access to the same quality of care as in urban areas by leveraging e-health technology. Recent legislation requires that medical insurance companies establish telemedicine consultation services in rural areas that lack adequate medical provider coverage. The goal is to eventually provide fully remote teleconsultation services to individuals living in the countryside.

Technology is also seen as a solution for rural areas in the United States. The Department of Veterans Affairs' Office of Connected Care is working to bring digital technology to veterans and health care professionals in remote communities, extending access to care beyond the traditional office business. The Office of Connected Care focuses on improving health care through technology by engaging veterans and care teams outside of traditional health care visits, including telehealth.

Mobile services, such as Airbnb, are helping older people in villages in Japan to open their homes to visitors from around the world and generate income, which helps revitalize remote communities and curb the migration to cities. The Yoshino Cedar House, a collaboration between the Tokyo-based architect Go Hasegawa and the local community, came about as a response to the shrinking rural population in the rapidly aging country. Airbnb also has programs that focus on older hosts in rural Korea and Taiwan.

The ride-sharing app Uber has made serving rural Japan and its elders central to its business model in that country. In 2015, the company entered the Japanese market in some rural areas in Hokkaido and Kyoto Prefecture. Uber is particularly helpful for older residents with mobility challenges, as well as tourists wishing to access more remote areas, which is generally very difficult to do without a car. Uber also employs a diverse group of people, including retirees, students, and even stay-at-home parents. It has plans to expand throughout Japan by partnering with the existing taxi infrastructure wherever possible.

Regarding rural communities that are past the point of no return and beginning to vanish, towns such as Cammarata, located in the interior of Sicily, Italy, may offer a solution. Not long ago, Cammarata's government, as well as others in Italy, began offering houses for sale starting at one euro to draw in younger buyers and offset population aging and decline. Cammarata also happens to be home to Italy's largest concentration of centenarians. Buyers typically have to begin renovations on the homes within one year. The response, according to Cammarata's mayor, has been overwhelming.

Time will tell if Cammarata's decision will halt the out-migration of young people, as well as the brain drain that this and other communities are experiencing. Like other towns with similar demographics, Cammarata witnessed a possible reversal of fortune as younger people returned "home" during the pandemic. There is also hope that "neorurals," people who choose to move back to them or into such communities for the first time, might become a reality. The pandemic may be speeding up a shift in which people want to live, or at least aspire to live, outside cities. According to the real estate site Redfin, before the pandemic one in ten homebuyers said they were searching for a home in a rural area. Now one in five say they have looked at rural options. This change follows the disruption of the traditional workweek and office life, which, for a time during the pandemic, existed almost exclusively in a virtual world. Those who have the means may opt to maintain both a country home and an urban pied-à-terre, while others may forgo city life forever.

Even some US cities with unique geographic and demographic challenges are offering financial incentives for people to move into them. Tulsa, Oklahoma, which has been suffering from perennial outward migration that outpaces birth rates and inward migration, grants $10,000 for relocation expenses plus $1,000 from the George Kaiser Family Foundation for housing expenses for skilled individuals who are already engaged in remote work, which is paid out over the course of a year. Some US states that have already entered the Super Age, including Maine and Vermont, have been more explicit in their desire to recruit younger workers in an effort to offset some degree of population aging and bolster the tax base by actively marketing to younger populations and offering them direct cash payments, as well as tax incentives.

In order to address the demographic challenges in rural communities, we must be willing to get past our idea that investing in aging rural communities is bad for business, because it is far too easy to buy into the idea that urban areas with younger customers, larger customer bases, and higher pricing margins do better. Oftentimes, rural-based businesses do incredibly well, whether they be agriculture, agricultural technology (agtech), cottage industries, rural outsourcing, solopreneurs and small consultancies, or even community-based and cooperative retail outlets. Even though rural businesses tend to be smaller and grow more slowly, they're also likely to be more profitable than those in the city and have better survival rates. Entrepreneurs may have an easier time accessing investment capital in the countryside, too.

In his book *Reprogramming the American Dream: From Rural America to Silicon Valley—Making AI Serve Us All,* Microsoft's chief technology officer, Kevin Scott, offered an optimistic view of a future in which technology is leveraged to supplement and enhance the older rural workforce. He argued, and rightfully so, that robotics in particular can extend the working lives of individuals in labor-intensive jobs. This approach is already being utilized in Super Age countries such as Germany that are struggling with skills shortages in their manufacturing sector. Scott made the case that with investments to improve broadband access, as well as tax incentives to lure businesses, AI-driven manufacturing could thrive in the heartland.

Then there is the question of small-business succession, a hot topic in aging rural communities around the world. RedTire, short for Redefine Your Retirement, is located in the University of Kansas School of Business and works to secure succession arrangements in the state's rural areas without charge. The Center for Rural Entrepreneurship, based in Lincoln, Nebraska, works with communities across the United States and Canada to make them more enticing to a new generation of potential small-business owners.

Japan, which is facing some of the greatest challenges in business succession, enlisted the Japanese Small and Medium Enterprise Agency (SMEA) to create a Five-Year Plan for Business Succession, which encourages business owners to be aware of business succession and develop an environment that will motivate the next generations to succeed them. Without succession planning, many of Japan's traditional craft industries may cease to exist in the next decade.

Private equity firms are increasingly on the lookout for small and medium-sized businesses across Japan and other rural areas around the world that may have great products but haven't had access to the capital needed in the past. They are particularly keen to find businesses that don't have family succession or a buyer. Sometimes they buy such businesses outright, and sometimes they take a partial ownership stake with an eye on taking control at a later date. Such relationships have proved to be valuable for both the business owner and the investor.

These governments and corporations are clear-eyed and pragmatic in their response to the realities of the Super Age, and they are leveraging public resources and private innovation to meet the demands of a distinctly different demographic future. But simply reacting to change is not going to be enough to carry us toward excellence. We need to mitigate and address the bias that blinds us.

Bias, whether implicit or explicit, is a real problem, and when it is levied at historically marginalized groups, older people, or rural populations, it is particularly damaging and creates unnecessary barriers to progress. It holds society back from achieving its true potential and gets in the way of economic growth. A whole-of-society approach that focuses on equity and inclusion while leveraging the unique strengths that a diverse group of individuals and geographic locations bring can help make the Super Age a truly spectacular period for humanity; there is hope. But we have to do the work and leverage the contributions of all groups, generations, and geographic locations to transition to a more positive version of the future.

The continued failure to address inequalities early and often could exacerbate some of the bigger socioeconomic challenges that we face today. The longevity gap could widen even further than now, wealth may continue to concentrate in upper income groups, and the divide between urban and rural areas has the potential to expand to a chasm that cannot be bridged. This path could lead to a demographic dystopian future that will be impossible to recover from.

PART THREE

A New Demographic Order

| 8 |

A Novel Reality Emerges

The biggest misconception that people have about the Super Age is that it is all about old people all of the time. Though it is true that there are more people over the age of 65 alive on this planet than ever before, the exponential growth of this demographic has overshadowed the reality that extended longevity is altering the entire life course. The United Nations estimates that at least three-quarters of the global population will reach the age of 65 this year—the fraction was less than half that in 1960—and a growing number of people are living past that traditional retirement age. Octogenarians and above are now the fastest-growing demographic in the world.

Increasing life span doesn't mean just tacking on extra years at the end of life but stretching out the healthy, active years in the middle. This provides unique opportunities for businesses, in particular, to tap into new and emerging life stages, much as they did with teenagers and retirees in the last century. The scientific advances that have helped propel humanity into the Super Age are also helping people remain physically and mentally fit for longer than previous generations did. This progress may also have created social and economic conditions that have triggered younger generations to delay or reject traditional milestones, such as purchasing a home or a car or getting married and having children. All of these factors are coming together and forcing us to rethink our expectations about what it means to be 30, 50, 70, and beyond.

New products and services are also being developed and deployed to serve not only older populations but also multigenerational groups who are keen on living in good health for greater periods of time. Many companies are reconsidering their approach as social and economic realities change for large swaths of the population. Some of the innovations enable people who are living with chronic conditions and noncommunicable diseases to feel more "normal," but they are also helping to recalibrate the definition of the word *old*, since a growing number of people reject being defined by this term. And some of the most successful businesses are creating products and services that address the fears of decline that many people face, doing so in a non-threatening way. They are moving away from an age-based model of design and marketing and "threading the needle" masterfully between designing products and services that address consumers' needs while catering to their desire to be perceived as youthful and relevant. They are including generationally diverse and older populations in their design process, and they are making aging and longevity central to their human resource strategies and marketing and communications plans.

The First Wave of the Super Age

My father, Gary, is a Super Age consumer who is actively seeking out products and services that help him retain his health and his ability to engage in normal activities, such as driving, despite the fact that he suffered a stroke on Christmas Day 2017. Rather than bemoan his condition, he did the work of occupational therapy and sprang to action to identify and purchase products and services that would help him retain his dignity, independence, and purpose, while looking and feeling good.

Gary is not alone in this journey. Each year, hundreds of thousands of people in the United States suffer strokes, and by 2030, it is projected that 3.88 percent of the US population, or approximately 14 million people over the age of 18, will have had one. That's a lot of people who will be considering whether to slip into decline or utilize products and services that could help them live a fulfilling life.

One of the first things my father purchased was a new and safer automobile that is especially good for someone with his condition, which includes a slight decrease in his peripheral vision. He bought a Porsche Macan, a sporty crossover vehicle that is outfitted with a number of age-friendly and safety features, including push-button start, front- and rearview cameras, a "surround view" function, and drive-assist technology.

Like most adult children, I was worried about his safety, and the prospect of his buying a vehicle from a company best known for its sports cars horrified me. Yet the automobile turned out to be amazing. It gave him license to feel good about himself once again, but more important, it enabled him to retain his mobility and kept him safe. Since then, he's upgraded to a Tesla Model S with "autopilot" technology, which enables him to travel longer distances in comfort and with peace of mind.

As people live longer, it isn't unusual for them to develop a number of health issues or experience physical or cognitive setbacks, as my father did with his stroke. By the age of 50, approximately half of the population will be living with one condition, one-fifth with two conditions, and around one in ten with three. However, by the time people turn 80, the numbers jump dramatically; nine out of ten have at least one condition, and more than a third have three or more.

Statistically speaking, the longer people live, the more likely they are to get sick or suffer from a health problem and the more likely they are to die. But this doesn't mean that people are worse off today than they were in previous generations. People living longer today are showing signs that they are biologically younger than previous generations were, meaning that they are both physically and mentally stronger. This suggests that the bias many people have against older people, specifically that they are frail or forgetful, might be completely out of touch with reality.

In 2020, researchers at the University of Jyväskylä in Finland found that older people today have notably higher physical and cognitive capacities than the previous generation did. They examined two groups of people aged 75 to 80 who were born twenty-eight years apart—the first born in 1910 and 1914 and the second in 1938 or 1939 and 1942 or 1943—and found that the latter cohort showed "markedly and meaningfully higher results in the maximal functional capacity tests, suggesting that currently 75- and 80-year-old people in Finland are living to older ages nowadays with better physical functioning."

This kind of research indicates not only that older people may be "younger" today than they were a generation ago but also that some life stages might be changing or extending and others might be emerging. It also suggests that people can be healthy, even if they suffer from one or two health conditions. This means that more people today will have more good-health years in the middle of their lives to live and work than previous generations did. Therefore, many of our preconceived notions and biases about older people should be rethought. Maybe there's something to the adage "50 is the new 30," at least in biological years.

The Life Course Is Changing

Chronological and biological aging are inevitable, but the way individuals age—biologically, economically, and socially—can be influenced by any number of factors, including personal behaviors and individual choices, employment status, medical and scientific interventions, government programs, and private sector innovations. All of these can enhance or detract from quality of life and independence and can add or subtract healthy years from the life span.

What's less discussed and understood is how longer lives are having a profound effect on social and economic norms over the entire life course, not just the last few years. Younger people today not only are going to live a lot longer but are living differently from the way their parents and grandparents did just one or two generations ago. They are earning less and delaying or eschewing life's major milestones. They are also confronted with the reality that much of the government support that was enjoyed by previous generations, such as Social Security and Medicare, may not be there for them in the future.

For perspective, a recent Bloomberg report showed that Millennials make up the largest share of the American workforce, yet they control only 4.6 percent of the country's total wealth. They would have to quadruple their savings over the next two years to catch up to the wealth the boomers had at the same point in the 1980s. Younger people can also expect to be in the workforce for more years, due in part to this earning discrepancy but also to the fact that they will live longer than previous generations, and the last years of their life may need to be funded privately through either personal wealth or family contributions. These realities present unique challenges for young people's long-term prospects and personal longevity strategies, as well as potential opportunities for business.

The home is changing, too. For most of human history, people lived in extended-family households, meaning that multiple generations, including grandparents, parents, brothers, sisters, aunts, uncles, and cousins, lived under one roof; just over a third of the global population still lives in such an arrangement today. Those family units were economic in nature and historically based in agrarian societies. As recently as 1800, three-quarters of Americans lived and worked on farms, and a quarter were engaged in family-owned and -operated businesses. That all began to change with the modernization of society, evolved with the creation of the "nuclear family"—a family unit consisting of two parents and their children—and led to the current state of affairs, where a growing number of people of all ages are living in unmarried households and often without children.

The move to unmarried homes impacts the income and purchasing power of households, the types of housing and services that are needed in communities, and the way health resources are apportioned, and it also shifts consumer behaviors: single people simply don't need to buy as much. Couple this with living longer and having fewer kids, and we are looking at a domino effect of radical transformation in all parts of the economy. Home sizes are shrinking, and exponential growth has been witnessed in categories such as single-serve and flexible packaging of alcohol and food, which have become very popular for an increasing number of people who live alone.

For years, another somewhat contradictory trend has been happening: a growing number of younger single people have been returning home to live with their parent(s), and for longer periods of time, because they have found it economically unfeasible to live alone. This has been attributed to poor or flat wages, as well as increased costs of things such as health care and housing. That trend sped up during the covid-19 pandemic and subsequent economic downturn, and now a majority of young adults aged 18 to 29 in the United States are living with their parents—the first time this has happened since the Great Depression. The loss of this population living independently means that vacancies could rise and rents decrease, which has the potential to positively affect housing affordability but also to negatively impact the economy of the surrounding community.

At the very least, family and living experiences are becoming more diverse. On the one hand, wealthier individuals, who are able to buy services such as cleaning, cooking, and caregiving, have continued to live alone or in nuclear families. On the other, poorer people have tended to remain in traditional extended-family homes or have moved into generationally diverse households that function more cohesively as a social and economic support unit. This is particularly true of immigrant families.

Other individuals, particularly those living in urban areas, are leveraging what is commonly referred to as "chosen family," a term that developed in the LGBTQ+ community during the late nineteenth century, to create an environment similar to that of a traditional extended-family unit, with friends and neighbors filling the roles of blood relatives. Whether by choice or by necessity, people are tailoring their family and living experiences to meet the new realities of the

Super Age. (As regards the term "chosen family," while there isn't a hard start date, the term was born in the Harlem Ball scene, which began in the 1860s. The term was popularized in the late twentieth century, likely after the release of *Paris is Burning* in 1991.)

Shifting Milestones

Much of the new normal for younger people comes down to basic economics: not only do they earn less than their parents, but they are also hampered by increased debt from education, as well as growing housing and health care costs. These financial burdens impact all of their economic decisions, but especially the largest and most conse-quential ones.

In 2020, the median age at first marriage was almost 30 for men and almost 28 for women. Though historically women married at an age that was three years younger than men's, that gap has been slowly but steadily narrowing. Now they are separated by only two years, on average. A half century ago, in 1970, the median ages were just over 23 for men and nearly 21 for women. Today, about one-third of young adults aged 18 to 34 are married, but just over forty years ago, in 1978, two-thirds of young adults in the same age group were married.

Young people are delaying having children, too, which corre-sponds roughly to their delay in marrying. The average age of first-time mothers in the United States is up from 21 to 26 since the 1980s, whereas for first-time fathers, it has increased from 27 to 31. The ages are even higher when marriage and educational statuses are factored into the equation; those who are married and with a higher educa-tional attainment tend to wait longer to have children. The covid-19 pandemic pushed many people to wait even longer to have children in 2020, which had the lowest birth rate in the US on record. This pattern has also been observed during other difficult periods.

The delay in first childbirth isn't limited to Americans. Women in other developed countries are also waiting longer, on average, to have children, with the average age of new mothers now 31. This means that a growing number of people are delaying parenthood until well after they have begun their careers. This delay impacts birth rates, which, as discussed earlier, are falling at a precipitous rate in most of the developed world and parts of the developing world as well.

Young homeowners are vanishing from the marketplace, too, and those who are not being forced to move back home with their parents are being forced to rent. The median age of first-time home buyers has increased to 33 since 1981, according to the National Association of Realtors, but this tells only part of the story. The median age of all buyers is increasing, too, and now stands at 47, increasing for the third straight year and well above the median age of 31 in 1981. The median age of repeat buyers is now 55—it was 36 just forty years ago—which may signal that more people are willing to take on a mortgage and debt later in life, because they understand that they will live and work longer than previous generations did.

Average first-time home buyers are also more likely to be single than in previous generations. Their median income is $54,340, which is about the same as what first-time home buyers made in the 1970s when adjusted for inflation, even though home prices have increased dramatically over the same period. The inability of people to enter the housing market at a young age means that they are losing out on one of the key drivers of wealth and financial security later in life. It also means that more of the wealth has become concentrated in the older and whiter parts of society.

Younger people today are much more likely to participate actively in the shared economy, for financial reasons as well as functional ones. Getting a driver's license and owning a car, which used to be hall-marks of moving into adulthood, are being delayed, largely because of family economics but also because of the trend toward more online shopping and on-demand delivery of products and services, which makes it easier for people to get what they want, when they want it, without ever having to get into a vehicle. When they require a car, they can easily hail one from a rideshare service for a point-to-point ride or rent one for a longer period. This also goes for bicycles and scooters in many urban environments today.

The shift to online shopping and on-demand delivery of products and services has the potential to remake many of the industries that will support a longer life, if only because it will be easier for individuals to opt in to and out of the products and services they need throughout their lives. The senior housing industry calls these "instrumental activities of daily living" (IADLs), but the reality is that people have always needed specialized products at different ages, and the second half of life is no different.

Rethinking the End

We may have to begin to rethink death, too. Living is expensive. Living a long life, especially one in poor health, is even more so, and it raises serious social and economic justice issues if people are not allowed to choose how and when they expire. In many cases, the costs of care in later life can push individuals and entire families into bankruptcy. Countries such as the Netherlands have begun to allow euthanasia (aka doctor-assisted suicide) as an option for individuals and families who are suffering due to health decline.

A December 2020 article by Dutch physicians in *JAMA Internal Medicine* noted that most requests for euthanasia have come from terminal cancer patients, but a growing number are coming from individuals with multiple geriatric syndromes (MGS). They found that an accumulation of MGS was not enough of a reason to request euthanasia, but those who did had also encountered some type of major health or life tipping point, including a fall or the loss of a partner or loved one. Such a change signaled a future of decline that could be dominated by dependence and isolation and a life that they no longer wanted to lead.

A growing number of Americans—nine out of ten—are interested in having greater control of their end of life. One way to do this is through advance care planning (ACP), a process that includes discussing values and goals of care by an individual, his or her family, and his or her physician in determining or executing treatment directives, as a way to help ensure that wishes about end-of-life care are honored. ACP manifests in the creation of a living will and/or medical power of attorney. These often include a "do not resuscitate" (DNR) order in the event of a major medical event.

ACP is generally utilized by older members of society—those over the age of 85—who also happen to be more affluent and whiter and are more often living in a congregate care setting. However, younger people, BIPOC, and lower-income people should consider it as well, since personalized control over health and health-related decisions is becoming de rigueur. Not only may ACP prevent terribly difficult decisions having to be made later on, it may also help people avoid an incredible amount of expense and confusion after a major medical event. Hundreds of thousands of people encountered this reality during the pandemic, since just over a third of Americans had advance medical directives.

Personalized control over the way one's remains are handled after death has also become more popular today and likely will continue to do so in the future. Individuals are now able to go outside the traditional processes of burial and cremation, as well as the dated funeral home, and opt in to new-age services. In 2019, for example, Washington became the first state to pass a law allowing composting as an alternative. Recompose, the first company to offer this service, will return a body to the earth naturally and without environmentally damaging chemicals for $5,500—a steal given that the median cost of a funeral with a viewing and burial was $7,640 in 2019, according to the National Funeral Directors Association.

The funeral industry is changing in other ways, too. In 2019, the hospitality entrepreneur Oliver Peyton launched a design-focused funeral home in London, England, called Exit Here, with the goal of making people more comfortable with the concept of death. His first shop was located in west London. The space is light filled, modern, and outfitted with comfortable furniture, warm colors, and reflection spaces. It offers what can only be described as "hip" casket and urn options, with all of the traditional services of a classic funeral home.

Caitlin Doughty, a mortician and the founder of the Order of the Good Death, argues that death should be part of everyone's life and that more open, honest engagement with death is needed. More people, she says, should address death fears, as well as accept that death itself is natural but the death anxiety of modern culture is not. Understanding and accepting mortality could help greater numbers of people become more conscious of their day-to-day lives, which could have a positive impact on overall health and longevity.

Preserving Health Across Generations

Above all, and regardless of their age, people are looking for products and services that will help them live a better life. A growing number of these products are in the health space, because a growing number of people want to take greater control of their health and monitor their biometrics throughout their lives. They understand that behaviors including diet and exercise, as well as leveraging technology, can lead to not only a fitter life but one that is less marked by physical decline. A significant number of them are older, and some leading businesses are meeting them in the marketplace with innovative products and services that would have been considered science fiction a generation ago.

Devices such as the Apple Watch, for example, help users take greater control of their health. Nearly 80 percent of owners use the device to track their health data, but a growing number of them are also using such wearables to monitor their biometrics and manage their chronic health conditions, including sleep apnea, atrial fibrillation, diabetes, and hypertension. This makes sense because although roughly half of all Apple Watch customers are in the 35-to-55 age cohort, a full third of the people using the device are over the age of 55. Regardless of their age, the number of US smartphone users using fitness apps jumped by more than 25 percent in one year, from nearly 69 million in 2019 to just over 87 million in 2020.

In 2020, Apple doubled down on its approach to health by making it even more central to its strategy. It added new functions, including one that measures the oxygen saturation of the users' blood so they can better understand their overall fitness and wellness. Oxygen saturation, or SpO_2, represents the percentage of oxygen being carried by red blood cells from the lungs to the rest of the body and indicates how well the oxygenated blood is being delivered throughout the body. This was a particularly remarkable and timely innovation, considering that covid-19 causes some people to experience dangerous, life-threatening drops in their blood oxygen levels. Apple also introduced Apple Fitness+, which connects fitness classes—both live and recorded—with all of its devices.

This interest in health metrics and monitoring may be one reason that men age 65 and older spend more on Apple devices than does any other demographic group in the United States. Another reason could be that they are buying these devices for their children, grandchildren, and even great-grandchildren. Regardless, it is impossible to dismiss the fact that older customers exist and are making some pretty significant purchasing decisions for both themselves and their families; they are flexing their economic muscle.

Apple hasn't been the only one to get into the health and biometric monitoring game. A relative newcomer, Peloton, an exercise equipment and media company founded in 2012, achieved notoriety in late 2019 for a sexist and incredibly memeworthy ad campaign. It achieved household name status shortly thereafter in 2020, after many fitness centers closed, either temporarily or permanently, due to the pandemic. The company, which had a shaky IPO in September 2019, is now valued at over $10 billion, and its products can be found in a growing number of homes, including the White House. Peloton currently has north of 3 million subscribers, with more than 1 million being connected fitness subscribers—a 113 percent increase year over year and a number that is expected to double by the end of 2021.

What few people realize about Peloton is that its target users are not younger people, even though the look and feel of its products may be "young." On average, according to a 2016 interview with its CEO, John Foley, younger people in their twenties and early thirties have more time and desire to go to the gym and boutique fitness classes. This is borne out by statistics, with 33 percent of Millennials, 24 percent of Gen Xers, and 22 percent of baby boomers accounting for all gym memberships in the United States. Gen Zers and the Silent Generation make up the remaining 21 percent.

Younger people may also struggle with the price tag of a Peloton, which starts at around $2,000 plus a monthly fee for the classes. This makes Peloton's target demographic multigenerational and unabashedly 35- to 65-year-olds (and older) who are working and tend to have children, higher incomes, and larger homes. They often have the money and the interest in their health but rarely have time to go to a gym, even in a nonpandemic period.

Both Apple and Peloton have embraced older customers as central to their business strategies. In addition, they are thinking about their consumers differently by not pegging them to a particular age or generation. Rather, they have grouped customers by their ability to spend, as well as their goal of remaining healthy as long as possible. They are part of a growing cadre of companies that are looking past chronological age, realizing the importance of older consumers, and/ or embracing multigenerationalism.

Appealing to a Generationally Diverse Market

Even with the ability to remain healthier longer through improved health behaviors, vision is one of the first things to go, and three-quarters of the population requires some vision correction. The likelihood of needing corrective eyewear increases with age, and it is more likely that older people will suffer from presbyopia, which can be corrected by reading glasses.

Until recently, presbyopia was common only among individuals over the age of 40, since the internal anatomy of the eye changes naturally in later life, the lens losing its flexibility to adjust to varying viewing distances. Perhaps this is why many people have assumed that reading glasses, which correct for this condition, are only for older people and why most of the products in the marketplace are found in pharmacies.

Normalizing products that were once considered to be only for the old, such as reading glasses, is one way to tap into the burgeoning market of Super Age consumers. A new eyewear company, Caddis Eye Appliances, is challenging the perception that reading glasses aren't or shouldn't be cool. It has reinvented the look of these glasses and intentionally crafted them to "crush age stereotypes," but they function nearly the same way as they have for more than eight hundred years, ever since the thirteenth century when Venetian craftsmen began making the *roidi da ogli*, "round glass for the eyes." The difference with Caddis is its intentional inclusion of real older people—not some Madison Avenue stereotype—into design, as well as marketing and communications. It has even taken a cheeky approach with its advertising by aggressively mocking age stereotypes. My favorite is its general information email address, helpivefallenandicantgetup@caddis life.com, which is a play on the 1980s infomercials for Life Alert, a nationwide company that to this day provides services that help elderly people contact emergency services, such as the fire or police department. Life Alert's tagline was "Help! I've fallen and I can't get up," which, when paired with the image of an older woman flailing helplessly on the floor, stoked fear into seniors for two generations.

Tim Parr, the founder and CEO of Caddis, shared with me that he and his team were amazed that no one had yet tapped into the current demographic shift in population and culture. "One of the more interesting thoughts from launching this brand is in analyzing how we got here [as a culture]," he told me. "What was going on in corporate culture, and of course pop culture, that allowed such a white space to exist?" Tim saw the solution not just in his eyewear but in the marketing and brand positioning of other categories.

Reading glasses aren't just for older people anymore. Thanks to technological innovations and the near-constant screen time—on computers or smartphones or both—that has lately become a reality, nearsightedness has become much more common among younger people. The viewing of digital devices causes undue strain, which makes it harder for the eyes to relax; they essentially "lock up." The longer the gaze is fixed, the more likely the eyes will fatigue and fail to focus.

Perhaps this is why Caddis isn't the only eyewear company that is working to capture older customers and generationally diverse audiences. The stalwart Millennial brand Warby Parker, which disrupted the eyewear industry more than a decade ago, now sells reading glasses as well as progressives. A newcomer, the New Orleans–based eyewear brand KREWE, which has been worn by the likes of Beyoncé, Serena Williams, Gigi Hadid, Blake Lively, Emma Watson, Kendall Jenner, Selena Gomez, David Byrne, and Lil Wayne, introduced reading glasses into its ultrahip collection in late 2020, perhaps in an effort to reach a broader audience.

These companies took classic products and made them better. They addressed ageist bias in certain product lines and added features that appeal to a wider and more generationally diverse audience.

Morning Consult, which releases an annual list of these companies, found that Zoom dominated all age groups in 2020, due largely to the need for connection during the pandemic. The report showed that some companies have the unique ability to cut across generations. In 2020, these included pandemic all-stars such as the online and app-based grocery delivery service Instacart and the media-streaming service Peacock from NBCUniversal.

In 2019, the story was a bit different; the top brands among boomers included a number that would be typically associated with younger consumers, including the plant-based meat producer Impossible Foods, the smart-doorbell and home security company Ring, the direct-to-consumer mattress company Purple, and the alcoholic seltzer brand White Claw. Younger consumers, on the other hand, took to legacy brands such as Häagen-Dazs ice cream, Jif peanut butter, the fruit and vegetable producer Dole Food Company, the drugmaker Bayer, the pharmacy and convenience store Walgreens, and the exploration-driven media organization National Geographic.

All of this research suggests that there is incredible value in appealing to older and generationally diverse audiences. Companies have one of three options during this transformative period: they can risk doing nothing and hope to survive, they can retool for a new group of customers, or they can consider how to appeal to a greater swath of the population. Businesses that are willing to be generationally inclusive in both design and marketing stand to win the biggest prizes.

New Visuals Bring in the Generations

Our attitudes toward older people are already beginning to change. They are showing up more prominently in popular culture and not just in the traditional "fuddy-duddy" space that they occupied for generations. They are starting to appear cool. Nowhere is this more evident than in social media, where the "Instagranny," a term for older female influencers, thrives, even though many of the women aren't actually grandmas. Some of them are embracing the term, unafraid to share and show off their age.

My earliest exposure to the Instagranny came through the New York–based photographer Ari Seth Cohen and his pre-Instagram blog, *Advanced Style*. Ari hunted the streets of New York and the world, snapping photos of older women wearing wildly colorful and garishly beautiful outfits. His book by the same name is a bestseller, and his Instagram account (@advancedstyle) has nearly 300,000 followers. In many ways, Cohen expressed the beauty and relevancy of older women to the larger world, since traditional media, and specifically fashion media, had ignored them for years.

One of the more successful fashion influencers is Lyn Slater, who is better known by her Instagram handle, Accidental Icon (@icon accidental). Slater, who has a "day job" as a professor at the Graduate School of Social Service at Fordham University, has more than three-quarters of a million followers on Instagram. Because of her influence, she not only regularly models and writes on the subject of fashion but is also "repping" some major brands via paid partnerships—a feature that allows influencers to "clearly" disclose that they're publishing sponsored content. Her sponsors include but are not limited to La Marca prosecco, La Prairie skin care, Canada Dry ginger ale, Kate Spade, Visa, and Bally.

Even more impressive than Slater is the Japanese couple Bon and

Pon (@bonpon511), who boast more than 800,000 followers. They are known for their matching outfits, which are super-*kawaii*, Japanese for "cute." Their influence is so great that they have published two books and were invited to develop a fashion line for the venerable Tokyo-based international department store Mitsukoshi, which launched in 2018.

Even larger, at least in terms of followers, is Fashion Grandma, who is on Douyin, the Chinese version of ByteDance's short-video platform, TikTok. Fashion Grandma features older Chinese women modeling traditional outfits, such as cheongsams—a type of high-necked body-hugging dress of Manchu origin—at sites throughout China and around the world. It has more than 2.9 million followers, many of whom are young women, and is believed to be redefining the image of the *da ma*—Chinese for "grandma"—for a new generation.

The grandmother of all influencers, in my opinion, is Helen Ruth Elam, better known by her Instagram handle, Baddiewinkle (@baddiewinkle). Elam, who launched her social media presence at the age of 85 with the help and encouragement of her granddaughter, has more than 3.6 million followers today. She is best known for her tagline, "stealing your man since 1928." Baddiewinkle has been featured by two major cosmetics lines and appeared on the 2016 MTV Video Music Awards in a bedazzled nude bodysuit. In 2017, she released a book, *Baddiewinkle's Guide to Life*, and she regularly engages in paid partnerships with Svedka vodka, Polaroid, and Caspar.

What makes these social media mavens and masters unique is not just the fact that they have a remarkable number of followers but that so many of their followers are young. Perhaps this is because everyone wants a positive vision of the future; I know I do. These influencers are also illustrating that a growing number of companies see age—especially advanced age—as more of an asset than a liability. These influencers are leveraging their lines (i.e., wrinkles) to make an incredible impact through paid sponsorships, book deals, and collaborations.

These older women and men are showing younger people that they can live a longer life with dignity and purpose and also remain relevant up to and past traditional retirement age. This is increasingly important for Millennials and Gen Zers, who see the normal life course of their parents and grandparents disappearing—a trend that has been in progress for more than a generation. They are seeing new life stages emerge and are able to imagine a future that breaks with the traditions of the past.

The Middle-Plus

As life spans continue to lengthen, it is inevitable that people will have the opportunity to do more. It is also likely that they will need to work longer. This will likely lead to the emergence of new life stages, as happened with teenagers and retirees in the 1950s.

The "middle-plus" is emerging; this is a group of people who are around middle age, but their age extends past traditional retirement age. I peg this group roughly between the ages of 50 and 74, but age is only a guideline. Middle-plus people can be younger or older than this, as long as they meet some basic criteria, such as work status and whether they have children living in their home.

I noticed this age bracket expansion in the early 2000s when reviewing demographic data on 50-plus women. In particular, I observed that a woman in her fifties or sixties could be both a mother and a grandmother, and many of them were engaged in full-time or part-time work. This represented the future of longevity, the shifting consumer landscape, and the opening of the middle-plus group. Market segmentation should be less about age and more about stage—economic condition, health status, outlook—and pegging people to their age is outdated. Mothers will always need the right tools to raise a child, whether they are 16 or 60-plus.

Recent research by J. Walter Thompson echoed these observations. The company found "A 55-year-old woman might be a grandmother or a new mother, a college leaver or an entrepreneur, a wild motorcyclist or a multi-marathon runner. Her lifestyle is not governed by her age, but by her values and the things she cares about;

her passions, ambitions and goals." More than that, the company's observations confirmed for me that this wasn't a new life stage only in the United States but globally.

The middle-plus, as a whole, is an economically active, aspirational group of people, meaning that they are engaged in some type of work and full of life. They may have dependent children and grandchildren, and they may be the primary or secondary caregivers for their parents. They just happen to be a bit older and, like my father, may have encountered some kind of health setback during or just after the traditional middle years (45 to 65). Like most, they have a fear of being seen as frail, disabled, old, or elderly and will do whatever they can to combat that perception. They have the resources to buy products and services to enhance their lives, as well as the lives of the people around them. They are wealthier than average, because they have had the ability to work in higher-paying jobs and have been proactive in their saving strategies.

Companies would be wise to consider this consumer group, because unlike previous generations, this group isn't interested in the beige-colored, function-over-form, poorly designed products and services that have plagued the longevity marketplace for decades. They are using the power of their pocketbook to entice brands to design for the dynamic lives they lead. They are insisting that products be built for them or, at the very least, with them in mind.

Businesses would also be smart to consider that just because people are living longer than previous generations, it doesn't mean they are old. As the saying goes, age is just a number, and middle-plus consumers don't like being seen as old and frail. From beginning to middle to end, the Super Age is upending all parts of life and death. It will be a wildly complex and transformative period for humanity. It will provide enormous opportunities for businesses to look past chronological age and focus on consumers' wants and needs. Some companies are already doing this, but there is more than enough room for others to enter the market and meet the wants and needs of an increasingly age-diverse population.

| 9 |

Make Age Work

Much of the workplace transformation that had been under way in a few innovative organizations became reality for most in just a few short months during the covid-19 pandemic. The workplace has changed forever, but two things remain constant: the generational composition of the workforce continues to change, and the participation rate of older people continues to increase.

It has become clear that flexible work and working from home are possible and should be encouraged, especially for employees who are caregivers—whether for children, loved ones, or parents. These individuals were slipping through the cracks before the pandemic and were constantly forced to make a choice between work and home. Although both flexible work and working from home can be challenging for managers at times, such arrangements are possible and can lead to more productivity. There's also the probability that workers confronted with caregiving responsibilities will demand flexible work arrangements in the future.

Coming out of the pandemic, the physical workplace will likely look a lot different. Offices will probably shrink their physical footprint and limit their use of space primarily to in-person meetings and collaboration, at least in the short-term, which could, in turn, reshape commercial districts and transportation networks. Companies will likely leverage a number of health technologies to monitor workers' body temperature and improve air filtration. And office design will move away from the despised, ill-conceived "open plan."

The success of working from home has proved that digital transformation is not only possible for small, medium, and large businesses but essential for all organizations. The change showed that all generations of employees can connect and collaborate in a digital space. Older employees showed a greater level of resilience and took on the challenge with gusto. As Jacques van den Broek, the CEO of Randstad Holding, told me, "Technology has been the great equalizer during the pandemic," and the work product became more important than the age of the person producing it.

Businesses that were primarily consumer facing were forced to pivot their models and adapt to the digital marketplace, whether online or through apps. They began to be thoughtful about the way they engaged consumers, while facing the daunting task of moving to online sales. They engaged established digital customers with new experiences, but perhaps more exciting, they were patronized by new ones, many of whom were older and engaging in online shopping and on-demand delivery of products and services for the first time. The pandemic may have changed some consumer behaviors, such as banking and grocery shopping, forever. It certainly forced some businesses to consider how they engaged with consumers in the digital space, and some are employing older workers to advise them in the process to grab even more market share.

Foresight for an Aging Workforce

All generations should be considered in workplace design, and there are a number of changes that should be made with the needs of an older population in mind. The growing generational diversity of consumers demands that there be greater representation of older people in the workforce. These workers can positively influence innovation, product development, and marketing and communications.

The concept of working past retirement was not considered to be feasible in a world in which there was an abundance of youths who needed jobs. In fact, the construct of retirement was specifically designed for a world with an abundance of young people and very few who were older. In many countries, retirement age was mandated by law. Prior to the first baby boomers entering the workforce, nearly half of individuals over the age of 65 were employed. However, a downward trend began shortly thereafter and bottomed out at 14 percent in 1990. The number has been on a slow but steady upward trend ever since.

I ran the AARP Best Employers International awards program (BEI), the international sister program of AARP's Best Employers for Workers over 50 award, which was conceived by my colleague Deborah Russell. Both programs worked to uncover and award organizations in the United States and abroad that excelled in creating age-friendly work environments, benefits, and work arrangements. They valued the contributions of all workers of all ages and attempted to create generationally diverse teams that fostered creativity, innovation, and workplace cohesion and effectiveness.

Our teams determined that the demographic makeup of the labor force was going to change over the coming quarter century, as participation rates began to grow fastest for the 65-and-over age group and began to shrink for others. In the next decade alone, the participation rate for both sexes aged 65 to 74 in the United States is expected to grow by 20 percent to just over a third, and the participation rate for both sexes over the age of 75 is expected to grow by a third, to nearly 12 percent. This is not just an American phenomenon; the labor force participation rate of 65-and-over workers worldwide has doubled since 1990 and is expected to continue to grow.

We realized that if nothing was done to foster an age-diverse workforce, many workers of talent would exit, often without choosing to do so; conservative estimates are that as many as ten thousand boomers could retire each day for the rest of this decade, and many more may be forced out of work due to the pandemic and the subsequent economic downturn. This loss of productive workers from the workforce could result in a decrease of economic opportunity for businesses. The loss of taxpaying citizens could be even more problematic for cities, states, and nations.

Many of the organizations that were highlighted in the BEI awards program employed skills development, as well as knowledge transfer and mentoring, to keep older workers on the payroll. Others invested in so-called softer skills, which are essential for the transition to a Super Age workplace, including communication, teamwork, adaptability, problem solving, critical thinking, conflict resolution, and team building, to create better enterprises. A hallmark of the award winners was their diversity of geography and industry, since they were located everywhere from rural towns to big cities and included both lower-skilled and highly skilled workers.

Perhaps the biggest surprise in both programs was that there was active participation by small mom-and-pop businesses, as well as large organizations and global consumer-facing brands. The US awardees were overwhelmingly connected to academic institutions, such as my alma mater, American University, and large health care institutions, such as the Veterans Health Administration. Financial sector organizations such as S&T Bank and the global tire manufacturer Michelin were perennial awardees, too. AARP even went so far as to formally partner with one of its awardees, the home improvement giant Home Depot, to recruit older workers and promote home modification. All of the organizations were employing people past the traditional retirement age in ways that made the organizations more productive, enhanced their offerings, and improved their bottom line. There was a compelling business case for each and every organization to do this.

Above all else, our team recognized in the early 2000s that a dramatic demographic shift that had begun in just a handful of countries would soon extend to the United States, and it would radically transform the workforce. Certain professions, such as nursing, were already having staffing crises, while others, such as technology, had a glut of applicants. For industries that struggled with recruiting and retaining qualified staff, hiring or rehiring older workers became paramount. Organizations that pursued generational diversity became more resilient and developed and delivered better products and services. In the case of some organizations, the inclusion of older workers opened their eyes to product and service design flaws, as well as marketing and communication missteps, while at the same time revealing new business opportunities.

Although BEI no longer exists, AARP has instituted a self-reporting program for companies that hire older workers, called the AARP Employer Pledge, and sponsors original and important research on the longevity economy. It has also developed Living, Learning, and Earning Longer (LLEL), a "learning collaborative" of fifty of the biggest global companies, in partnership with the Organisation for Economic Co-operation and Development and the World Economic Forum—two relationships that I helped the organization build. LLEL is working to get companies to share promising practices and, where knowledge gaps exist, collaborate on new research to help employers build, support, and sustain multigenerational workforces. It is promising work.

The companies participating in older-worker programs that are fostered by AARP and other leading organizations understand that the Super Age is changing the way they do business. They have awakened to the idea that there is incredible opportunity if they include older people in their diversity and inclusion strategies. They are becoming aware that approaching older people as assets could help future-proof their organization against skills shortages. This approach could also open the minds of their younger employees to the growing marketplace of older consumers.

A Super Age CEO

Nearly every company in the world employs a multigenerational workforce, and a "normal" organization today employs three to four generations. Some even have five generations on their payroll: the Silent

Generation, baby boomers, Gen Xers, Millennials, and the youngest Gen Z workers. But by the time the United States and most other nations enter the Super Age, the youngest members of Generation Alpha will be working, and some organizations will be employing six generations by then.

This kind of generational diversity will likely present new challenges for managers and human resource professionals, but plenty of strategies can be employed to get the most out of their employees, regardless of their age. This change will also create many opportunities for collaboration. However, many organizations will need to rethink the fundamentals of recruitment and retention. Both employers and workers would be wise to consider the future and nature of work and the implications of technology, as well as the growing generational diversity in their planning. This could help foster a culture of resilience in which generational differences are leveraged to the benefit of the entire enterprise, not just the bottom line.

The reality is that members of all generations mostly want the same things from life: personal achievement, fulfilling relationships, financial security, and control over their choices. They also want support from their employer as their needs shift over time. Yet since this generationally diverse workforce grew up in different eras, faced varying challenges and opportunities, and engaged with all types of technologies—analog, digital, and AI—their perspectives and skills may differ. Understanding these differences and leveraging them through pragmatic measures are essential to creating a highly functioning workforce, and a majority of companies agree that taking workers' differences into account can make their businesses stronger.

A Gartner report predicted that through 2022, three-quarters of companies with frontline decision-making teams reflecting a diverse and inclusive culture will exceed their financial targets. The study found that gender-diverse, inclusive teams outperform their less inclusive counterparts by 50 percent on average. Age should be just as important in diversity, equity, and inclusion (DEI) strategies as race, gender, and sexuality are, but often it is not.

Employees want to work in a multigenerational environment, too.

The global staffing firm Randstad found that nearly nine in ten workers prefer to work in age-diverse teams, "reflecting perhaps the different opinions and insights they gain from those older and younger than they are." Eighty-five percent believe that generational diversity contributes to innovation and the development of meaningful solutions to problems.

Although a generationally diverse workforce is key to business growth and success, fewer than one in ten global companies includes aging as part of its DEI strategy. Worse, more than a third of global companies still maintain a mandatory retirement age. Businesses and their leadership are literally getting into the way of their own success by not actively and aggressively engaging older workers and creating a generationally inclusive workforce. C-suites, boards of directors, and small businesses bear the responsibility of leading these changes, and often their members are older workers themselves.

The average age of CEOs of the biggest US companies has risen from 45 to 50 since 2012, and the average age of first-time hires for C-suite positions has risen by 15 percent since 2005, from 45 to 54. *Harvard Business Review* reported in its annual list, "The Best-Performing CEOs in the World," that on average, the CEOs on the list began their tenure at 45 and have been in office fifteen years, meaning that many of the best and brightest are well into their fifties, sixties, and beyond. The average age of a CEO across industries is 58, with the oldest average CEO age 60 in financial services and the youngest 55 in the technology sector. Furthermore, and outside the major corporate C-suites, research by Experian found that the average age of a small-business owner in the United States is over 50.

One would think that these executives and small-business owners would see their own age and experience as valuable to the operations of their organizations. One would also assume that they would realize the contributions of older workers as essential, too. However, all too often, corporate leadership in the transition to a Super Age workforce is limited to a few people who have the foresight and desire to unlock their potential. Even more, companies delay action until they are staring down the undeniable reality of the Super Age.

While I was in Germany to speak a number of years ago, I saw the power corporations have in tackling ageism head-on. The German automaker Mercedes-Benz launched an in-person and online exhibit called "Ey Alter"—"Hey, Buddy"—that was conceived to educate the public, as well as its own employees, about the changing demographics in Germany. Numerous tools helped tens of thousands of visitors and thousands of employees shift their perspectives about aging by highlighting the impact that older generations can have on business and German society.

The initiative, which was led by Markus Schäfer, Mercedes-Benz's chief operating officer, launched demographic surveys across the company. He encouraged employees and management to have open and frank conversations about the generational diversity of their teams and to identify ways to encourage and promote cooperation between young and old. It was a smart move, but it was prompted by the realization that Mercedes-Benz would need older workers—the average age of its employees was over 45 at the time—to be able to compete in the future against other automakers both at home and abroad.

One of the results of "Ey Alter" was the appreciation that there are, in fact, differences among generations. However, they shouldn't be seen as weaknesses, and they shouldn't be attributed to chronological age. The skills that are the main predictors of job performance, which are knowledge and expertise, flourish throughout younger years and well past the traditional retirement age, in some cases past the average life expectancy. There is also evidence to suggest that traits such as drive and curiosity, which are essential for new skill acquisition, exist well into later life.

If similar initiatives were carried out across entire industries or economies, the impact would be transformative. Not only would there be more people working and contributing to the economy as active consumers, but many of the products and services that would be produced would be more reflective of society's generational diversity. Older workers would, in nearly every way, contribute to this change.

An analysis of twenty studies covering nearly twenty thousand workers revealed that generational differences in job attitudes were few and far between; there was no prevailing positive or negative stereotype that held up across age or generational groups. There were, of course, differences in needs, interests, preferences, and strengths that developed over the working life but few overarching differences that were dependent on age or generation.

Age, as it turns out, is a pretty lousy predictor of job performance and workers' needs. Employers would be wise to reconsider their approach to recruiting and retaining candidates whom they may see as "too old" or "too young" for a job. They should ask instead if a current or future employee has the skills to get the job done. They should also get into the habit of rejecting the notion that someone may be "too experienced" for a job; there is no such thing.

It would also be smart to rethink benefits packages to be more inclusive of needs throughout employees' lives. Companies that offer an inclusive benefits package can appeal to a wider talent pool. Even the nomenclature and scope of existing programs, such as maternity and paternity leave, could be altered ever so slightly to be more inclusive of all workers who are caregivers. This is important to workers who may be later in life and may want or need to take on grandparenting responsibilities, for example.

Recruiting All Generations

Recruitment of an age-diverse workforce has been challenging for companies since the middle of the last century, if only because business leaders—both hiring managers and human resource professionals—peppered job advertisements and interviews with unintentionally ageist language and unnecessary measures such as "years of experience," which is possibly the most foolish measure of a potential employee's ability to do a job. Other typical job-posting terms, such as "digital native," are also counterproductive, since most workers have at this point been on a computer and the internet for most if not all of their careers. Asking for birth date or college graduation date also doesn't serve much purpose other than to cause anxiety for applicants.

Some companies have been explicit and intentional in their efforts to recruit older workers in particular, because they see the incredible market opportunity of the Super Age. They realize that they do not currently have the internal expertise or the correct age profile in their existing staff to design products and services that will meet the wants and needs of their customers. This includes businesses in countries such as China. Many people still see the country as being relatively young, yet it will have nearly half a billion inhabitants over the age of 50 by 2030, and half of those will be over the age of 65—it will be "older" on average than the US.

The Chinese retail giant Taobao, the eighth most visited website in the world and the largest retail site in China, has understood this and sees the older population as part of its business strategy in terms of both customers and employees. In 2018, it reported having over 30 million users over the age of 50, or about 7 percent of the total 50-plus population in China. To increase its relevance in the market, as well as market share, it posted an advertisement for "senior square dancers" who would advise the company on new products and services, as well as user experience, also known as UX. In this case, Taobao was explicit in asking for a member of the target demographic by age—60 and over—but was more focused on finding individuals who were seen as influencers in their communities and had at least one year of online shopping experience. The company received more than a thousand applications on the first day. Taobao also enlisted the help of older workers for its "Taobao College for Seniors," which helps older customers, some of whom may be new to online shopping, improve their digital skills.

Other companies have put older workers on the front lines of their retail experience. The British do-it-yourself (DIY) and home improvement company B&Q launched a pioneering age diversity pilot project more than thirty years ago by staffing its Macclesfield store in Cheshire, England, entirely with people aged over 50. This experiment resulted in greater profits, higher retention rates, and improved customer service. Since then, employing an age-diverse workforce has been central to its business strategy. The company achieves this by encouraging its three hundred stores to hire employees who reflect the makeup of the local community but with a focus on people over 50. This was due largely to customer demand for workers who had experience in DIY. This approach had the added benefit of avoiding the high cost of staff turnover, which was a particular problem among its younger workers.

Even in nations with a work culture that embraces retirement and rejects retaining older workers, such as Japan, companies such as Mitsubishi Heavy Industries (MHI) are making strides. In 2016, the company launched MHI Executive Experts, a company specifically for workers who are at or above the Japanese retirement age. MHI Executive Experts recruits veteran MHI employees, including engineers, managers, and executives. It then dispatches them as specialists to advise on current company projects and businesses. The employees provide years of intelligence and know-how, as well as on-the-job training, support, and guidance to newer employees, which helps foster the new generation of employees and the future of manufacturing. Older workers help MHI reduce risk and strengthen its management structure.

MHI's approach is important because it illustrates the necessity of retaining and transferring institutional knowledge. All too often, this important step in workforce development is overlooked, leaving younger employees to fend for themselves. It solves the outdated model of mandatory retirement in Japan by implementing a near-immediate retire/rehire program. Older workers transition, albeit abruptly, into a flexible work situation. This approach helps MHI retain essential manufacturing skills and craftsmanship while infusing the new techniques and approaches of younger employees. It leverages the best of new hires and retirees to improve the company and its products.

Building for Life

The shortage of skilled workers is causing manufacturers to think past their hiring practices and make capital investments that will benefit all workers and extend their working lives. The German automaker

Porsche made such investments at its Leipzig plant—the same plant that built the car that gave my father his poststroke mobility independence—to ensure that the longevity of its workforce would be the center of design. The company approached its factory design not through the lens of catering to older workers per se but rather through a human-centered one, which makes the entire car production process more ergonomic and easier on the body.

The innovations include everything from a Herman Miller–like office chair that enables workers to scoot under a vehicle without bending over to machinery that rotates the entire car chassis and a harnesslike exoskeleton that reduces the strain on a worker's shoulders and arms caused by repetitive overhead work. Workers move from station to station during the workday, spending no more than an hour at each one, in an effort to reduce the physical wear and tear that the repetition of a single task may cause.

Porsche's approach ensured that all people on the line would have a better experience building cars, and that their labor would be less intensive on the body. The design of the plant considered all parts of the car-manufacturing process, and investments both large and small made it easier for workers to build high-performance auto-mobiles. The approach not only directly improves product quality but also has a direct impact on extending working lives and may create some empathy with and awareness of older consumers, since younger employees are exposed to the realities some of their older coworkers may face.

This example is arguably extreme and extremely costly, but there is a business case for Porsche's expenditure, and the company expects that it will pay dividends in worker retention and overall product qual-ity. Many companies lack the foresight of Porsche, much less the abil-ity to invest hundreds of millions of dollars, if not more, into building a workplace that will meet the needs of the Super Age. However, that doesn't mean that organizations cannot make changes and meet the opportunities of this period. There are tried-and-true practices I've witnessed in action that consider the whole life through ergonomics, benefits, and education that nearly every enterprise can implement today. These workplace enhancements make the office, factory, or farm more welcoming not only to older workers but to all generations. They pay off in worker satisfaction, which leads to greater levels of performance and retention.

Considering the Whole Life

Businesses also need to consider that a generationally diverse Super Age staff will have different needs from one that is made up primarily of younger employees. Nearly three-quarters of adults, for example, live without children in their home, and that number is set to grow. Regardless, many organizations still have policies that favor parents over nonparents.

In the Super Age, individuals are delaying parenthood or not having children at all. This is one of the ways that workers' needs are shifting. Businesses that already have programs such as maternity and paternity leave would be wise to consider offering leave for other caregiving responsibilities, too. Companies need to be responsive to workers by offering flexible schedules, whenever possible, as well as leave to take care of family, friends, and even pets. It's time for them to address the disharmony created when parents and nonparents are treated differently by employers in terms of the key ways the work relationship is defined: time and money.

The reality is that any business can build the sleekest-looking workplace outfitted with the newest technology if it has the finances, but fewer, and arguably the best, organizations make investments directly in their workers through lifelong learning, financial compensation, and benefits packages that consider the whole life of their employees. I've found that the most impactful employee engagements are often driven by empathy and the recognition that workers are going to have shifting priorities outside work at various times in their lives. Giving employees the license to have open conversations with management and leadership about the pressures they face can lead to proactive solutions that improve retention and keep some of the best and brightest team members active and engaged in the enterprise for longer periods of time.

This happened at the Australian bank Westpac, which has proactively supported employees throughout their life course, perhaps better than any other company in the world. In the early 2000s, Westpac management realized that the bank was struggling to recruit and retain tellers, many of whom were older women. They learned that many of them were encountering challenges with balancing their employment and the demands of caregiving for their grandchildren.

Westpac responded by engaging them in a conversation, which led to its offering a first-of-its-kind grandparental leave—up to fifty-two weeks of unpaid leave to be a child's primary caregiver up to his or her second birthday. It also moved to support employees who are transitioning to retirement with flexible working arrangements, as well as three days of paid leave during their transition time to pursue activities related to their retirement. They provide employees with tools to envision their transition to retirement and offer flexibility throughout life for just about every reason possible. Its "career break," which allows employees to take up to twelve months' paid leave (salary amortized over four years) or three to twelve months' unpaid leave for whatever reason, is by far the most forward thinking and considerate of a longer working life.

US companies have taken note, too. CVS Caremark, the prescription benefit management subsidiary of CVS Health, offers a "snowbird" program in which several hundred older pharmacists and other employees from northern states are transferred each winter to pharmacies close to their winter homes in Florida and other warmer states. UPS welcomes its retired workers, also known as "alumni," back for seasonal holiday work, enabling the company to take advantage of a trained workforce during one of the busiest times of the year. And Michelin, the global tire manufacturer, has a "preretirement" program that allows workers age 55 and over to scale back to working part-time.

At the end of the day, a Super Age life is one that will likely involve extra years in the workforce. Companies can do a great deal to support the life transitions of their workers through benefits programs. However, one of the bigger challenges for both companies and employees, as well as one of the more promising opportunities, is keeping workers' hard and soft skills sharp throughout their work life. This will likely require investments by both employees and employers in education, training, and development. As I always say, if companies are willing to regularly invest in the upkeep of their physical plant, they should be willing to do the same for their human capital.

Investing in Education and Training

Our approach to education, which is based largely on a model developed during the Middle Ages, does not function properly, especially against the backdrop of lengthening work lives. Education and training are increasingly important for older workers the farther away they get from their university degrees or apprenticeship programs.

Older workers tend to stick around longer than younger workers do. They are often regarded as more loyal, too. In the United States, for example, in January 2020, the median tenure of workers aged 55 to 64 (9.9 years) was more than three times that of workers aged 25 to 34 (2.8 years).

These realities will require a paradigm shift within enterprises to account for the fact that their education and training investments during the last five to ten years of a worker's life will equal or exceed those of the first five to ten years. Such investments should be made throughout the life of an employee.

Education and training are particularly important in the public sector, where employees stay in their jobs nearly twice as long as employees in the private sector. According to Bureau of Labor Statistics data, in January 2020, public sector workers had a median tenure of 6.5 years, considerably higher than the median of 3.7 years for private sector employees. The fact that older workers tend to stay around longer means that public sector employees, especially older ones, have the potential to be great assets, but they need continuing education. It's imperative that public sector employees have the tools they need to succeed both early on and later in their careers.

Companies should also consider giving older workers pathways to employment through traditional internships, which are typically focused on college-age, graduate, and doctoral students, as well as "returnships," which are geared exclusively to workers who have left the workforce. Barclays, the British multinational investment bank and financial services company, launched Barclays Bolder Apprenticeships in 2015, making it the first UK company to extend such a program to people over the age of 24. Barclays' leadership recognized that the program was valuable to all people and should not be limited by age or social circumstances. Since its launch, the scheme has recruited more than eighty apprentices, growing the bank's number of older apprentices from 4 percent to 20 percent—a remarkable feat and one that illustrates the demand.

Make no mistake, internships and returnships for older people are new, and few organizations are establishing them at this point. Data from the Department of Labor's Registered Apprenticeship Partners Information Database System (RAPIDS) show that of apprentices employed from 2008 to 2019, fewer than one out of twenty-five was aged 50 or older. As more organizations promote their work and illustrate the return on investment, these programs will become commonplace in corporate environments.

Responsive to Reality

When I work with organizations that are interested in planning for their journey into the Super Age, I ask them to consider that many of the assumptions they may have about the current, near-future, and long-term labor and consumer markets could be fundamentally wrong. They often need to challenge their conventional thinking about diversity, equity, and inclusion and accept that generational differences and older workers might be assets, not liabilities.

Companies need to look at the foundation of their Super Age strategy as a three-legged stool: one leg is human resource practices; the second is research, design, and innovation; and the third is marketing and communication. Wise organizations know that if they do not have generational diversity in their hiring and human resource practices, they will fail to build age-inclusive innovation and design teams, and their marketing and communications strategies may exhibit ageist bias. If even one of the three legs is wobbly and does not consider generational diversity, the strategy may falter. The failure to retain and recruit older workers may lead to generational blind spots that could manifest throughout products' life cycles.

Despite its reputation as a Super Age–savvy company, at least in workplace and product design, BMW launched an ad campaign in November 2020 for its new sports utility vehicle, the iX, that seemingly attacked boomers for not liking the look of the design, suggesting that they were out of touch with modern-day styles and trends. It even went so far as to tweet, "OK, Boomer. And what's your reason not to change?"

BMW doubled down on that approach with a global ad campaign in advance of the 2021 Consumer Electronics Show (CES). In the commercial, the all-new iX sport utility vehicle faces off against the classic 7-series from 2001. The two vehicles engage in an expletive-laden "conversation" that is riddled with ageist dog whistles leaning into perceived generational conflict. At best, the commercials were offensive; at worst, they stoked negative and counterproductive generational narratives.

These two cases suggest that BMW is unaware that the average household income of a new BMW car or SUV buyer in 2020 was $124,800 per year, that buyer's average age was 56, and two-thirds of all BMW sales are to individuals over the age of 55. Perhaps no one made the connection that the iX was manufactured at the plant in Dingolfing that is the home of BMW's Super Age workforce strategy and some of the company's oldest and most skilled employees.

BMW sales dropped in 2020, and it is impossible to say if there is a direct connection between the sales numbers and the overtly ageist ad campaign. However, there is a correlation, and the move by the German automaker to go after older customers in a pejorative way not once but twice was an avoidable error. Unfortunately, the BMW example is an all-too-familiar cautionary tale of an organization that is working toward a cohesive Super Age strategy only to deliver a self-inflicted wound. This story is a warning to be conscious of the pitfalls that exist in this new era. Businesses need to recalibrate across the board and make sure that they are Super Age friendly in all aspects of their work.

If some workplaces and businesses are so intrinsically ageist and cannot see into the future, is there anything that can be done to change them from within? The short answer for many is yes, but the path is long and fraught with the challenges that have been faced by other marginalized groups in enterprisewide diversity, equity, and inclusion strategies. Some companies, particularly those that have embedded youth as central to their ethos, will likely struggle to consider age diversity "a thing."

Adapting to the Super Age in the workplace requires a shift in organizational mindset, and it must occur in every component of the organization, much like current diversity, equity, and inclusion strategies for historically marginalized groups. The first and most logical step for enterprise leaders to tackle is to audit for demographic change, so they understand how it is influencing their companies' bottom line. Once they understand the economic benefits of responding to age diversity, they can better respond to its challenges and implement incremental change and capital improvements that will take advantage of the opportunities of a new workplace dynamic and an expanding customer base.

| 10 |

Make Home and Community Gray Again

For the past few years, I've been fixated by the large numbers of older people moving into urban environments, the growth of older people as a proportion of the suburban population, and the decline of "senior housing," an omnibus term that can mean anything from independent living to twenty-four-hour skilled nursing care but always focuses on the needs of an older population. The covid-19 pandemic started, introduced new variables, sped up or enhanced some trends, and challenged my thinking on what to expect in the future. All kinds of change that would directly impact the future of home and community in the Super Age were gathering steam well before the pandemic began in 2020. Public and private leadership will need to address demographic change throughout the built environment.

For example, the National Investment Center for Seniors Housing & Care, a nonprofit organization that provides data and analytics on older adults and their housing needs used by housing investors and operators, reported that in the third quarter of 2020, the average senior housing occupancy rate in its thirty-one primary markets fell to 82.1 percent—a precipitous 5.6-point decline from the first quarter of 2020 thanks to the pandemic. The decline would likely have happened in any case. However, it would have been drawn out over a longer period of time. Preferences are simply shifting away from institutional living, a trend that is happening all around the world.

This shift away from institutionalized settings has paved the way for a host of new companies, such as Papa, Home Instead Senior Care, and Visiting Angels, to offer concierge-like services that can be delivered at home through either dedicated personnel or apps. Other companies, such as UpsideHōM, offer one- to three-bedroom apartments in existing market-rate apartments for people they call "tweeniors," those between adult and senior in the 60-to-85 age group. Some people live alone; others have roommates. The company is offering a housing-plus-services solution that allows its tenants to live independently in an intergenerational community.

The trend toward urbanization is also universal, and although the percentage of older people living in cities has declined over the past thirty years, the overall number of older urbanites is growing. This is due to the sheer size of the boomer population. The only place where the older population grew faster was in suburban areas, where the shift in age structure is negatively impacting education, labor, and housing, as well as the tax structure. According to the Pew Research Center, "While the population is aging in all three county types, this is happening more rapidly in US suburban and small metro counties. The 65-and-older population grew 39% in the suburbs since 2000, compared with 26% in urban and 22% in rural counties."

Although there is some thinking that the pandemic may have altered people's choice to live in urban, suburban, or rural areas, it is way too early to know if this is a temporary or permanent trend. There are also significantly more challenges, as discussed earlier, related to the delivery of services as well as the mobility of the suburban and rural population. The issue of mobility will tick up in importance, especially for suburban and rural areas that do not currently have accessible and extensive transportation networks.

The number of people over the age of 50 who are renting has also seen a dramatic increase of more than 50 percent over the last decade, outpacing that of other age groups. This growth is attributed to changing preferences, as well as the shifting economic realities following the Great Recession—they haven't earned or saved enough to be able to buy a home. This trend presents unique opportunities for developers and public officials, as well as businesses that operate where older people live.

The increase in older renters should trigger developers to think about how older populations will interact with existing and newly built housing stock. Developers should also consider how to incorporate elements such as barrier-free design, which involves designing to remove or replace the things that keep people from accessing or using their home the way they need to, in their properties. Local governments may need to consider if their building codes are adequate and support individuals who live independently for longer periods of time.

There was also a good amount of migration prior to the pandemic; nearly a million people over 60 moved across state lines in 2018, an increase of about 16 percent from five years earlier. Expensive states such as California and New York witnessed a net loss of older people, while more affordable southern states such as Arizona and Florida continued to see growth. Texas, South Carolina, Idaho, Tennessee, and Delaware also saw an increase, and all of those states have tax policies that are attractive to an older population.

In the last decade, urban areas such as Las Vegas, Raleigh, Atlanta, Austin, and Phoenix all saw double the normal rate of growth in the 55-to-64 population. Other cities with substantially above-normal growth over the same period included my adopted hometown of Washington, DC, as well as Portland, Albuquerque, Dallas, and Orlando.

Large numbers of middle- to higher-income older people are moving into neighborhoods like mine, looking for homes that require little upkeep and in some cases have concierge services. Many of them are also looking to free themselves from the burden of cars, home maintenance, and seasonal tasks such as shoveling snow, raking leaves, and landscaping. They want to live in areas that are walkable and have access to public parks, as well as biking and hiking trails. They want to live in multigenerational settings or generationally diverse communities. And they are looking for housing that supports them but rejecting the idea of being pigeonholed as needing senior housing.

The verdict is still out on whether the pandemic may have temporarily or permanently reversed that trend, but it also exposed another trend that was lying just beneath the surface at the near-opposite end of the age spectrum. Young people aged 18 to 29 moved home en masse for the first time since the Great Depression; by July 2020, a majority of them (52 percent) were living with at least one of their parents. This trend was consistent across all major racial and ethnic groups, men and women, and metropolitan and rural residents, with growth being sharpest in the 18-to-24 age group, as well as among young White adults.

This trend is happening at the opposite end of the age scale, too. Large numbers of older adults have not saved enough for retirement, and a growing number of them are moving in with their adult children, many of whom are Millennials. This presents a clear conundrum for the younger generation, which has struggled to gain an economic footing for years. They are now confronted with the reality of providing housing and in some cases financial support and care for their older parents. Many of these adult children are further delaying their own retirement savings, which could be catastrophic for them in the long run. At the very least, it will require them to remain employed for more years.

All of this adds up to a reversal of the trend that started in the middle of the last century, when the first generation of retirees moved to exclusive enclaves in places such as Sun City in Arizona and the Villages in Florida, lured by a manufactured concept of retirement as well as marketing campaigns that told them how to live the good life. Homes and communities today are starting to reflect the age diversity that all but disappeared nearly three-quarters of a century ago. This remarkable shift in the way people are living will require pragmatic action in the way homes and communities are designed and built, the way mobility and transportation are conceptualized and constructed, and the way services are developed and delivered.

Home and Community

The first and foremost consideration is the home, which has functioned as shelter, workplace, gym, and school for many people throughout the pandemic. This has forced many to consider their living space and ask themselves "Does my home work for me and my needs?" The pandemic gave some a reason to consider their living space, but more should contemplate not only what their immediate postpandemic wants and needs are but also the type of home they will desire and require for the next ten, twenty, or even thirty or more years.

Though it is true that average Americans born today can expect to live to about 79 years, most can expect to live to only about 68 both illness and injury free. This means that the initial conversations about home modifications or new home construction should begin between ages 50 and 60. This may sound jarring, especially considering that these ages are relatively young. However, it would be prudent for people to consider these things, especially if they want to safeguard themselves against a future move into a long-term care setting. The industry refers to this as "aging in place."

I prefer the term "living in place," because the vast majority of the population is hardwired to enjoy living and reject aging. Developers, architects, and general contractors, as well as the associated industries within the building trades, have an incredible opportunity, if not an obligation, to design and sell products that help people live at home as long as possible. These can be innovative analog solutions or new technologies, such as Internet of Things (IoT) technology that can predict falls.

Design for living at home must consider our later years as much as our younger ones. It must address changing life needs in advance, rather than after a major detrimental event. At present, discussion about modifying a home to meet an older individual's future needs is taboo. This doesn't jive with the fact that most people want to live at home for as long as possible and occurs because many people refuse to engage in conversations about getting old.

Researchers at AARP found that "Nearly 90 percent of people over age 65 want to stay in their home for as long as possible, and 80 percent believe their current residence is where they will always live." However, for older adults to age in place, their physical and service environment must be accommodating; retrofitting a home to meet the needs of old age can take months, if not longer, and building a new one can take years. A major medical event won't wait for that to happen, so future-proofing a home to the greatest extent possible is the best option for those with adequate financial resources.

The greatest area of risk is falls. They are preventable, to some extent, with the right retrofit, and there's an economic imperative to tackling them head-on. At least 3 million Americans over the age of 65 are treated for falls annually, requiring 800,000 hospitalizations and resulting in 300,000 hip fractures. About $50 billion is spent each year on medical costs for falls that are nonfatal, and a good amount of that cost is covered by Medicare, but that doesn't cover everything, including home modifications, nor does it cover pain, suffering, recuperation time, and loss of income—all things that a rational consumer would want to avoid. The cost of fall fatalities is over three-quarters of a million dollars per year.

Other countries have taken a more hands-on approach to this challenge. In Germany, only 5 percent of older citizens live in barrier-free apartments, and 83 percent of them live in older buildings that are generally less accessible than more recent construction is. Structural inefficiencies in private homes account for about one-quarter of falls experienced by older Germans. In response, the government has allocated funds to facilitate the conversion of buildings and apartments into barrier-free living spaces through programs such as the Age-Appropriate Rebuilding Program.

Just over a decade ago, the United Kingdom published its "Housing our Ageing Population: Panel for Innovation (HAPPI)" report, which examined best-in-class design principles from across the European continent. That report, combined with growing demands by older Britons, has led to improvements in the livability of homes. In short, consumers are more design aware than they were just a generation ago. The new generation of consumers, much like their American counterparts, has no interest in retreating to an old people's home.

I've engaged in conversations of home modification with my own parents. In fact, they've often led the dialogue and have laid out their comprehensive plan to build a new home rather than modify their existing one. The new home will likely be in their current town and will be one that will aid them in their quest to remain independent as long as possible. My parents' desires aren't unique, but their approach is, since they are actively engaged in a property search that they know could take years. They are cognizant of the realities of their longevity and factoring those into their design choices, such as first-floor living, and investing the time and effort it will take to build something new.

As I have mentioned several times, the fastest-growing age group in the United States is people over the age of 80. In 1900, there were only 100,000 Americans who lived this long, but that number has swelled to nearly 6 million today. By 2050, it's anticipated that there will be nearly 20 million people in this age group—a 220 percent increase in just under thirty years.

Nearly nine out of ten home renovations were done by baby boomers and Gen Xers in 2019, up from 83 percent in 2018. More than half of those—55 percent—were undertaken by boomers, and the main areas of renovation were the kitchen and bathrooms. Given the fact that two-thirds of falls happen inside the home and the vast majority of those most harmful occur in the bathroom, that room is one of the best places to start modifications.

Most people don't like the look of grab bars or walk-in tubs, because they make the bathroom feel as though it belongs in a hospital or nursing home. More bath fittings companies and builders should consider ways to integrate and incorporate grab surfaces in their designs. Walk-in tubs should look as seamless and sleek as possible, and roll-in showers with benches should be more commonplace. The "institutional" look of these can be offset with quality materials and modern design. Architects should make lighting central to home design and include motion-sensing floor-level lighting. Storage should be incorporated throughout to keep floors and surfaces clear of clutter.

There are also opportunities in the rental market. In the past ten years, the number of renters in the United States over the age of 60 grew by more than a third, while those that were 34 and younger grew by only 3 percent, according to a 2019 analysis of US Census Bureau data by RENTCafé. The percentage of older renters making $60,000 a year or more increased to 15 percent, a growth of 4 percent, between 2006 and 2016. The growth in the number of older people, especially those with more disposable income, in the rental marketplace means that property owners and developers need to be tuned in to the wants and needs of this growing demographic.

New construction, as well as home modification and renovation, of both homes and apartments is beginning to consider the life course, as well as the growing trend toward multigenerationalism. Modifications could include finishing basements as living quarters, adding in-law suites onto existing homes, or constructing "granny pods"— preferably referred to as accessory dwelling units, built from scratch or modular—on existing property. In Singapore, I observed different generations of the same family renting within the same complex— Mom and Dad on one floor and adult grandchildren on another. There is a growing desire to build multigenerational homes from the ground up, a trend that has been observed around the world. Designs range in size and scope, but the most promising ones incorporate a whole-of-life approach. They include central areas in which to gather, but perhaps more important, they also incorporate places to which to retreat. The biggest challenge with these homes is their size and cost, which are prohibitive for most people and many urban environments.

Module, a modular housing company based in Pittsburgh, Pennsylvania, believes that right-sized homes that grow with the family are a prime way to address the issues of multigenerational living and attainability. The company's units start as small as five hundred square feet, roughly the size of an urban studio apartment. If a family grows, for example, and needs more room for children, in-laws, or extended family, Module has a ready-made design to meet their needs. The two most important considerations of this approach are the urban environment—the design has an intentionally small footprint for small lots and dense neighborhoods—and the speed at which these homes can be built, making the buildings more responsive to life events.

Some multigenerational housing innovation is taking on the problem of affordability, too, but without design or the needs of an extended family in mind. In Israel, an initiative called "Here We Live" was launched in 2014 as an experiment to make higher education more accessible while enhancing the social connectedness of older people living alone. Students who participate in the project enjoy subsidized housing and tuition in exchange for socializing with their elderly landlords. The program isn't unique to Israel, and similar ones have popped up across Europe and in the Americas.

Community

It's important that civic leaders around the world consider the growing generational diversity in their communities, especially as more older people choose to remain in their homes and in the workforce. The communities in which they live need to be modified from traditional ones that considered only the young and able to ones appropriate to the needs of all generations and all abilities today and in the future. This extends to reimagining or reconfiguring historic districts to embrace the needs of a multigenerational population, and in the development of new neighborhoods and communities. They include both physical structures and the public institutions that contribute to community life.

I often consider an illustration by a Vermont-based artist, Kevin Ruelle. In it, a man is shoveling the snow from the stairs of a public school, next to which there is a ramp covered with snow. A number of students, including one in a wheelchair, are waiting to enter. The caption reads, "Clearing a path for people with special needs clears the path for everyone!" and makes the not-so-fine point that if the man cleared the ramp first, all of the children would be able to enter at once. This lesson is especially true when we consider accessibility. Take the ubiquitous curb cut in sidewalks around the world, which has become one of the prevailing symbols of inclusive design. Though it was designed for people in wheelchairs, it is used daily by virtually everyone, from the parent with a child in a stroller to the delivery person with a pushcart.

The central goal of accessibility modifications is to create an environment that is welcoming to as many people as possible. Considering an older population in the design of communities may be novel, but there are good guidelines and best practices that can help most communities understand the paths forward. Above all, local elected officials and civil servants would be wise to consult members of older generations at the onset of every municipal decision that could impact them. Much like businesses, governments would be wise not to assume what the wants and needs of older people may be.

The World Health Organization's Global Network for Age-friendly Cities and Communities is beginning to challenge local governments to embrace aging and has begun to give municipalities some guideposts. Loosely defined, an age-friendly community is one in which older people are valued, engaged, and supported by a physical and social environment that accommodates their interests and needs. Today, more than seven hundred cities and communities in thirty-nine countries participate in the network, with the number having doubled in just the past few years.

Though membership in the program doesn't guarantee that a municipality is actually age friendly, it does indicate that it is committed to engaging the community, especially its oldest members, to create a place that is more welcoming to all people, regardless of age. Membership in the program connects towns, cities, states, and national governments and organizations through a growing list of best practices and inspirations.

One of the earliest and most impressive member cities is Akita, a city of just over 300,000 people located in Japan's Honshu province. This city, which entered the Super Age long ago, now boasts a population where more than a third of its residents are over the age of 65. This astonishing demographic reality underscores what happens when the two megatrends of urbanization and population aging collide. However, unlike other localities around the world with similar demographic challenges, Akita chose to meet its head-on and turn it into an opportunity for reinvention and innovation.

The city's forward-thinking mayor, Motomu Hozumi, as well as his dedicated age-friendly staff, have focused on improving Akita's infrastructure to meet the needs of an age-diverse population. They have built a fully accessible, human-centered city hall that considers all life stages. It doubles as a community center and has become a favorite gathering place of older Akitans. It is outfitted with child care facilities, as well as hooks for walking canes and parking for strollers and wheelchairs. They have also endeavored to build a strong community that embraces all ages, with the goal of becoming a more attractive place for all people, by partnering with local businesses to improve service delivery, such as grocery delivery, as well as mobility options, such as a fixed-rate public transportation system. Both of these initiatives, as well as others, are working to ensure that social connectedness is central to the civic life of Akita—a key component of combating isolation, which is linked to serious health conditions and death.

New York City, the largest US city by population, is also doing its part to meet the demands of an increasingly older population. It has added 1,500 benches and 3,500 new or improved bus shelters throughout the city in the last decade and has worked closely with the oldest citizens to ensure that their placement has the maximum impact. Nottingham, England, has enrolled more than three hundred businesses in its "Take a Seat" program, which welcomes all people with mobility impairments into shops for a rest; they are identified by a "We are age-friendly" decal on the front window. And the German city of Griesheim—the "seatable city"—has built various places to rest, including benches and leaning stations, noting that sitting isn't always the best option.

Perhaps what's least understood about an age-friendly community is that many of the facilities may already exist and some require only modifications to meet the needs of the Super Age. Existing infrastructure, such as schools, can be adapted for reuse. Community engagement through cultural opportunities, recreation, public services, and religious institutions can be expanded. Access to college and further training can be broadened, as well as options for volunteering and job creation. Housing, cost of living, mobility, and transportation can be made more convenient and affordable.

Mobility and Transportation

The loss of mobility is one of the most important challenges that needs to be addressed later in life. It is one of the main triggers of social isolation, which can lead to loneliness. This happens when individuals are not able to connect to their community through established daily routines, such as going to the grocery store, visiting the post office, or attending religious services. It also limits their ability to work and earn a living, as well as volunteer and participate in social activities— all things that contribute to a good quality of life.

The challenges associated with the loss of mobility increase the farther an individual is removed from a town or city. Urbanites, for example, have to travel relatively short distances to access stores and services and can generally do so by foot or via multiple mobility choices (e.g., bike, bus, rail, taxi, ride-hailing app). Suburbanites have to travel longer distances, often by car, since there are fewer transportation options. Country dwellers, apart from those who live in small towns, almost always require a car as their sole means of transportation and often have to travel long distances.

A growing number of areas have access to ride-hailing services, such as Uber, which now operates in more than 450 cities in more than seventy countries around the world. There are country and region-specific options, too, such as Lyft and Curb (United States), Ola (India), Didi (China), GrabTaxi (Malaysia, Indonesia, Thailand, Philippines), Free Now (Europe), Line Taxi (Japan), Blue Bird (Indonesia), and Kakao T (Korea).

Innovative companies, such as GoGo Grandparent in the United States, have created bridge technologies that allow registered riders to book rides through a "dumb phone"—an analog or basic push-button mobile with no apps or camera and often no internet access. An Uber driver in Washington, DC, put me onto this service years ago when he told me that it was the only way his mother, an octogenarian, would utilize a ride-hailing app. Sadly, the viability of these services requires them to operate within somewhat densely populated areas, so they tend to be limited to urban and suburban environments.

The loss of mobility and access to critical services, as well as daily interactions, is often due to physical impairment, which can occur suddenly. The probability of this happening increases with age, and many government jurisdictions across the United States and around the world have age-based requirements for driver's licenses, including mandating skills tests at certain points in later life. Driving also becomes more expensive as people age; despite their years of experience and safe driving, insurers view older drivers as higher risk and raise their rates accordingly. However, a growing number of mobility options are coming online, many of which remove the need to drive altogether.

This shift will usher in a new era of independence by enabling people to stay in their homes for longer periods of time, which will allow them to remain members of the communities that they love for more years, as well as stay socially connected well past what is possible today. This may sound like science fiction, but these changes are in place or under way in urban areas already and may move quickly into the suburbs and the countryside.

Take Pittsburgh, for example, where my story began. Today, there are no fewer than five organizations dedicated to developing autonomous vehicles there. They include household names such as Uber, which has approximately twenty vehicles operating with fare-paying passengers on city streets during daylight hours; Dallas, San Francisco, Washington, DC, and Toronto are also testing grounds. The other four organizations—Aptiv, Argo AI, Aurora, and Carnegie Mellon University—are testing another forty or so cars in thirty-two of Pittsburgh's neighborhoods and suburbs. One in ten cars around the globe is anticipated to be autonomous by 2030, but self-driving cars are only part of the mobility revolution.

In 2019, during the Tokyo Motor Show, Mitsubishi Electric introduced its concept of "Mobility for Better Days," which included advances in technologies across the board, from the cars we drive to the adaptation of the wider social infrastructure. Not surprisingly, much of the discussion was about its self-driving cars, which have been at the top of many consumers' minds.

The interior of Mitsubishi's concept car, "EMIRAI," is notable because it features a number of health-monitoring innovations, including contactless heart rate monitoring, face tracking that senses when the driver is falling asleep, and a sensor that continually monitors body surface temperature. These health-monitoring innovations enable the onboard system to diagnose driver conditions such as fatigue, drowsiness, and sudden sickness in order to intervene with advanced autonomous driving modes or warn the police or fire department or EMS of a health emergency.

Municipal governments also play a major role in the delivery of mobility options. However, all too often, urban infrastructure was built decades ago or longer, for example in the case of the subway systems in London, Budapest, Glasgow, New York, Paris, and Buenos Aires, all of which were built more than a century ago. Retrofitting them would be incredibly expensive. However, many municipalities have made great strides in making buses, trains, and even the interiors of train stations and bus shelters more accessible and age friendly.

The United States now boasts that nearly 99 percent of its fixed-route buses and 90 percent of its rail fleet is accessible. However, these same municipal governments have failed to make the paths and entrances that lead to them accessible. Riders are confronted with the reality that many stations—more than a quarter of them—lack an accessible entrance. This makes getting around via public transportation, which most people take for granted, incredibly difficult, if not impossible, for an increasingly older population.

Paratransit, a term commonly used in the United States and Canada to describe affordable or no-cost transportation options that supplement bus and rail transportation that is not accessible, is available in cities and towns across the United States and is required by the Americans with Disabilities Act. However, it, too, has its barriers. Users have long complained about advance booking times—sometimes a day before—and drivers who arrive late or not at all. Some municipalities are initiating pilot programs to address this by leveraging technology or by linking to and subsidizing existing on-demand transportation options.

Service Design and Delivery

Making home and community gray again will require us to confront some of the biggest challenges that both younger and older people face, including social isolation. This is a tough subject but one that needs attention. A recent national study of 2,010 people conducted by the AARP Foundation and United Health Foundation found that two-thirds of adults across all age groups are suffering from social isolation. Additional studies have shown the negative effects of social isolation to be on a par with obesity and smoking. Connecting these vulnerable populations in a better way will create not only stronger communities but healthier ones.

Loneliness tends to develop when people are no longer able to engage in regular social interactions. It creates a litany of health issues that can build up very quickly if left unchecked. The costs associated with social isolation multiply, too, and are often paid for by family, friends, and publicly funded social welfare institutions. Isolation, if not corrected for, could lead to a future in which an individual is no longer able to live independently and will be forced into institutional care.

One of the more obvious approaches to connecting people with their communities is to make sure they don't become disengaged in the first place. This subject is top of mind not only for individuals and families but also for doctors and nurses, businesses, and advocacy organizations, as well as the public sector enterprises that are affected by its outcomes. In 2018, the UK government, realizing the epidemic of loneliness in the country, established and appointed the world's first minister for loneliness to address the crisis and seek solutions.

The good news is that various organizations around the world are tackling this issue head-on. Their goal is to keep people connected to their communities and living in their homes. The challenge is that the most innovative options are few and far between and not readily accessible to a majority of people. The lack of offerings plus the demand for improved service delivery and design presents a unique market opportunity for existing public and private sector organizations, as well as enterprising start-ups.

The covid-19 pandemic has played a role in the development of loneliness, and it has opened up even more opportunities for organizations that provide instrumental activities of daily living (IADLs). In addition to transportation, which has been discussed at length, IADLs include companionship and mental support, as well as assistance with shopping, meal preparation, managing a household, managing medications, communicating with family and friends, and managing finances. The need to deliver these services during the health crisis created innovation sandboxes—environments in which businesses solve complex challenges with free-form exploration and even playful experimentation—around the world. Some governments even backed off certain regulations, such as telehealth and digital health. Existing organizations that were already working to support individuals at risk of isolation did particularly well.

Participants in the Program of All-Inclusive Care for the Elderly (PACE) in the United States faced a daunting challenge during the pandemic but managed to excel. They provide comprehensive medical and social services to certain frail, elderly people who are still living in the community. The goal is to keep them out of institutional settings, and prior to the pandemic, most of the care was delivered at centers that provide social activities, meals, and therapies. PACE organizations, which are largely publicly funded, were allowed to pivot away from center-based care to in-home care as well as online social services during the pandemic, with little to no interruption of their funding.

A relative newcomer, the London-based "tech for good" company onHand, grew during the pandemic as the demand for support grew. onHand connects a community of volunteers who provide help at the click of a button to a growing number of older people who need assistance. onHand volunteers are vetted and verified to help with activities such as shopping, errands, prescription collection, and even companionship. The app has the added benefit of relieving the strain on the National Health Service, the UK's public health system, as well as local councils. onHand's approach is so innovative that in 2020, its founder, Sanjay Lobo, was awarded the Entrepreneur for Good Award at the Great British Entrepreneur Awards.

Many of the on-demand services that were already available became even more ubiquitous during the pandemic and have radically transformed the way the "future old" will live; on-demand and à la carte product, service, and care delivery will be readily available. The fact that even throughout the pandemic, I could reasonably expect to have a car at my home within minutes, restaurant delivery within a half hour, groceries delivered within two hours, my clothes picked up, washed, and delivered within a day, and packages delivered from Amazon within a few days, all with a few taps and swipes of my finger, is nothing short of amazing. The future old will have a lot more independence to look forward to thanks to these innovations and the ones that will follow.

| 11 |

Eldernomics

I've spent my career changing the global narrative on the older population from one that was gloom and doom, to a more positive one. I took on the challenge with gusto and have spent nearly a quarter of my life championing the rights of older people, extolling their value in the workplace, and calling for their inclusion in the development of products and services, as well as their active participation in our communities. I've argued that businesses and governments should tap into and exploit the "longevity dividend"—benefits derived from the productivity of older employees—which can lead to an increase in the purchasing power of older consumers, better social inclusion, and improved health outcomes.

I've done this by developing original research, hosting global meetings with major businesses, such as the *Financial Times* in London and the Nikkei in Tokyo, and working within the halls of power with national governments in China, France, Germany, Japan, the Netherlands, and Singapore, to name a few. I've collaborated with organizations such as the OECD, the World Economic Forum, and the United Nations and have shared my insights with major businesses, such as Dow Jones, Zurich Insurance Group, Fortune Brands, and

Shin Kong Group. All of them have taken to the idea that demographic change can bring positive changes to business, economy, and society.

Throughout all of this work, I've emphasized one simple truth: everyone wants to be part of something. All people want to belong and to be seen as normal, if not extraordinary. They want to have purpose, and they want to contribute to something—anything—that is bigger than they are. This goes for all people, regardless of age, all around the world and in all economic groups. In fact, it may be more important to people the longer they are alive.

When I speak about belonging, it isn't limited to a specific social, religious, or ethnic group. It extends deep into the fabric of society and includes being seen as a productive member—a vital cog that helps keep the greater engine of humanity running. This means that people can find value not only by contributing to income-generating activities but also by doing nonpaid work, such as caregiving and volunteering.

A lack of purpose is one of the main drivers of suicide, and the suicide rate is particularly high among older men, especially men aged 85 and over. Suicide attempts by older adults are also far more likely to result in death. The cost of each suicide is over $1 million, with the vast majority of the cost attributed to loss of productivity. In addition to the incalculable personal cost, the annual national cost of suicides is nearly $100 billion each year—much of it due to loss in productivity—a good portion of which could be mitigated by interventions.

A number of businesses are delivering assistance to those seeking purpose, including Jeff Tidwell's Next for Me, a start-up that is helping people face transitions at work and at home and find purpose in what they do. Social platforms and podcasts such as Paul Long's ProBoomer and Elizabeth Ribons's *NEXT* inspire older adults to be resilient and realize their value as contributors to society. Nonprofits such as Marc Freedman's Encore.org extol the values of people over the age of 50 who remain active and engaged in the community and help share their experiences within the community. Organizations such as these serve the growing demand for older people to be seen and recognized for their contributions and their needs.

Key Investments

My good friend and former AARP colleague Ramsey Alwin, the current chief executive officer of the National Council on Aging, is a relentless champion of the inclusion of older people in the economy. For years she had the Twitter handle @eldernomics, which she conceived as a term to promote the economic security and employability of older adults. I've always thought it was clever and expressed a pragmatic and inclusive approach to ensuring that older people had access to economic opportunity, as well as a hand in the economic prosperity of our society.

Though Ramsey has since given up that handle, she gave me her blessing to use it as the title of this chapter. I believe it encapsulates the thesis of this book: validate all people throughout all life stages in order to build a more vibrant and equitable society in which more individuals, businesses, and governments will win in the new demographic reality of the Super Age.

One way to achieve this is by ensuring that all people have digital access and digital literacy, as well as education and training throughout life. It is even more important today, as the pandemic has shown us, when so many individuals were relegated to their homes to conduct work and maintain their social lives virtually. All people need digital literacy to work, but they also need to be active participants in the digital world.

Online shopping is growing so fast in the United States that it is anticipated that 91 percent of the population, or over 300 million people, will be digital customers by 2023. Approximately a quarter of Americans shop online each month, and about two-thirds of them buy clothing. Nearly half of all online shoppers buy their first items on

Amazon. This provides opportunities to get more people online, consuming information, socializing, and transacting as regular shoppers.

Companies such as Careovacy, GetSetUp, Senior Planet, and Older Adults Technology Services (OATS) are helping older people to move online and feel comfortable with technology. They offer in-person and remote classes that connect older people with their peers to take lessons about frequently used online tools. The coursework includes the basics but also advanced topics such as marketing oneself (on LinkedIn and MailChimp), building websites (on Squarespace and Wix), and running an e-commerce marketplace (on Etsy and Shopify).

Other companies are instituting technologies that link customers who don't have access to smartphone technology to the services they need. One of these is Silberdraht, a phone service in Germany funded by Vodafone that connects older people to information that is otherwise available only online, such as podcasts and current, relevant news. Silberdraht exists because so few older Germans are connected the way Americans are. Every solution should be tailored to the needs of the local population.

There are also a growing number of entrepreneurs in the 55-to-64 age group. A quarter century ago, this population accounted for only 15 percent of new entrepreneurs. By 2016, that number had jumped to nearly one in four, according to the Kauffman Indicators of Entrepreneurship. People over 65 are more likely to be self-employed, according to the Bureau of Labor Statistics, with nearly 16 percent fitting that description. This growing group of people is important, not only because they are staying engaged outside the traditional workforce but also because their ventures tend to outperform those of younger ones.

Today, the average age of a successful entrepreneur is 45, and a 50-year-old founder is 1.8 times as likely as a 30-year-old founder to create one of the highest-growth firms. Founders in their early twenties have the lowest likelihood of building a top-growth firm. Yet the decks are stacked against funding for older entrepreneurs, especially since ageism is so prevalent. Paul Graham, a prominent venture capitalist, once quipped that when he evaluates entrepreneurs, the cutoff age is 32. Where's the vision in that?

The Cost of Doing Nothing

Meeting the basic need to belong, regardless of age, will become even more essential in the Super Age. Failure to do so could create a series of crises that could threaten business stability, weaken social cohesiveness, and disrupt national economies. Economies could stagnate, or worse, they could fall into recession or depression. If that happens, their governments would likely lose their position in the global economy, their credit rating and borrowing power would come under scrutiny, and their social welfare systems could collapse. The result would be an older, sicker, and poorer society. It is simply bad business not to consider that the older population, when properly engaged, can propel societies and economies into the future.

What stands in the way? For one, a mix of dated historical attitudes, poor public policy, and ageism—both implicit and explicit—that negatively impacts business decisions and economic productivity. If nothing is done to combat these things, taxpayers will be left to foot the bill for the hidden (and not so hidden) costs that result from the loss of economic productivity, as well as the increased health care costs associated with joblessness and isolation. If governments and businesses stand still, the current path presents an existential threat to economic growth and political stability.

By the time the first thirty-five countries are part of the Super Age in 2030, the global talent shortage could exceed 85.2 million people, which will cost trillions of dollars in economic activity if something isn't done to recruit and retain older talent. The industries that are projected to be hardest hit include many that are considered to have knowledge-intensive jobs, such as those in the financial services sector, where the lack of workers could result in $435 billion in unrealized economic output.

Even the Organisation for Economic Co-operation and Development (OECD), which to this day maintains a mandatory retirement age, agrees with the idea. Its own research projects that OECD nations can expect to see their GDP contract by an average of 10 percent over the course of the next three decades if businesses and governments do nothing to address this demographic change; some economies could contract by nearly 20 percent.

Even with age-inclusive changes, it may be too late for some countries, such as Iceland, South Korea, Japan, and Singapore, to turn their economic contraction around because of other factors that normally contribute to growth, such as immigration. Countries that lack pro-immigration policies may grow more reliant on robots, and their domestic demand for goods and services may contract with fewer people available to purchase. These economic projections should be a cautionary tale, not only for those in the OECD but also for the other 150 or so countries in the world.

Without action, demographic change can have a catastrophic effect on a nation's credit rating, a subject that isn't often discussed. Rating agencies provide global investors with information on the ability of corporations and countries to pay back debt—for example, how likely they are to make interest payments on time or to default. It should come as no surprise that the demographic outlook of a nation is directly linked to a number of economic risk factors. Rating agencies look closely at debt incurred via social welfare programs, such as health care and pensions. The debt of these programs is directly influenced by the dependency ratio, a term that expresses the number of people who are working to support the people who are not. It is intimately linked to the ageist policies that have systematically removed older people from the workforce since the middle of the last century.

Ten countries currently have a triple-A rating, the highest rating, which directly affects their borrowing power. They are Canada, Denmark, Germany, Liechtenstein, Luxembourg, the Netherlands, Norway, Singapore, Sweden, and Switzerland. Each of these countries is already in the Super Age or will be entering it this decade, and they face a downgrading of their credit score if they do not do more to tackle their problems head-on. Being downgraded has a big impact on a country's ability to borrow money. Investors see it as a riskier bet and demand a higher return to lend to it.

If any of these countries loses its high credit rating, it will likely be due to its inability to adjust its economy and social security systems to the new reality. The shrinkage in workforce participation due to population aging and outdated and ageist policies and practices has already put most of these countries on a path to facing labor shortages over the course of the next decade. This has already made it difficult for some companies to find enough of the right talent.

One option, which has been exercised in the past, is to increase the retirement age for pension beneficiaries and force people to work longer. Many countries, including the United States, have done this gradually. However, many experts, including myself, believe that this is like using a sledgehammer to crack a nut; there are always better, more equitable, and more nuanced ways to approach the demographic challenge, and I believe that businesses, especially large corporations, can play an oversized transformative role in making changes. Governments should financially support their citizens' skill and career transitions throughout the life course, and businesses should work to make themselves as ergonomic and generationally friendly as possible, so that the contributions of each individual can be maximized for as long as possible.

This is why I ask every organization that I work with to commit to a set of principles that encourages it to tackle ageism head-on, support its employees' life needs, and hold other businesses in its supply chain accountable. It's an approach that my good friend Fabrice Houdart at Out Leadership shared with me when he was working with the Office of the United Nations High Commissioner for Human Rights on its LGBTQ+ strategy with corporations. They include:

- Respect all people, regardless of age, as contributors and customers.
- Work to eliminate age-based discrimination in the workplace.
- Support employees through caregiving leave and continuous education.
- Refuse to support or engage with known ageist organizations, including those in the supply chain.
- Encourage and establish the development of policies, practices, products, and services that help people live better longer.

This approach isn't some Pollyanna vision of the future; it's pragmatic and underscores the reality of the demographic change that is happening at a quickened pace every minute of every hour of every day.

Real Talk

I'm a realist, and I am fully cognizant of the fact that it would be impossible to undo more than two thousand years of written human history and lived experience that has rather consistently marginalized older people. I also understand that undoing more than a century of calamitous public policy that has systematically sidelined or removed older people from the workplace and the community won't happen overnight. Change doesn't have to be earth shattering, but it does need to be progressive, inclusive, and deliberate.

The introduction of women into the formal labor market in the last century was one of the most significant changes to the US economy in the past hundred years. The female labor force participation rate doubled from 1950 till today, and women's working became the norm in 1978, when more than half of women were part of the workforce. Sadly, these gains are at risk, due largely in part to women bearing more of the burden for caregiving, as well as challenges incurred due to the pandemic—housekeeping, homeschooling, and so on. However, pro-longevity workforce policies that shift demands throughout the life course would help change this. Women's participation in the workforce is essential to continued economic growth.

Likewise, the systematic removal of older workers starting in the 1950s would have had an equal, albeit calamitous, effect on the economy had it not been for the introduction of young baby boomers into the workforce and the robust retirement industry. To provide some context, the labor force participation rate of men over the age of 65 in the United States in 1950 was nearly 50 percent, but it dropped precipitously from then until 1990, when it hit its lowest point at 16 percent, due to ageist public policies and a strong retirement system.

This finding aligns with mandatory retirement policies that were widespread in the United States and other developed nations in the 1960s and 1970s and are still common in many countries. These policies were instituted to get older people out of the labor market to make room for the glut of baby boomers. It wasn't until 1978 that Congress, with an amendment to the Age Discrimination in Employment Act (ADEA), outlawed mandatory retirement before the age of 70 and in 1986 the mandatory retirement age was abolished. This change has helped get older people working again, but it hasn't been enough to undo ageist work cultures, since it is notoriously difficult to enforce.

There is some positive news regarding the labor participation rate of older people, but it is really just a start. Between 2000 and 2018, the labor force participation rate of people over the age of 65 in high-income economies increased from 9.9 percent to 13.7 percent. In the United States, that rate was 20.2 percent in 2019. In Iceland and Indonesia, the two countries with the highest labor force participation rate, the figures were 35.2 percent and 41.7 percent, respectively.

In Luxembourg and Spain, the countries with the lowest labor force participation rate, the figures were 2.3 percent and 2.5 percent, respectively. The labor force participation rate in the European Union was only 6.6 percent. As birth rates continue to plummet and longevity continues to increase, the inclusion of older people in the economy will be paramount for continued growth, because when fewer older people participate in the labor force, the economy operates without the talents and abilities of a growing percentage of the population and begins to slow.

Prosperity Unites Generations

Baby boomers are expected to transfer a huge amount of wealth to subsequent generations. Most experts estimate that the value of boomer assets will be between $30 trillion and $40 trillion. This shockingly high amount has led many experts to refer to the event that will happen over the next decade or so as the "Great Wealth Transfer."

A lot of attention has been directed to Millennials as the key beneficiaries of the Great Wealth Transfer. However, it is far more likely that widows and Gen Xers are already starting to gain from the transfer of familial riches. The decisions that today's older adults make regarding their estates will have profound effects on the lives of their adult children, as well as those of future generations.

Make no mistake: this shift will have earth-rattling consequences that could impact entire sectors of the economy, especially when as much as $68 trillion could move between the generations over the next quarter century. Companies, especially those in the financial services sector, need to walk a tightrope between servicing the demands of their current clients and addressing the desires of the inheritors of wealth. This is an opportune time for all businesses to rebalance and create more generationally inclusive products and services.

One of the prevailing challenges facing small-business owners in the Super Age is that a growing number of them will struggle to transfer ownership to their adult children or find a buyer. This is more likely in rural areas. However, there is a growing trend of privately held companies transferring ownership to their employees, an ownership structure more commonly known as a cooperative.

Nearly half of all Americans are employed by a small business, and boomers make up 41 percent of the more than 30 million small-business owners in the United States. They are second only to Gen Xers, at 44 percent. As these owners prepare to retire in the coming years, it is anticipated that nearly three-quarters of their businesses will change hands. Unfortunately, changing hands usually includes liquidation or closure, which is far less advantageous than transitioning to a cooperative for some owners, employees, and the communities they serve, thereby keeping capital local.

Nearly eight hundred employee-owned cooperatives exist in the United States today; the numbers are higher in Europe. However, this is more than double the 350 that existed more than ten years ago. Cooperatives employ thousands of people and drive nearly half a billion dollars in revenue each year, according to the US Federation of Worker Cooperatives. Perhaps the coolest thing about a cooperative is that there is no limit to the size or scope of the business, meaning that it can employ a handful of people or a couple hundred or more. The largest cooperative in the United States is Cooperative Home Care Associates in New York, which employs nearly two thousand workers.

The immediate benefit of transferring to cooperative ownership is that an older sole proprietor is able to sell the business quickly or over time, which directly contributes to his or her retirement prospects. A secondary, and perhaps more impactful, benefit is that cooperative ownership is believed to contribute to a business's performance because more of its workers feel responsible for its success; this enhances the long-term durability of the enterprise, too. Some European regulations require that cooperatives hold money aside in a "rainy day" fund. However, the third and most dramatic benefit of the transfer from sole ownership to cooperative ownership is that it may help redistribute wealth through a market-based approach, which could narrow the wealth gap. Establishing a cooperative is one strategy an older entrepreneur can employ to exit from a business and make a profit while keeping important services in the community.

Research by Virginie Pérotin of Leeds University Business School in England supports this assertion. She examined research on labor-managed firms across the United States, Europe, and Latin America and found that a number of psychosocial benefits were associated with the arrangement. However, on the whole, she found that worker cooperatives were more productive than conventional businesses, that their staff worked better, and that they were organized more efficiently.

The Tip of the Spear

Japan's experience in the Super Age offers some valuable lessons for the rest of the world. The concomitant trends of rapid automation and population aging may often seem at odds with each other. Yet like all things in Japan, balancing the two is an attempt to find harmony, much as with *inyodo*, opposite or contrary forces that may actually be complementary, interconnected, and interdependent.

In Japan, where tradition is an art form, entire cottage industries and trades are disappearing due to the confluence of changing tastes, shifting demographics, and technology. Efficiencies caused by technological advances, for example, have wiped out more than half of the country's sushi restaurants, according to the government. Today, it is more common to eat the Japanese staple in a technology-driven environment that limits human interaction and delivers food produced by a robot chef via conveyor belt than in a traditional eatery.

The oldest Japanese sushi chefs, some of whom have been in business since the 1960s, have been forced to close thanks to these trends, as well as the pandemic. Others have turned their expertise of crafting handmade sushi into a luxury product, which increases their profit margins and helps with business sustainability. This may be the future of other cottage or artisanal industries that are owned by older people, as well as those that can't yet be replicated by machine.

Japan, unlike most of the other countries entering the Super Age, has never had a proactive immigration policy, which hastened its ascension to the Super Age and its reliance on technology. This has left the country with a monoculture that is growing ever more reliant on robotics to do jobs once held by humans, including high-touch settings such as health care and long-term care, in which artificial intelligence is being utilized for patient monitoring and robots, also equipped with AI, are being used to provide some degree of social interaction for residents.

Japan's use of technology, particularly robots that assist with physical work, is a vitally important lesson for the United States and other countries entering the Super Age. Research by the Center for Economic and Policy Research indicates that nearly half of workers over the age of 58 are engaged in physically demanding jobs, and it will be necessary to extend their working lives. Many of their jobs are in critical industries, such as delivery, construction, caregiving, and nursing, and a growing number of workers are forced to leave their good-paying jobs for lesser-paying ones simply because they are no longer physically able to do the job.

Some companies, such as Cyberdyne, are assisting with this challenge by developing exoskeletons to ease the strain of repetitive labor and increase overall physical "strength." Another company, Innophys, has developed a backpacklike suit that can be "charged" by squeezing a hand pump thirty times to fill pressurized air-powered "muscles." Larger companies, such as Panasonic and Toyota, are getting into the game with their own versions. These devices are being utilized at sites across the country and are helping individuals extend their working lives. The use of these devices will likely become ubiquitous across Japan and other Super Age countries.

Japanese businesses are adapting to the older consumers, and this includes all types of businesses, including the corner store. The Lawson convenience store chain in Japan has a number of locations across the country that are now specifically targeted toward the oldest members of society. They are equipped with blood pressure monitors and specialized products and staffed by social workers and other health care professionals. Some also operate mobile stores, which visit senior housing and nursing facilities around the country.

Leveraging the willingness of older people to work and to spend must be central to any Super Age strategy, but there has to be a willingness to change. Doing so can create an incredibly rich future.

A Rich Future

More than 80 percent of global GDP is generated by countries with rapidly aging populations. These countries are also home to some of the richest older populations in the world. With the worldwide over-65 population projected to double by 2050, these countries will soon control nearly three-quarters of disposable income. When coupled with the fact that older people are living healthier and more independent lives than ever before, this will create a level of business disruption unlike anything in living memory.

In 2016, AARP attempted to measure the size of the economic contributions of all people over the age of 50, also known as the "longevity economy." It estimated that it was $7.6 trillion per year. An update of the study in 2019 estimated that this economic activity was more than $9 trillion and included nonmonetary contributions, such as caregiving. AARP's estimate would make the US longevity economy the third largest economy in the world, just after the overall economies of the United States and China.

Older people are spending an incredible amount of money. Euromonitor International, a leading provider of strategic market research, has estimated that the global spending of people over 60 will surpass $15 trillion in 2020. The US population over the age of 50 spent $8.3 trillion in 2018, more than three-quarters of which was spent by people aged 50 to 74. The 50-to-74 age group spent approximately $6.3 trillion in 2018, about the same amount as the entire under-50 group, and people over the age of 75 spent $1.8 trillion.

Whether the starting line is 50 or 60, there's been an effort to classify everyone over a certain age in the same economic group, but this is problematic. Most organizations need better segmentation, because I would no sooner lump a centenarian with a 50-year-old than I would lump a newborn baby with a 50-year-old. The longevity economy is simply too big, and the wants and needs of people living past 50 are too diverse, for its meaning to have much impact. A life stage–based approach that considers similarities across generations may be more valuable. The age-based approach to segmentation is dead.

Rather than focusing on tailoring products and services exclusively for the longevity economy (i.e., people over the age of 50), national governments should be more focused on leveraging generational diversity. This may sound like a bit of wordplay, but the fundamental premise of the longevity economy is wrong, especially since it is buttressed by gross amounts of public spending, debt, and unpaid or nonmonetary contributions. The national bottom line would be healthier if we eschewed forced redundancy, created a work environment that embraced experience and encouraged longer working years, and fostered a community of innovators and businesses geared to helping people live their best lives regardless of age.

The more inclusive we are as a society, the more likely we are to see not only great economic benefits but deeply important social ones, too. Things just work better when more people are included and feel a part of something bigger than themselves. However, in order to create a society that is more welcoming to all people of all ages, leaders must pivot away from the dangerous ways of measuring success that brought us to where we are today, such as GDP, and look toward new, more positive social goals, such as well-being.

Our societies must be willing to cure or kill outdated institutions and systems, as well as belief structures, in order to meet the new realities of the Super Age. Perhaps the aphorism "A rising tide lifts all boats"—the idea that an improved economy will benefit all participants and that economic policy, particularly government economic policy, should therefore focus on broad economic efforts—best fits here.

The most progressive of all approaches is happening right now in New Zealand, where Prime Minister Jacinda Ardern and her government introduced a first-of-its-kind "well-being budget" in 2019. The budget focuses government spending on citizens' health and life satisfaction, not wealth or economic growth. She sees GDP alone as not a good enough measure for today and certainly not a good enough one for the Super Age. The budget requires all new public spending to support five goals: bolstering mental health, reducing child poverty, supporting indigenous peoples, moving to a low-carbon-emission economy, and flourishing in a digital age. Success is measured by sixty-one indicators tracking a host of issues, including isolation.

Approaches like the ones being undertaken in New Zealand underscore just how dramatic the transition to the Super Age is going to be and also highlight the incredible amount of opportunity that exists for individuals, organizations, and governments to innovate for a future in which there will be fewer children and an increasingly large number of older adults. A more equitable approach that considers all generations is good for both government and business.

The End Is Just the Beginning

Near the end of my tenure at AARP, I conceived and partnered with the Foreign Policy Group to produce "The Aging Readiness and

Competitiveness (ARC) Report." This groundbreaking report included an in-depth study of aging policy in twenty-two countries, both large and small. ARC examined the pressures and opportunities each of these countries faced, as well as their policy responses in four areas: community social infrastructure, productive opportunity, technological engagement, and health care and wellness. Consideration was given particularly to innovations aimed at engaging a healthier, more independent older population and unleashing its productive and economic potential. My goal, along with my counterpart Claire Casey at the Foreign Policy Group, was to help change the aging narrative from one that was consistently negative to one that was more realistic and positive by uncovering the good that was happening around the world.

On the whole, we found that no country excelled in all four areas. We also found that smaller countries were doing better than bigger ones. However, there were good examples of innovation in almost every nation, and every government was trying in some way to prepare for the Super Age. The bright spots in innovation were typically carried out by both the private and public sectors. They also tended to bubble up from local communities or organizations to the national and sometimes global level.

Many business sectors are beginning to realize that human longevity is one of the most significant forces shaping them. The shift to the Super Age could open up multitrillion-dollar opportunities to reshape societies, in many cases for the better. Perhaps the best modern-day example of this is climate change, which a growing number of corporate executives see as a pressing issue and an obstacle to their profitability—in the court of public opinion, as barriers to trade, or as the cost of doing business.

But none of these changes will be possible if individuals and organizations do nothing to address their negative bias toward older people at home, in the community, and in the workforce. If countries tackle ageism head-on and support age-friendly initiatives through direct financing and investment, tax incentives, and the creation of innovation districts to support longevity, they could see growth upward of 20 percent of GDP.

Businesses win when they embrace the issues of longevity head-on and engage an older and generationally diverse population in the workplace with the products and services that they want to buy, not just the ones they need to buy. They can do this in part by building workplaces that support human longevity through the design of physical spaces and benefits, as well as a culture that celebrates experience. Every sector can win in the Super Age.

Then there are the nonmonetary characteristics that erode over time, such as dignity and purpose. Bias blocks all too many people from seeing the whole person who exists behind the wrinkles, blue hair, and glasses.

Collective Purpose

Across cultures and generations, individuals are struggling to find purpose in our modern world. The French call it *raison d'être* and the Japanese call it *ikigai*, both of which translate as "reason for being." The Super Age will require the collective inspiration and might of all people of all colors and all creeds in all lands to come together to shape a world in which the oldest among us are valued as much as the youngest. This will require many of us to confront ageism head-on and bet on our future selves and our shared future. Our collective goal, at least in this time and place, may very well be to make the changes that are needed in our personal lives, our homes, our communities, our businesses, and our nations and economies in order to build a future that is more just and equitable.

The future may look gray, but it's incredibly bright.

Acknowledgments

My husband, Arthur Yampolsky;

My parents, Carol and Gary Schurman;

My brother, Christopher Schurman, his wife, Jennifer, and their children;

My relentless champion, collaborator, counsel, and friend, Claire Casey;

Rebecca Frankel and Lilian Myers, who encouraged me to pursue writing *The Super Age*;

My agent, Esmond Harmsworth, and the entire Aevitas Creative team;

My entire team at HarperCollins for their partnership, guidance, and patience, including Hollis Heimbouch, Rebecca Raskin, Wendy Wong, Leslie Cohen, Viviana Moreno, Penny Makras, Andrea Guinn, Rebecca Holland, Lynn Anderson, Pam Rehm, and Joe Jasko;

My research assistant, Nick Barracca;

A global network of advocates, experts, and mentors that have worked with me throughout my career to conceptualize and execute my vision for *The Super Age*, including Ramsey Alwin, Willemien Bax, Jee Eun "Geannie" Cho, Erica Dhar, Adam Cuthbert, Brian Elms, Kaye Fallick, Julia Farnen Feldmen, Alison Hernandez, Ellen Hunt, Kristian King, Almar Latour, Nancy LeaMond, Abel Lee, Frank Leyhausen, Ladan Manteghi, Edward Newburn, Henrique Noya,

Doug Pace, Nicola Palmarini, Geoff Pearman, Kim Sedmak, Adam Segal, Jeff Tidwell, Chris Vaughan, Arjan in't Veld, Tina Woods, Cynthia Wu, and Lisa Yagoda;

My chosen family and closest friends, including Giacamo Abrusci, David Bediz, Mark Bescher, Thomas Bowman, Delphine Francois Chiavarini, Orlando Croft II, Wesley Della Volla, Joaquin "Jocko" Fajardo, Bryce Furness, Matt Glassman, Jeffrey Gullo, Kyriacos Koupparis, Jake Kuhns, Kelly Lazcko, Luke Lewis, Tim Meinke, Maura Mitchell,Gary Mosher, Ski Rowland, Levi Schoenfeld, Tamo Sein, Eric Vermieren, Lynn Zdniak, and Mike Zdniak;

And, a special thank-you to those individuals who enhanced and expanded my understanding and perspectives on race, sexual orientation, gender, and rural life, including Jameson Beekman, Stefanie Cruz, Natalie Graves Tucker, Sheila Hooten Forney, Susan Kaminski, Jessica Kidd, Stephanie Tinsley Reganon, and CV Viverito.

Notes

| 1 | Underfoot and Everywhere

4   the number of persons: "Ageing," Global Issues, United Nations, https://www.un.org/en/sections/issues-depth/ageing.

6   "new technologies": Klaus Schwab, *The Fourth Industrial Revolution* (London: Portfolio Penguin, 2017), 6.

| 2 | How We Got Here

19   the average age: Benjamin F. Jones, et al., "How Old Are Successful Tech Entrepreneurs?," Kellogg Insight, May 15, 2018, https://insight.kellogg.northwestern.edu/article/younger-older-tech-entrepreneurs.

21   In 1914, the year: "Life Expectancy at Birth—USA," Human Mortality Database, University of California, Berkeley (USA) and Max Planck Institute for Demographic Research (Germany), https://www.lifetable.de/data/USA/e0.csv Sex Code 1; See "Life expectancy at birth" under Pooled Data Files at https://www.lifetable.de/cgi-bin/country.php?code=usa. The pooled resource pulls the data from Felicitie C. Bell and Michael L. Miller. Life Tables for the United States Social Security Area 1900-2100. Actuarial Study No. 116.

22   it is estimated: Karen Cokayne, "Old Age in Ancient Rome," Bath Royal Literary and Scientific Institution, March 21, 2005, https://www.brlsi.org/events-proceedings/proceedings/25020.

22   Researchers from the University of Reading: David Brown, "Linguists Identify 15,000-Year-Old 'Ultraconserved Words,'" *Washington Post*, May 6,

2013, https://www.washingtonpost.com/national/health-science/linguists-identify-15000-year-old-ultraconserved-words/2013/05/06/a02e3a14-b427-11e2-9a98-4be1688d7d84_story.html.

23 "From around the first century": Karen Cokayne, *Experiencing Old Age in Ancient Rome* (London: Routledge, 2003), 1.

23 Shulamith detailed : Shulamith Shahar, "Who Were Old in the Middle Ages?," *Social History of Medicine* 6, no. 3 (December 1993): 313–41, https://doi.org/10.1093/shm/6.3.313.

24 "A soldier would earn": Vauhini Vara, "The Real Reason for Pensions," *New Yorker*, December 4, 2013, https://www.newyorker.com/business/currency/the-real-reason-for-pensions.

24 In 1875, the American Express Company: Robert L. Clark, Lee A. Craig, and Jack W. Wilson, *A History of Public Sector Pensions in the United States* (Philadelphia: University of Pennsylvania Press, 2003), chap. 1, https://pensionresearchcouncil.wharton.upenn.edu/publications/books/a-history-of-public-sector-pensions-in-the-united-states/.

25 "those who are disabled": "Otto von Bismarck," Social Security Administration, https://www.ssa.gov/history/ottob.html.

26 The pensionable age was thirty years more: "Life Expectancy at Birth—Germany," Human Life Table Database. Retirement age set at 70 according to SSA.gov history: https://www.ssa.gov/history/ottob.html https://www.lifetable.de/data/DEU/e0.csv Year 1881; See "Life expectancy at birth" under Pooled Data Files at https://www.lifetable.de/cgi-bin/country.php?code=usa The pooled resource pulls the data from File 1: Bewegung der Bevölkerung im Jahre 1910, Statistik des Deutschen Reichs, Vol. 246, Berlin 1913, 16–17.

26 But as Angus Deaton: Julia Belluz and Alvin Chang, "What Research on English Dukes Can Teach Us About Why the Rich Live Longer," Vox, July 27, 2016, https://www.vox.com/2016/4/25/11501370/health-longevity-inequality-life-expectancy.

28 From 1990 to 2017: "Mortality and Causes of Death," World Health Organization, https://www.who.int/gho/child_health/mortality/neonatal_infant/en/.

28 women in 1950 had: "GBD 2017: A Fragile World," *Lancet* 392, no. 10159 (November 2018): 1683, https://doi.org/10.1016/S0140-6736(18)32858-7.

28 "The fertility rate in Niger": James Gallagher, "'Remarkable' Decline in Fertility Rates," BBC News, November 9, 2018, https://www.bbc.com/news/health-46118103.

29　The United Nations has even suggested: "Growing at a Slower Pace, World Population Is Expected to Reach 9.7 Billion in 2050 and Could Peak at Nearly 11 Billion Around 2100," Department of Economic and Social Affairs, United Nations, June 17, 2019, https://www.un.org/development/desa/en/news /population/world-population-prospects-2019.html.

29　China's population exploded: "Chinese Birth Rate Falls to Lowest in Seven Decades," BBC News, January 17, 2020, https://www.bbc.com/news /world-asia-china-51145251.

30　It's estimated that: Justin Parkinson, "Five Numbers That Sum Up China's One-Child Policy," BBC News, October 29, 2015, https://www.bbc.com/news /magazine-34666440.

30　Today, China's fertility rate: Joel Kotkin, "Death Spiral Demographics: The Countries Shrinking the Fastest," *Forbes*, February 1, 2017, https://www .forbes.com/sites/joelkotkin/2017/02/01/death-spiral-demographics-the -countries-shrinking-the-fastest/#68eb1b0eb83c.

30　the normal pension age: "China," in *Pensions at a Glance 2019: OECD and G20 Indicators*, OECD Publishing, Paris, https://www.oecd.org/els/public -pensions/PAG2019-country-profile-China.pdf. Also listed under Pensions at a Glance 2015 on pg. 233, https://www.oecd-ilibrary.org/social-issues-migration -health/pensions-at-a-glance-2015_pension_glance-2015-en.

32　"Classical authors such as": Tim G. Parkin, *Old Age in the Roman World: A Cultural and Social History* (Baltimore and London: Johns Hopkins University Press, 2003): In excerpt, https://jhupbooks.press.jhu.edu/title/old-age-roman-world.

33　"Old age will only": Cengage, "Status of Older People: The Ancient and Biblical Worlds," Encyclopedia.com, June 2, 2020, https://www.encyclopedia .com/education/encyclopedias-almanacs-transcripts-and-maps/status-older -people-ancient-and-biblical-worlds.

34　"People talk about aging": Quoted in W. Andrew Achenbaum, "Ageism, Past and Present," in *The Cambridge Handbook of Social Problems*, vol. 1, edited by A. Javier Treviño (Cambridge, UK: Cambridge University Press, 2018), 441–58.

35　"in condescending generalisations": Caroline Baum, "The Ugly Truth About Ageism: It's a Prejudice Targeting Our Future Selves," *Guardian*, September 14, 2018, https://www.theguardian.com/lifeandstyle/2018/sep/14/the -ugly-truth-about-ageism-its-a-prejudice-targeting-our-future-selves.

35　"Older women face marginalization": "Gendered Ageism: Trend Brief," Catalyst, October 17, 2019, https://www.catalyst.org/research/gendered-ageism -trend-brief/.

36 "greedy geezers": David Ingles and Miranda Stewart, "The Ghost of the 'Greedy Geezers' Hovers over Our Super Debate," The Conversation, June 9, 2016, https://theconversation.com/the-ghost-of-the-greedy-geezers-hovers-over-our-super-debate-60706.

36 Wage stagnation since the Great Recession: Megan Leonhardt, "Millennials Earn 20% Less than Baby Boomers Did—Despite Being Better Educated," CNBC, November 5, 2019, https://www.cnbc.com/2019/11/05/millennials-earn-20-percent-less-than-boomersdespite-being-better-educated.html.

36 "OK, millennials": Sara Fischer, "The Boomers' Media Behemoth," Axios, November 12, 2019, https://www.axios.com/the-boomers-media-behemoth-412b5106-f879-477d-806d-6130148956bf.html.

36 more than two out of three: Katie Sehl, "20 Important TikTok Stats Marketers Need to Know in 2020," Hootsuite, May 7, 2020, https://blog.hootsuite.com/tiktok-stats/.

37 According to CNN exit polls: "Exit Polls 2016," CNN, November 23, 2016, https://www.cnn.com/election/2016/results/exit-polls.

38 In the 2016 presidential election: Thom File, "Voting in America: A Look at the 2016 Presidential Election," US Census Bureau, May 10, 2017, https://www.census.gov/newsroom/blogs/random-samplings/2017/05/voting_in_america.html.

38 In 2016, there was: Simon Shuster, "The U.K.'s Old Decided for the Young in the Brexit Vote," Time, June 24, 2016, https://time.com/4381878/brexit-generation-gap-older-younger-voters/.

| 3 | The Altar of Youth

41 Around 25 percent: "Family Life," The Roman Empire in the First Century, PBS, 2006, https://www.pbs.org/empires/romans/empire/family.html.

42 Legends of healing waters: Jesse Greenspan, "The Myth of Ponce de León and the Fountain of Youth," History, April 1, 2020, https://www.history.com/news/the-myth-of-ponce-de-leon-and-the-fountain-of-youth.

42 "the equivalent of today's major medical centers": David Clay Large, The Grand Spas of Central Europe: A History of Intrigue, Politics, Art, and Healing (Lanham, MD: Rowman & Littlefield, 2015): In excerpt, https://rowman.com/isbn/9781442222366/the-grand-spas-of-central-europe-a-history-of-intrigue-politics-art-and-healing.

43   in 2018, youth advertising: A. Guttmann, "Kids Advertising Spending Worldwide 2012–2021, by Format," Statista, April 7, 2020, https://www .statista.com/statistics/750865/kids-advertising-spending-worldwide/.

43   In 2015, 500 percent: Marty Swant, "Infographic: Marketers Are Spending 500% More on Millennials than All Others Combined," *Ad Week*, November 17, 2015, https://www.adweek.com/digital/infographic-marketers-are -spending-500-more-millennials-all-others-combined-168176/.

45   "Overall, adults": "The Age Gap in Religion Around the World," Pew Research Center, June 13, 2018, https://www.pewforum.org/2018/06/13/the -age-gap-in-religion-around-the-world/.

46   only one out of ten: Ibid.

46   "protect the educational opportunities": "Youth and Labor," US Department of Labor, https://www.dol.gov/general/topic/youthlabor.

46   By 1900, thirty-four US states: P. A. Graham, *Community and Class in American Education, 1865–1918* (New York: Wiley, 1974).

47   "24 states and the District of Columbia": Stephanie Aragon, "Free and Compulsory School Age Requirements," Education Commission of the States, May 2015, https://www.ecs.org/clearinghouse/01/18/68/11868.pdf.

47   by 1940, 50 percent: Jurgen Herbst, *The Once and Future School: Three Hundred and Fifty Years of American Secondary Education* (New York: Routledge, 1996).

47   "Boys and girls in their teens!": Quoted in Allan A. Metcalf, *From Skedaddle to Selfie: Words of the Generations* (New York: Oxford University Press, 2016), 100.

48   "The teenager emerged": Derek Thompson, "A Brief History of Teenagers," *Saturday Evening Post*, February 13, 2018, https://www.saturdayeveningpost .com/2018/02/brief-history-teenagers/.

48   According to a two-part profile: Dwight Macdonald, "A Caste, a Culture, a Market," *New Yorker*, November 22, 1958, https://www.newyorker.com/magazine /1958/11/22/a-caste-a-culture-a-market.

49   "Its editorial content": John McDonough and Karen Egolf, *The Advertising Age Encyclopedia of Advertising* (Routledge, 2015), 1693. Edited from page here, https://books.google.com/books?id=HZLtCQAAQBAJ&pg=PA1693 &lpg=PA1693&dq=Seventeen+provided+a+new+medium+for+advertisers .+Its+editorial+content,+fashion+pages+and+special+features,+combined +with+a+rapid+circulation+growth,+created+a+perfect+vehicle+for+advertisers +to+reach+young+consumers.&source=bl&ots=HBYrPiwwC4&sig=A CfU3U1ujW_Dcua0OOiS4WNMwMNxsPYa-w&hl=en&sa=X&ved=2

ahUKEwiIyIXQk4TqAhWjTDABHbptCIIQ6AEwAHoECAoQAQ#v
=onepage&q&f=false.

50 "Berry injected a cocksure": "Chuck Berry Didn't Invent Rock n' Roll, but He Turned It into an Attitude That Changed the World," *Billboard*, March 18, 2017, https://www.billboard.com/articles/columns/rock/7728712/chuck-berry -rock-roll-pioneer-attitude.

50 "When the youngest boomer graduated": Louis Menand, "The Misconception About Baby Boomers and the Sixties," *New Yorker*, August 18, 2019, https://www.newyorker.com/culture/cultural-comment/the-misconception -about-baby-boomers-and-the-sixties.

55 "young people are just smarter": Margaret Kane, "Say What? 'Young People Are Just Smarter,'" CNET, March 28, 2007, https://www.cnet.com /news/say-what-young-people-are-just-smarter/.

55 "When you are 50 to 60 years old": Zameena Mejia, "Self-Made Billionaire Jack Ma: How to Be Successful in Your 20s, 30s, 40s and Beyond," CNBC, January 30, 2018, https://www.cnbc.com/2018/01/30/jack-ma-dont -fear-making-mistakes-in-your-20s-and-30s.html.

56 Today, the US beauty: Pamela N. Danziger, "6 Trends Shaping the Future of the $532B Beauty Business," *Forbes*, September 1, 2019, https://www .forbes.com/sites/pamdanziger/2019/09/01/6-trends-shaping-the-future-of -the-532b-beauty-business/?sh=1a2a13a3588d.

56 It's understood that Cleopatra: Joe Schwarcz, "Why Did Cleopatra Supposedly Bathe in Sour Donkey Milk?," Office for Science and Society, McGill University, March 20, 2017, https://www.mcgill.ca/oss/article/science-science -everywhere-you-asked/why-did-cleopatra-supposedly-bathe-sour-donkey -milk.

56 Women in Elizabethan England: Taylor Stephan, "A Slightly Terrifying History of Facial Beauty Treatments—from Poison to Blood Injections," E Online, October 26, 2015, https://www.eonline.com/news/710329/a -slightly-terrifying-history-of-facial-beauty-treatments-from-poison-to-blood -injections.

56 According to AARP: Colette Thayer and Laura Skufca, "Media Image Landscape: Age Representation in Online Images," AARP, September 2019, https://www.aarp.org/content/dam/aarp/research/surveys_statistics/life -leisure/2019/age-representation-in-online-media-images.doi.10.26419 -2Fres.00339.001.pdf.

57 Today, more than one-third: Katie Kilkenny, "How Anti-Aging Cosmetics Took over the Beauty World," *Pacific Standard*, August 30, 2017, https://psmag .com/social-justice/how-anti-aging-cosmetics-took-over-the-beauty-world.

57 "In 2020, the global": M. Ridder, "Value of the Global Anti-aging Market 2020–2026," Statista, January 27, 2021, https://www.statista.com/statistics /509679/value-of-the-global-anti-aging-market/#:~:text=In%20 2020%2C%20the%20global%20anti,percent%20between%202021%20 and%202026.

57 "We are making a resolution": Michelle Lee, "*Allure* Magazine Will No Longer Use the Term 'Anti-aging,'" *Allure*, August 14, 2017, https://www.allure .com/story/allure-magazine-phasing-out-the-word-anti-aging.

| 4 | Building on Longevity Gains

59 a tortoise named Harriet: "176-Year-Old 'Darwin's Tortoise' Dies in Zoo," NBC News, June 24, 2006, http://www.nbcnews.com/id/13115101/ns/world _news-asia_pacific/t/-year-old-darwins-tortoise-dies-zoo/#.Xtj44PJ7mgQ.

59 It is believed: Elizabeth Pennisi, "Greenland Shark May Live 400 Years, Smashing Longevity Record," *Science*, August 11, 2016, https://www.science mag.org/news/2016/08/greenland-shark-may-live-400-years-smashing -longevity-record.

60 They include the Methuselah tree: "Bristlecone Pine," Bryce Canyon National Park, National Park Service, February 24, 2015, https://www.nps.gov /brca/learn/nature/bristleconepine.htm.

61 "The knowledge of death": Ernest Becker, *The Denial of Death* (New York: Free Press, 1973), 27.

61 It wasn't until recently: Bridget Alex, "Chimps Know Death When They See It," *Discover*, September 28, 2018, https://www.discovermagazine.com /planet-earth/chimps-know-death-when-they-see-it.

63 Preliminary 2020 data: Marisa Fernandez, "American Life Expectancy Fell by 1 Year in the First Half of 2020," Axios, February 18, 2021, https:// www.axios.com/us-life-expectancy-2020-pandemic-ba166c4b-c29d-4064 -9085-4ef6c94fc2df.html.

63 by nearly two years: https://www.npr.org/2021/06/23/1009611699/the -pandemic-led-to-the-biggest-drop-in-u-s-life-expectancy-since-ww-ii-study-fi.

63   more than seventy thousand people died: "Overdose Death Rates," NIH, January 29, 2021, https://www.drugabuse.gov/drug-topics/trends-statistics /overdose-death-rates. Correct statistical although the in text referenced to CDC instead of NIH (pre-submission) "Drug Overdose Deaths," Centers for Disease Control and Prevention, March 3, 2021, https://www.cdc.gov/drug overdose/deaths/index.html.

63   pulled down the US life expectancy: Steven H. Woolf and Heidi Schoomaker, "Life Expectancy and Mortality Rates in the United States, 1959–2017," JAMA 322, no. 20 (November 26, 2019): 1996--2016, https://doi .org/10.1001/jama.2019.16932.

63   In the groundbreaking study: *Fair Society, Healthy Lives: The Marmot Review*, Institute of Health Equity, https://www.instituteofhealthequity.org /resources-reports/fair-society-healthy-lives-the-marmot-review/fair-society -healthy-lives-full-report-pdf.pdf.

63   improvements to life expectancy: Ibid.

64   It also led to the discovery: Meagan Flynn, "The Man Who Discovered That Unwashed Hands Could Kill—and Was Ridiculed for It," *Washington Post*, March 23, 2020, https://www.washingtonpost.com/nation/2020/03/23 /ignaz-semmelweis-handwashing-coronavirus/.

65   The "Spanish flu": Barbara Jester, Timothy Uyeki, and Daniel Jernigan, "Readiness for Responding to a Severe Pandemic 100 Years After 1918," *American Journal of Epidemiology* 187, no. 12 (2018): 2596–602, https://pubmed.ncbi .nlm.nih.gov/30102376/.

65   "Rules for Influenza": Quoted in W. Stull Holt, *The Great War at Home and Abroad: The World War I Diaries and Letters of W. Stull Holt* (Sunflower University Press, 1999), 263, https://www.google.com/books /edition/The_Great_War_at_Home_and_Abroad/053vAAAAMAAJ ?hl=en&gbpv=0&kptab=overview; Keith Martin, "The Pandemic Poet and Other Tales From a NIST 'Genealogy' Project" *National Institute of Standards and Technology*, Medium, May 19, 2021, https://nist.medium .com/the-pandemic-poet-and-other-tales-from-a-nist-genealogy-project -9c10d3b5d0d0.

66   "The modern bathroom developed": Elizabeth Yuko, "How Infectious Disease Defined the American Bathroom," Bloomberg CityLab, April 10, 2020, https://www.bloomberg.com/news/articles/2020-04-10/the-war-against -coronavirus-comes-to-the-bathroom.

67   The US Department: https://optn.transplant.hrsa.gov/news/organ-donation -again-sets-record-in-2019/.

67   In the United States: "2017 Profile of Older Americans," US Department of Health and Human Services, April 2018, "U.S.—Seniors as a Percentage of the Population 1950–2050," Statista, last modified January 20, 2021, https://www.statista.com/statistics/457822/share-of-old-age-population-in-the-total-us-population/.

68   In 2020, the US population: "Share of Old Age Population (65 Years and Older) in the Total U.S. Population from 1950 to 2050," Ibid.

68   In 1900, 30 percent: "Patterns of Childhood Death in America," in *When Children Die: Improving Palliative and End-of-Life Care for Children and Their Families*, edited by Marilyn J. Field and Richard E. Behrman (Washington, DC: National Academies Press, 2003), 41–72, https://www.ncbi.nlm.nih.gov/books/NBK220818/pdf/Bookshelf_NBK220818.pdf.

68   In fact, since 1990: "Children: Reducing Mortality," World Health Organization, September 19, 2019, https://www.who.int/news-room/fact-sheets/detail/children-reducing-mortality.

68   According to the National Council on Aging: "Get the Facts on Healthy Aging," National Council on Aging, January 1, 2021, https://www.ncoa.org/article/get-the-facts-on-healthy-aging.

68   "60 percent of [all] American adults": Doug Irving, "Chronic Conditions in America: Price and Prevalence," RAND, July 12, 2017, https://www.rand.org/blog/rand-review/2017/07/chronic-conditions-in-america-price-and-prevalence.html.

69   A 2018 report: Hugh Waters and Marlon Graf, "The Costs of Chronic Disease in the U.S.," Milken Institute, August 28, 2018, https://milkeninstitute.org/reports/costs-chronic-disease-us.

69   according to a 2015 study: Julianne Holt-Lunstad et al., "Loneliness and Social Isolation as Risk Factors for Mortality: A Meta-Analytic Review," *Perspectives on Psychological Science* 10, no. 2 (March 2015): 227–37, https://journals.sagepub.com/doi/10.1177/1745691614568352.

70   The other, known as: Kunlin Jin, "Modern Biological Theories of Aging," *Aging and Disease* 1, no. 2 (October 2010): 72–74, https://www.ncbi.nlm.nih.gov/pmc/articles/PMC2995895/.

74   "We want to increase": Interview with author.

| 5 | Perception Versus Reality

79   Davis not only helped: Eric Schurenberg and Lani Luciano, "The Empire Called AARP Under Its Nonprofit Halo, the American Association of Retired

Persons Is a Feared Lobbyist and an Even More Awesome Marketer," *Money*, October 1, 1988, https://money.cnn.com/magazines/moneymag/moneymag _archive/1988/10/01/84702/.

82   a personal fortune of $230 million: "Obituary: AARP Founder, Philan-thropist Leonard Davis, 76," USC News, January 24, 2001, https://news.usc .edu/6078/Obituary-AARP-founder-philanthropist-Leonard-Davis-76/.

81   In January 1960: Trevor Perry, "Sun City: A Revolution," https://saltriver stories.org/items/show/402.

83   Yet the dominant narrative: Kriston McIntosh et al., "Examining the Black-White Wealth Gap," Brookings, February 27, 2020, https://www.brookings.edu /blog/up-front/2020/02/27/examining-the-black-white-wealth-gap/.

83   The reality is: William E. Gibson, "Nearly Half of Americans 55+ Have No Retirement Savings" AARP, March 28, 2019, https://www.aarp.org/retirement /retirement-savings/info-2019/no-retirement-money-saved.html.

83   "Over 15 million": "Get the Facts on Economic Security for Seniors," NCOA, March 2, 2021, https://www.ncoa.org/article/get-the-facts-on-economic -security-for-seniors.

84   The 630 billionaires: Tommy Beer, "The Net Worth of America's 600-Plus Billionairs Has Increased By More Than $400 Billion During the Pan-demic," *Forbes*, May 21, 2020, Accessed August 23, 2021, https://www .forbes.com/sites/tommybeer/2020/05/21/the-net-worth-of-americas-600 -plus-billionaires-has-increased-by-more-than-400-billion-during-the-pandemic /?sh=356a2ef84a61.

85   Stanford University's Raj Chetty: "Geography, Income Play Roles in Life Expectancy, New Stanford Research Shows," Stanford News, April 11, 2016, https://news.stanford.edu/2016/04/11/geography-income-play-roles-in-life -expectancy-new-stanford-research-shows/.

86   Researchers at the Department of Population Health: "Large Life Ex-pectancy Gaps in U.S. Cities Linked to Racial & Ethnic Segregation by Neighborhood," NYU Langone Health, June 5, 2019, https://nyulangone.org /news/large-life-expectancy-gaps-us-cities-linked-racial-ethnic-segregation -neighborhood.

87   Gender plays a significant role: Louise Sundberg et al., "Why Is the Gender Gap in Life Expectancy Decreasing? The Impact of Age- and Cause-Specific Mortality in Sweden 1997–2014," *International Journal of Public Health* 63, no. 6 (2018): 673–81, doi: 10.1007/s00038-018-1097-3.

88 Nearly half of all older bisexual: "Older Women & Poverty," Justice in Aging, December 2018, https://www.justiceinaging.org/wp-content/uploads /2018/12/Older-Women-and-Poverty.pdf.

89 Black women earned 62 cents: Jasmine Tucker, "It's 2020, and Black Women Aren't Even Close to Equal Pay," National Women's Law Center, July 27, 2020, https://nwlc.org/resources/its-2020-and-black-women-arent-even -close-to-equal-pay/.

89 All of this translates: Amanda Fins, "Women and the Lifetime Wage Gap: How Many Woman Years Does It Take to Equal 40 Man Years?," National Women's Law Center, March 2020, https://nwlc-ciw49tixgw5lbab .stackpathdns.com/wp-content/uploads/2020/03/Women-and-the-Lifetime -Wage-Gap.pdf.

89 If the United States continues: "Age and Sex Composition in the United States: 2019," US Census Bureau, 2019, https://www.census.gov/data/tables /2019/demo/age-and-sex/2019-age-sex-composition.html.

89 the population of older women: "U.S.—Seniors as a Percentage of the Population 1950–2050," Statista, September 24, 2020, https://www.statista.com /statistics/457822/share-of-old-age-population-in-the-total-us-population/; https://justiceinaging.org/wp-content/uploads/2020/08/Older-Women-and-Poverty.pdf.

90 Only 29 percent: "U.S. Financial Health Pulse: 2019 Trends Report," Financial Health Network, November 2019, https://s3.amazonaws.com/cfsi -innovation-files-2018/wp-content/uploads/2019/11/13204428/US-Financial -Health-Pulse-2019.pdf.

90 A shockingly high 22 percent: "Planning & Progress Study 2019," Northwestern Mutual, 2019, https://news.northwesternmutual.com/planning-and -progress-2019.

90 According to the Transamerica Center: 19th Annual Transamerica Retirement Survey: A Compendium of Findings About U.S. Workers, Transamerica Center for Retirement Studies, December 2019, https://www.transamerica center.org/docs/default-source/retirement-survey-of-workers/tcrs2019_sr _19th-annual_worker_compendium.pdf.

90 According to the Social Security Administration: "Actuarial Life Table," Social Security Administration, 2019, https://www.ssa.gov/oact/STATS/table 4c6.html.

92 Though workers over the age of 85: Andrew Van Dam, "A Record Number

of Folks Age 85 and Older Are Working. Here's What They're Doing," *Washington Post*, July 5, 2018, https://www.washingtonpost.com/news/wonk /wp/2018/07/05/a-record-number-of-folks-age-85-and-older-are-working -heres-what-theyre-doing/.

93   the Kellogg School of Management at Northwestern University: Pierre Azoulay et al., "Age and High-Growth Entrepreneurship," *American Economic Review: Insights* 2, no. 1 (2020): 65–82, https://pubs.aeaweb.org/doi/pdfplus /10.1257/aeri.20180582.

93   This holds true: "Despite Lower Revenues and Slower Growth, Women-Owned Businesses Survive at Same Rate as Male Entrepreneurs, According to New JPMorgan Chase Institute Data," JPMorgan Chase & Co., February 7, 2019,   https://institute.jpmorganchase.com/institute/news-events/institute -women-owned-businesses-survive-at-same-rate-as-male-entrepreneurs.

93   According to a 2019 survey: Harry Campbell, "Lyft & Uber Driver Survey 2019: Uber Driver Satisfaction Takes a Big Hit," The Rideshare Guy, February 24, 2021, https://therideshareguy.com/uber-driver-survey/.

| 6 | The Drag of Ageism

96   For reference, the average age: Jennifer E. Manning, "Membership of the 116th Congress: A Profile," Congressional Research Service, December 17, 2020, https://fas.org/sgp/crs/misc/R45583.pdf.

96   People aged 18 to 34: Mobilewalla, "New Report Reveals Demographics of Black Lives Matter Protesters Shows Vast Majority Are White, Marched Within Their Own Cities," PR Newswire, June 18, 2020, https://www .prnewswire.com/news-releases/new-report-reveals-demographics-of-black -lives-matter-protesters-shows-vast-majority-are-white-marched-within-their -own-cities-301079234.html.

96   Protesters in the 35-to-54 age group: Ibid.

97   In fact, the United Nations: *Report of the World Assembly on Aging*, United Nations, Vienna, July 26–August 6, 1982, https://www.un.org/esa/socdev/ageing /documents/Resources/VIPEE-English.pdf.

97   A 2006 study: Ed Snape and Tom Redman, "Too Old or Too Young? The Impact of Perceived Age Discrimination," *Human Resource Management Journal* 13, no. 1 (2006): 78–89, https://doi.org/10.1111/j.1748-8583.2003. tb00085.x.

98 According to the 2020 study: Alison L. Chasteen, Michelle Horhota, and Jessica J. Crumley-Branyon, "Overlooked and Underestimated: Experiences of Ageism in Young, Middle-Aged, and Older Adults," *Journals of Gerontology, Series B*, April 3, 2020, https://doi.org/10.1093/geronb/gbaa043.

99 "volunteer to die": Bess Levin, "Texas Lt. Governor: Old People Should Volunteer to Die to Save the Economy," *Vanity Fair*, March 24, 2020, https://www.vanityfair.com/news/2020/03/dan-patrick-coronavirus-grandparents.

99 Unlike the Spanish flu: Justin Fox, "Coronavirus Deaths by Age: How It's like (and Not like) Other Disease," Bloomberg Opinion, May 7, 2020, https://www.bloomberg.com/opinion/articles/2020-05-07/comparing-coronavirus-deaths-by-age-with-flu-driving-fatalities.

100 The Kaiser Family Foundation found: Nancy Ochieng et al., "Factors Associated with COVID-19 Cases and Deaths in Long-Term Care Facilities: Findings from a Literature Review," Kaiser Family Foundation, January 14, 2021, https://www.kff.org/coronavirus-covid-19/issue-brief/factors-associated-with-covid-19-cases-and-deaths-in-long-term-care-facilities-findings-from-a-literature-review/.

100 According to a 2018 AARP report: Rebecca Perron, "The Value of Experience: Age Discrimination Against Older Workers Persists," https://www.aarp.org/content/dam/aarp/research/surveys_statistics/econ/2018/value-of-experience-age-discrimination-highlights.doi.10.26419-2Fres.00177.002.pdf.

101 "56 percent [of older workers] are laid off": Peter Gosselin, "If You're over 50, Chances Are the Decision to Leave a Job Won't Be Yours," ProPublica, December 28, 2018, https://www.propublica.org/article/older-workers-united-states-pushed-out-of-work-forced-retirement.

101 "Employees, just like": Quoted in Bradley Schurman and T. J. Londagin, "Viewpoint: The Public Sector Needs to Invest in Older Workers," SHRM, May 3, 2019, https://www.shrm.org/resourcesandtools/hr-topics/employee-relations/pages/public-sector-must-invest-in-older-workers.aspx.

102 According to the 2019 report: L. Smith et al., "Inequality in 1,200 Popular Films: Examining Portrayals of Gender, Race/Ethnicity, LGBTQ & Disability from 2007 to 2018," Annenberg Foundation and University of Southern California, September 2019, http://assets.uscannenberg.org/docs/aii-inequality-report-2019-09-03.pdf.

103 According to a 2007 study: Tara L. Gruenewald et al, "Feelings of

Usefulness to Others, Disability, and Mortality in Older Adults: The MacArthur Study of Successful Aging," *The Journals of Gerontology*, January 1, 2007, https://academic.oup.com/psychsocgerontology/article/62/1/P28/572495.

103 In a 2018 study: Becca R. Levy et al., "Ageism Amplifies Cost and Prevalence of Health Conditions," *Gerontologist* 60, no. 1 (January 24, 2020): 174–81, https://doi.org/10.1093/geront/gny131, https://academic.oup.com/gerontologist/article/60/1/174/5166947.

104 the World Health Organization asked her to lead: Michael Greenwood, "Harmful Effects of Ageism on Older Persons' Health Found in 45 Countries," *Yale News*, January 15, 2020, https://news.yale.edu/2020/01/15/harmful-effects-ageism-older-persons-health-found-45-countries.

105 finding ways to minimize: M. S. North and S. T. Fiske, "A Prescriptive Intergenerational-Tension Ageism Scale: Succession, Identity, and Consumption (SIC)," *Psychological Assessment* 25, no. 3 (2013): 706–13, https://doi.org/10.1037/a0032367.

105 A 2018 report: "PwC Golden Age Index: Unlocking a Potential $3.5 Trillion Prize from Longer Working Lives," PwC, June 2018, https://www.pwc.com/gx/en/news-room/docs/pwc-golden-age-index.pdf.

108 a 2018 survey by AARP: Kenneth Terrell, "Age Discrimination Common in Workplace, Survey Says," AARP, August 2, 2018, https://www.aarp.org/work/working-at-50-plus/info-2018/age-discrimination-common-at-work.html.

108 study of Stack Overflow members: Matt Shipman, "Older Is Wiser: Study Shows Software Developers' Skills Improve over Time," *NC State University News*, April 29, 2013, https://news.ncsu.edu/2013/04/wms-murphyhill-age-2013/.

108 the world's twenty-eighth largest employer: M. Szmigiera, "Largest Companies in the World Based on Number of Employees 2019," Statista, March 20, 2021, https://www.statista.com/statistics/264671/top-50-companies-based-on-number-of-employees/.

108 "make room for" younger ones: Peter Gosselin, "The U.S. Equal Employment Opportunity Commission Confirms a Pattern of Age Discrimination at IBM," *Propublica*, September 11, 2020, https://www.propublica.org/article/the-u-s-equal-employment-opportunity-commission-confirms-a-pattern-of-age-discrimination-at-ibm.

108 "As we've studied": EEOC Acting Chair Lipnic Releases Report on the State of Older Workers and Age Discrimination 50 Years After the ADEA,"

US Equal Employment Opportunity Commission, June 26, 2018, https://www.eeoc.gov/newsroom/eeoc-acting-chair-lipnic-releases-report-state-older-workers-and-age-discrimination-50.

110 "I'm not a crusader": Jennifer Delton, *Racial Integration in Corporate America, 1940–1990* (Cambridge, UK: Cambridge University Press, 2009), 47.

110 According to Boston Consulting Group: Rocío Lorenzo et al., "How Diverse Leadership Teams Boost Innovation," Boston Consulting Group, January 23, 2018, https://www.bcg.com/publications/2018/how-diverse-leadership-teams-boost-innovation.

113 "they are projected to spend": Wolfgang Fengler, "The silver economy is coming of age: A look at the growing spending power of seniors," January 14, 2021, Brookings, https://www.brookings.edu/blog/future-development/2021/01/14/the-silver-economy-is-coming-of-age-a-look-at-the-growing-spending-power-of-seniors/.

| 7 | Canaries in the Coal Mine

115 It is also playing out: Jon Emont, "The Growing Urban-Rural Divide Around the World," *Atlantic*, January 4, 2017, https://www.theatlantic.com/international/archive/2017/01/electoral-college-trump-argentina-malaysia-japan-clinton/512153/.

116 the Chinese government enacted a law: XinQi Dong, "Elder Rights in China," NCBI, August 12, 2020, https://www.ncbi.nlm.nih.gov/pmc/articles/PMC7422934/.

116 "do not have": "Family Farms," National Institute of Food and Agriculture, https://nifa.usda.gov/family-farms.

116 Rural communities must also grapple: "Rural America at a Glance: 2018 Edition," Economic Research Service, United States Department of Agriculture, November 2018, https://www.ers.usda.gov/webdocs/publications/90556/eib-200.pdf.

117 However, nearly nine in ten: Ibid.

118 Over a third of US rural counties: University of New Hampshire, "Shrinking population in more than a third of rural U.S. counties," *Science News*, February 6, 2019, https://www.sciencedaily.com/releases/2019/02/190206115611.htm.

118 A whopping two-thirds: Art Cullen, "Rural America Is Ready for Some Sort of a New Deal, Preferably Green," *Guardian*, March 15, 2019, https://

www.theguardian.com/commentisfree/2019/mar/15/rural-america-is-ready
-for-some-sort-of-a-new-deal-preferably-green.

120 "Valley of Dolls": Austa Somvichian-Clausen, "Life-Size Dolls Have
Taken over This Near-Deserted Town," *National Geographic*, October 10, 2017,
https://www.nationalgeographic.com/news/2017/10/japan-dolls-population
-artist-nagoro-spd/.

121 Overall, rural seniors: "Rural America at a Glance," US Department of
Agriculture, November 2018, https://www.ers.usda.gov/webdocs/publications
/90556/eib-200.pdf; "Rural Health," CDC, July 1, 2019, https://www.cdc
.gov/chronicdisease/resources/publications/factsheets/rural-health.htm; "Gender Differences in Social Isolation and Social Support among Rural Residents,"
University of Minnesota Rural Health Research Center, August 2018, https://
rhrc.umn.edu/wp-content/files_mf/1532458325UMNpolicybriefsocial
isolationgenderdifferences.pdf.

121 Birth rates are falling: "Trends in Fertility and Mother's Age at First Birth
Among Rural and Metropolitan Counties: United States, 2007–2017," CDC,
October 2018, https://www.cdc.gov/nchs/products/databriefs/db323.htm.

121 The loss would have been much larger: Kim Parker et al., "What Unites
and Divides Urban, Suburban and Rural Communities," Pew Research Center,
May 22, 2018. https://www.pewsocialtrends.org/2018/05/22/demographic-and
-economic-trends-in-urban-suburban-and-rural-communities/.

122 Immigrants account for approximately: Andrew Schaefer and Marybeth J.
Mattingly, "Demographic and Economic Characteristics of Immigrant and
Native-Born Populations in Rural and Urban Places," Carsey Research National Issue Brief no. 106, University of New Hampshire, Fall 2016, https://
scholars.unh.edu/cgi/viewcontent.cgi?article=1283&context=carsey.

123 These so-called deaths of despair: Anne Case and Angus Deaton, *Deaths
of Despair and the Future of Capitalism* (Princeton, NJ: Princeton University
Press, 2020), 40.

123 "have been directly impacted": "Rural Opioid Epidemic," American Farm
Bureau Federation, https://www.fb.org/issues/other/rural-opioid-epidemic/.

123 Rural areas led urban areas: "Urban–rural Differences in Drug Overdose
Death Rates, by Sex, Age, and Type of Drugs Involved, 2017," CDC, August
2019, https://www.cdc.gov/nchs/products/databriefs/db345.htm.

123 Mortality data: Asha Z. Ivey-Stephenson et al, "Suicide Trends Among
and Within Urbanization Levels by Sex, Race/Ethnicity, Age Group, and

Mechanism of Death — United States, 2001–2015," *MMWR* Surveillance Summary 2017; 66(No. SS-18):1–16, http://dx.doi.org/10.15585/mmwr.ss6618a1, https://www.cdc.gov/mmwr/volumes/66/ss/ss6618a1.htm.

124 In 2018, suicide rates: "Suicide Statistics," American Foundation for Suicide Prevention, March 1, 2020, https://afsp.org/suicide-statistics/.

124 The suicide rate rose: Danielle L. Steelesmith et al., "Contextual Factors Associated with County-Level Suicide Rates in the United States, 1999 to 2016," *JAMA Network Open* 2, no. 9 (2019): e1910936, doi:10.1001/jamanetworkopen.2019.10936.

125 Over the past decade: "The Rural Health Safety Net Under Pressure: Rural Hospital Vulnerability," The Chartis Group, February 2020, https://www.ivantageindex.com/wp-content/uploads/2020/02/CCRH_Vulnerability-Research_FiNAL-02.14.20.pdf.

125 prompting the American Hospital Association: "The Rural Health Safety Net Under Pressure: Understanding the Potential Impact of COVID-19," The Chartis Group, April 2020, https://www.chartis.com/resources/files/CCRH_Research_Update-Covid-19.pdf.

125 453 rural hospitals: Ibid.

128 The rural health care workforce: Lucy Skinner et al., "Implications of an Aging Rural Physician Workforce," *New England Journal of Medicine* 381 (July 25, 2019): 299–301, doi: 10.1056/NEJMp1900808.

129 In the summer of 2020: "2020 Survey of America's Physicians: COVID-19 Impact Edition," The Physicians Foundation, August 2020, http://physiciansfoundation.org/wp-content/uploads/2020/08/20-1278-Merritt-Hawkins-2020-Physicians-Foundation-Survey.6.pdf.

129 Since the start of the Great Recession: Olugbenga Ajilore, "Economic Recovery and Business Dynamism in Rural America," Center for American Progress, February 20, 2020, https://cdn.americanprogress.org/content/uploads/2020/02/20114441/DynamismRural-brief.pdf.

130 One of the most devasted areas: Board of Governors of the Federal Reserve System, "Perspectives from Main Street: Bank Branch Access in Rural Communities," Federal Reserve, November 2019, https://www.federalreserve.gov/publications/files/bank-branch-access-in-rural-communities.pdf.

131 The plan implements funding: "Biden-Harris Administration Extends Moratorium on Residential Evictions in USDA Multifamily Housing Communities

in Accordance with CDC Guidance," United States Department of Agriculture, March 29, 2021, https://www.usda.gov/media/press-releases/2021/03/29/biden -harris-administration-extends-moratorium-residential.

132 Japan Post's Watch Over Service: Japan Post Group, Annual Report, Year Ended March 31, 2018, https://www.japanpost.jp/en/ir/library/disclosure /2018/pdf/all.pdf, 26.

132 Veiller Sur Mes Parents: Jane Hanks, "Postal Workers Will Watch over Your Elderly Parents," Connexion, May 15, 2017, https://www.connexionfrance .com/French-news/Postal-workers-will-watch-over-your-elderly-parents.

132 Other postal services: Ibid.

132 There is even a growing demand: Christopher W. Shaw, "Postal Banking Is Making a Comeback. Here's How to Ensure It Becomes a Reality," *Washington Post*, July 21, 2020, https://www.washingtonpost.com/outlook/2020/07/21 /postal-banking-is-making-comeback-heres-how-ensure-it-becomes-reality/.

132 England's Newcastle Building Society: Kevin Peachey, "A New Rural Bank Branch Opening! What's Going On?," BBC News, February 9, 2020, https://www.bbc.com/news/business-51372724.

132 One of the pioneering sites: "What does KOTOEN mean?," © 2016, Kotoen, http://www.kotoen.or.jp/about/english.

133 The German government is focused: Laura Richter and Tobias Silberzahn, "Germany's e-Health Infrastructure Strengthens, but Digital Uptake Is Lagging," McKinsey & Company, December 11, 2020, https://www.mckinsey .com/industries/pharmaceuticals-and-medical-products/our-insights /germanys-e-health-infrastructure-strengthens-but-digital-uptake-is-lagging.

133 The Department of Veterans Affairs' Office of Connected Care: "Improving Health Care Through Technology," US Department of Veterans Affairs, https://connectedcare.va.gov/terms/connected-health/single/About.

133 The Yoshino Cedar House: "Space for Sharing," Yoshino Cedar House, https://www.yoshinocedarhouse.com/.

133 In 2015, the company entered: Masatsugu Horie, "Uber embarks on unconventional strategy in Japanese countryside," *JapanTimes*, October 24, 2016, https://www.japantimes.co.jp/news/2016/10/24/business /uber-embarks-unconventional-strategy-japanese-countryside/.

133 Not long ago, Cammarata's government: Cailey Rizzo, "This Italian Town Will Give You a Free House and Pay You to Raise a Child There,": *Travel & Leisure*, November 4, 2019, https://www.travelandleisure.com/travel-news

/cammarata-sicily-italy-paying-families-to-move-there; Julia Buckley, "The Millennials Using Covid to Change Sicily's €1 Home Schemes," CNN Travel, May 25, 2021, https://www.cnn.com/travel/article/cammarata-sicily-1-euro -homes-streetto/index.html.

134 Tulsa, Oklahoma, which has been: "Hi, Remote Workers! We'll Pay You to Work from Tulsa. You're Going to Love It Here," Tulsa Remote, © 2021, https://tulsaremote.com/.

135 Even though rural businesses: "2016 Small Business Credit Survey: Report on Rural Employer Firms," Federal Reserve Bank of Richmond and Federal Reserve Bank of Atlanta, December 2017, https://www.richmondfed .org/-/media/richmondfedorg/community_development/resource_centers /small_business/pdf/credit_survey/sbcs_report_rural_employer_firms_2016.pdf.

135 Japan, which is facing: "Five-Year Plan for Business Succession Formu- lated," Ministry of Economy, Trade, and Industry, Japan, July 7, 2017, https:// www.meti.go.jp/english/press/2017/0707_001.html.

| 8 | A Novel Reality Emerges

139 The United Nations estimates: "Survival to Age 65, Male (% of Cohort)," The World Bank, November 2019, https://data.worldbank.org/indicator/SP .DYN.TO65.MA.ZS.

142 In 2020, researchers at: Kaisa Koivunen et al., "Cohort Differences in Maximal Physical Performance: A Comparison of 75- and 80-Year-Old Men and Women Born 28 Years Apart," *Journals of Gerontology, Series A*, Septem- ber 4, 2020, glaa224, https://doi.org/10.1093/gerona/glaa224.

144 now a majority of young adults: Richard Fry, Jeffrey S. Passel, and D'Vera Cohn, "A Majority of Young Adults in the U.S. Live with Their Parents for the First Time Since the Great Depression," Pew Research Center, September 4, 2020, https://www.pewresearch.org/fact-tank/2020/09/04/a-majority-of- young-adults-in-the-u-s-live-with-their-parents-for-the-first-time-since-the- great-depression/.

145 Young people are delaying: Quoctrung Bui and Claire Cain Miller, "The Age That Women Have Babies: How a Gap Divides America," *New York Times*, August 4, 2018, https://www.nytimes.com/interactive/2018/08/04/upshot/up -birth-age-gap.html.

146 The median age of home buyers: Reade Pickert, "Young Homebuyers Are Vanishing from the U.S.," Bloomberg, November 8, 2019, https://www

.bloomberg.com/news/articles/2019-11-08/young-homebuyers-vanish-from
-u-s-as-median-purchasing-age-jumps.

146 The median age of repeat buyers: Jessica Lautz, "Age of Buyers Is Sky-rocketing . . . But Not for Who You Might Think," National Association of Realtors, January 13, 2020, https://www.nar.realtor/blogs/economists-outlook
/age-of-buyers-is-skyrocketing-but-not-for-who-you-might-think.

146 Their median income is $54,340: "Zillow: Average First-Time Home-buyer 33 Years of Age," National Mortgage Professional, August 20, 2015, https://nationalmortgageprofessional.com/news/55433/zillow-average-first
-time-homebuyer-33-years-age.

147 A December 2020 article: Vera van den Berg et al., "Euthanasia and Physician-Assisted Suicide in Patients with Multiple Geriatric Syndromes," *JAMA Internal Medicine* 181, no. 2 (2021): 245–50, doi: 10.1001/jamaintern
med.2020.6895.

148 Recompose, the first company: "Precompose," Recompose, https://recompose.life/precompose/.

148 the median cost of a funeral: "Statistics," The National Funeral Directors Association, July 18, 2019, https://nfda.org/news/statistics.

148 In 2019, the hospitality entrepreneur: Natasha Levy, "Exit Here funeral parlour is designed to have 'the eclectic feel of home'," *De-zeen*, October 30, 2019, https://www.dezeen.com/2019/10/30/exit-here
-funeral-parlour-death/.

148 Caitlin Doughty, a mortician: "Welcome to the Order. Welcome to Your Mortality," Order of the Good Death, © 2021, http://www.orderofthegood
death.com/about.

149 Nearly 80 percent: Mikey Campbell, "Apple Watch, Other Wearables Increasingly Used to Manage Chronic Health Conditions, Study Says," Apple Insider, August 18, 2018, https://appleinsider.com/articles/18/08/30/apple
-watch-other-wearables-increasingly-used-to-manage-chronic-health-conditions
-study-says.

149 although roughly half: Bernard Desarnauts, "One Year In and Only Now Are We Getting to Know Apple Watch Owners," Medium, April 19, 2016, https://medium.com/wristly-thoughts/one-year-in-and-only-now-are-we
-getting-to-know-apple-watch-owners-db60d565d041.

149 the number of US smartphone users: Alicia Phaneuf, "The Number of Health and Fitness App Users Increased 27% from Last Year," eMarketer,

July 20, 2020, https://www.emarketer.com/content/number-of-health-fitness
-app-users-increased-27-last-year.

150 Peloton, an exercise equipment: Martin Belam and Joanna Partridge, "Peloton loses $1.5bn in value over 'dystopian, sexist' exercise bike ad," *The Guardian*, December 4, 2019, https://www.theguardian.com/media/2019/dec/04/peloton-backlash-sexist-dystopian-exercise-bike-christmas-advert; Lauren Thomas, "Peloton thinks it can grow to 100 million subscribers. Here's how," *CNBC*, September 15, 2020. https://www.cnbc.com/2020/09/15/peloton-thinks-it-can-grow-to-100-million-subscribers-heres-how.html.

150 On average, according to: Uptin Saiidi, "Pedaling to dominate the stationary bike industry," *CNBC*, January 11, 2016, https://www.cnbc.com/2016/01/08/pelotons-race-for-home-cycling.html.

150 This is borne out: Rachel Valerio, "Fitness Industry Roundup: Millennials Are Good for Business," IHRSA, October 4, 2019, https://www.ihrsa.org/improve-your-club/industry-news/fitness-industry-roundup-millennials-are-good-for-business/.

152 ever since the thirteenth century: "Eyeglasses Timeline," Luxottica, © 2020, https://www.luxottica.com/en/about-us/museo-dellottica/eyeglasses-timeline.

153 Morning Consult, which releases: "The Fastest Growing Brands of 2020," Morning Consult, © 2021, https://morningconsult.com/fastest-growing-brands-2020/.

156 Recent research by J. Walter Thompson: "Elastic Generation: The Female Edit," Wunderman Thompson, January 2018, https://intelligence.wunderman thompson.com/trend-reports/elastic-generation-female-edit/.

156 "A 55-year-old woman": Marie Stafford, "Elastic Generation: The Female Edit," The Innovation Group, December 2017, https://marcommnews.com/wp-content/uploads/2018/01/234000_Elastic-Generation-The-Female-Edit.-FINAL.pdf.

| 9 | Make Age Work

161 In the next decade alone: "Civilian Labor Force Participation Rate by Age, Sex, Race, and Ethnicity," US Bureau of Labor Statistics, September 1, 2020, https://www.bls.gov/emp/tables/civilian-labor-force-participation-rate.htm.

164 A Gartner report predicted: Manasi Sakpal, "Diversity and Inclusion Build High-Performance Teams," Smarter with Gartner, September 20, 2019,

https://www.gartner.com/smarterwithgartner/diversity-and-inclusion-build-high-performance-teams/.

165 "reflecting perhaps": "Accelerating Business with an Age-Diverse Workforce," Randstad, February 26, 2020, https://www.randstad.com/workforce-insights/future-of-work/accelerating-business-with-an-age-diverse-workforce/.

165 Although a generationally diverse workforce: "Age Diversity: How to Engage Different Age Groups in Your Workplace," CV Library, June 7, 2019, https://www.cv-library.co.uk/recruitment-insight/engage-different-age-groups-your-workplace/.

165 fewer than one in ten: "Accelerating Business with an Age-Diverse Workforce," Randstad.

165 The average age of CEOs: Oliver Staley, "How the Average Age of CEOs and CFOs Has Changed Since 2012," Quartz, September 11, 2017, https://qz.com/1074326/how-the-average-age-of-ceos-and-cfos-has-changed-since-2012/.

165 the average age of first-time hires: "Volatility Report 2020," Crist|Kolder Associates, https://www.cristkolder.com/media/2697/volatility-report-2020-americas-leading-companies.pdf.

165 Harvard Business Review reported: Jane Johnson, "70 Is the New 50: Aging CEOs Provide Both Opportunities and Challenges for Businesses," Business Transition Academy, June 12, 2019, https://www.businesstransition academy.com/strategic-business-planning-blog/70-is-the-new-50-aging-ceos-provide-both-opportunities-and-challenges-for-businesses; "Crist/Kolder Associates: Volatility Report 2018," Crist|Kolder Associates, https://www.crist kolder.com//media/2135/volatility-report-2018-americas-leading-companies..pdf; "Spotlight Series – The CEO 100, 2019 Edition," Harvard Business Review, November 2019, https://hbr.org/2019/11/the-best-performing-ceos-in-the-world-2019.

165 The average age of a CEO: "Providing More Insight into the Small Business Owner," Business Information Solutions, Experian, September 2007, https://www.experian.com/whitepapers/BOLStudy_Experian.pdf.

166 An analysis of twenty studies: David P. Costanza et al., "Generational Differences in Work-Related Attitudes: A Meta-analysis," Journal of Business and Psychology 27 (2012): 375–94, https://doi.org/10.1007/s10869-012-9259-4.

168 In 2018, it reported: "Alibaba Targets China's Aging Population With 'Taobao for Elders'," Alizila, February 1, 2018, https://www.alizila.com/alibaba-targets-chinas-aging-population-with-taobao-for-elders/.

168 To increase its relevance: Liu Caiyu, "Taobao Job Ad Seeking Two Square Dancing Senior Citizens Goes Viral," *Global Times*, January 18, 2018, https://www.globaltimes.cn/content/1085533.shtml.

168 Taobao also enlisted the help: Tara Francis Chan, "Alibaba Said It Would Hire Staff Older Than 60 and Received 1,000 Applications in 24 Hours," *Insider*, January 22, 2018, https://www.businessinsider.com/taobao-hiring -senior-staff-like-the-intern-movie-2018-1.

169 The British do-it-yourself: "B&Q and Ageing Workers," *Occupational Medicine*, © 2021, https://www.som.org.uk/bq-and-ageing-workers.

169 In 2016, the company launched: Shunichi Miyanaga, "The Business Case for Older Workers," AARP International, January 1, 2017, https://www.aarp international.org/the-journal/current-edition/journal-articles-blog/2017/01 /the-business-case-for-older-workers.

169 The German automaker Porsche: Patrick McGee, "Germany Invests to Prolong Employees' Working Lives," *Financial Times*, January 17, 2019, https://www.ft.com/content/f1b294b8-9cbe-11e8-88de-49c908b1f264.

172 This happened at the Australian bank: Miklos Bolza, "How Two Aussie Firms Are Winning over Older Workers," Human Resource Director, August 8, 2016, https://www.hcamag.com/au/specialisation/diversity -inclusion/how-two-aussie-firms-are-winning-over-older-workers/146545.

172 CVS Caremark: CVS Caremark Snowbird Program, The Center on Aging and Work, © 2012, http://capricorn.bc.edu/agingandwork/database /browse/case_study/24047.

172 UPS: "Hiring Older Workers Is Suddenly In Season," Next Avenue, November 17, 2017, https://www.forbes.com/sites/nextavenue/2017/11/17 /hiring-older-workers-is-suddenly-in-season/?sh=81e1022e8808.

172 And Michelin: Paul Davidson, "Older Workers Get Flexible Hours, Work-At-Home Options to Keep Them from Retirement," *USA Today*, May 22, 2018, https://www.usatoday.com/story/money/2018/05/21/retirement-delayed-firms -keep-older-workers-hire-retirees/613722002/.

173 Older workers tend: "Employer Tenure Summary," US Bureau of Labor Statistics, September 22, 2020, https://www.bls.gov/news.release/tenure.nr0.htm.

173 "Employees, just like": Quoted in Bradley Schurman and T. J. Londagin, "Viewpoint: The Public Sector Needs to Invest in Older Workers," SHRM, May 3, 2019, https://www.shrm.org/resourcesandtools/hr-topics/employee -relations/pages/public-sector-must-invest-in-older-workers.aspx.

173 According to Bureau of Labor Statistics data: Ibid.

174 Barclays, the British multinational: "'I'm Proof That Age Is Not a Barrier for Apprenticeships,'" Barclays, May 30, 2019, https://home.barclays /news/2019/05/-i-m-proof-that-age-is-not-a-barrier-for-apprenticeships-/.

174 Data from the Department of Labor's: "FY 2019 Data and Statistics," US Department of Labor, https://www.dol.gov/agencies/eta/apprenticeship /about/statistics/2019.

175 the average household income: "New BMW Owner Demographics: Income, Age, Gender and More," Hedges & Company, March 2019, https:// hedgescompany.com/blog/2019/03/new-bmw-owner-demographics/#bmw _owner_demographics_average_age_of_a_bmw_owner.

| 10 | Make Home and Community Gray Again

177 For example, the National Investment Center: Chuck Sudo, "Senior Housing Occupancy Falls to Another Record Low in Q3," Senior Housing News, October 15, 2020, https://seniorhousingnews.com/2020/10/15/senior -housing-occupancy-falls-to-another-record-low-in-q3/.

178 "While the population is aging": Kim Parker et al., "Demographic and Economic Trends in Urban, Suburban and Rural Communities," Pew Research Center, May 22, 2018, https://www.pewresearch.org/social-trends /2018/05/22/demographic-and-economic-trends-in-urban-suburban-and -rural-communities/.

178 The number of people: Jennifer Molinsky, "The Future of Renting Among Older Adults," Joint Center for Housing Studies of Harvard University, February 3, 2016, https://www.jchs.harvard.edu/blog/the-future-of-renting-among -older-adults.

179 nearly a million people: Stephanie Horan, "Where Retirees Are Moving—2020 Edition," SmartAsset, March 10, 2020, https://smartasset .com/financial-advisor/where-retirees-are-moving-2020.

179 In the last decade: "Empty Nest? Leave the Boring 'Burbs Behind and Move Back to the City for a Better Social Life," High50, March 2, 2015, https://high50.com/homes/why-empty-nesters-are-moving-back-to-the-city.

180 Young people aged 18 to 29: Richard Fry, Jeffrey S. Passel, and D'Vera Cohn, "A Majority of Young Adults in the U.S. Live with Their Parents for the First Time Since the Great Depression," Pew Research Center, September 4, 2020, https://www.pewresearch.org/fact-tank/2020/09/04/a-majority-of-young

-adults-in-the-u-s-live-with-their-parents-for-the-first-time-since-the
-great-depression/.

182 "Nearly 90 percent of people": Nicholas Farber et al., "Aging in Place: A State Survey of Livability Policies and Practices," National Conference of State Legislatures and AARP Public Policy Institute, December 2011, https://assets .aarp.org/rgcenter/ppi/liv-com/ib190.pdf.

182 At least 3 million Americans: "Important Facts About Falls," Centers for Disease Control and Prevention, February 10, 2017, https://www.cdc.gov/home andrecreationalsafety/falls/adultfalls.html.

182 In Germany, only 5 percent: "The Aging Readiness & Competitiveness Report," AARP International, https://arc.aarpinternational.org/File%20Library /Full%20Reports/ARC-Report---Germany.pdf.

182 Just over a decade ago: "Housing our Ageing Population: Panel for Innovation (HAPPI)," 2009, https://www.housinglin.org.uk/_assets/Resources/Housing/Support _materials/Other_reports_and_guidance/Happi_Final_Report.pdf.

183 Nearly nine out of ten: Erin Carlyle, "Baby Boomers and Gen Xers Drove Remodeling and Spending in 2019," Houzz, June 30, 2020, https://www .houzz.com/magazine/baby-boomers-and-gen-xers-drove-remodeling-and -spending-in-2019-stsetivw-vs~137253690.

184 In the past ten years: Irina Lupa, "The Decade in Housing Trends: High-Earning Renters, High-End Apartments and Thriving Construction," RENT-Café, December 16, 2019, https://www.rentcafe.com/blog/rental-market /market-snapshots/renting-america-housing-changed-past-decade/.

184 Module, a modular housing company: "Home Page" Module Housing, https://www.modulehousing.com/.

185 In Israel, an initiative: "The Aging Readiness & Competitiveness Report," AARP International, https://arc.aarpinternational.org/countries/israel

186 The World Health Organization's: "About the Global Network for Age-friendly Cities and Communities," World Health Organization, https://ex-tranet.who.int/agefriendlyworld/who-network/.

186 One of the earliest: "Case Study: The Age-friendly Programme in Akita City," World Health Organization, https://extranet.who.int/agefriendlyworld /resources/age-friendly-case-studies/akita-city/.

187 New York City: "Better Benches and Bus Stop Shelters," AARP, Au-gust 2015, https://www.aarp.org/livable-communities/network-age-friendly -communities/info-2015/domain-2-new-york-city-bus-bench-program.html.

187 Nottingham, England: https://www.architecture.com/-/media/gather content/age-friendly-handbook/additional-documents/alternativeagefriendly handbook2014pdf.pdf.

187 And the German city of Griesheim: Sophie Handler, *An Alternative Age-Friendly Handbook* (Manchester, UK: The University of Manchester Library: 2014), https://www.architecture.com/-/media/gathercontent/age-friendly -handbook/additional-documents/alternativeagefriendlyhandbook2014 pdf.pdf.

191 A recent national study: "The Pandemic Effect: A Social Isolation Report," AARP Foundation and United Health Foundation, October 6, 2020, https://connect2affect.org/the-pandemic-effect/.

192 In 2018, the UK government: Jason Daley, "The U.K. Now Has a 'Minister for Loneliness.' Here's Why It Matters," *Smithsonian Magazine*, January 18, 2019, https://www.smithsonianmag.com/smart-news/minister-loneliness -appointed-united-kingdom-180967883/

192 Participants in the Program: "Caring for Older Adults with Complex Needs in the COVID-19 Pandemic: Lessons from PACE Innovations," Better Care Playbook, June 2020, https://www.bettercareplaybook.org/resources/caring-older-adults-complex-needs-covid-19-pandemic-lessons-pace-innovations.

193 A relative newcomer: "onHand founder wins Entrepreneur for Good Award," onHand, December 15, 2020, https://www.beon hand.co.uk/onhand-blog /onhand-founder-wins-entrepreneur-for-good-award.

| 11 | Eldernomics

197 Online shopping is growing: Tugba Sabanoglu, "U.S. Fashion and Accessories E-retail Revenue 2017–2024," Statista, November 30, 2020, https://www.statista.com/statistics/278890/us-apparel-and-accessories-retail-e -commerce-revenue/.

197 Nearly half of all online shoppers: "NPR/Marist Poll of 1,057 National Adults," May 18, 2020, http://maristpoll.marist.edu/wp-content/misc/usa polls/us180423_NPR/NPR_Marist%20Poll_Tables%20of%20Questions _May%202018.pdf, 2.

198 One of these is Silberdraht: "Founders Stories #5: Access All Areas (Silberdraht)," Vodafone Uplift, December 17, 2020, https://vodafoneuplift.de /founders-stories-5-access-all-areas-silberdraht/.

198 By 2016, that number: Robert Fairlie, Desai Sameeksha, and A. J.

Herrmann, "2018 National Report on Early-Stage Entrepreneurship," Kauffman Indicators of Entrepreneurship, Ewing Marion Kauffman Foundation: Kansas City, 2019, https://indicators.kauffman.org/wp-content/uploads/sites/2/2019/09/National_Report_Sept_2019.pdf.

198 People over 65: "Self-employment in the United States," US Bureau of Labor Statistics, March 2016, https://www.bls.gov/spotlight/2016/self-employment-in-the-united-states/home.htm.

198 Today, the average age: Pierre Azoulay et al., "Research: The Average Age of a Successful Startup Founder Is 45," *Harvard Business Review*, July 11, 2018, https://hbr.org/2018/07/research-the-average-age-of-a-successful-startup-founder-is-45.

199 By the time the first: "The Global Talent Crunch," Korn Ferry, https://infokf.kornferry.com/global_talent_crunch_web.html?_ga=2.95076255.2053081181.1610813922-1378629803.1610813922.

199 Its own research projects: OECD (2020), *Promoting an Age-Inclusive Workforce: Living, Learning and Earning Longer*, OECD Publishing, Paris, https://doi.org/10.1787/59752153-en.

203 Between 2000 and 2018: David Baxter, "Re-thinking Older Workforce Potential in an Aging World," Population Division, Department of Economic and Social Affairs, United Nations Secretariat, November 2018, https://www.un.org/development/desa/pd/sites/www.un.org.development.desa.pd/files/unpd_egm_201811_egm_david_baxter.pdf.

203 In Luxembourg and Spain: "Labour Force Participation Rate," OECD Employment Outlook, https://data.oecd.org/emp/labour-force-participation-rate.htm.

204 Cooperatives employ: "About the USFWC," United States Federation of Worker Cooperatives (USFWC), December 7, 2020, https://www.usworker.coop/about/.

205 Research by Virginie Pérotin: "What Do We Really Know About Worker Co-operatives?," Co-Operatives UK, pg. 20, http://efesonline.org/LIBRARY/2016/worker_co-op_report.pdf.

206 Research by the Center: Hye Jin Rho, "Hard Work? Patterns in Physically Demanding Labor Among Older Workers," Center for Economic and Policy Research, August 2010, https://www.cepr.net/documents/publications/older-workers-2010-08.pdf.

207 In 2016, AARP attempted: "World Population Ageing 2019: Highlights,"

United Nations, Department of Economic and Social Affairs, Population Division, 2019, pg. 1, https://www.un.org/en/development/desa/population /publications/pdf/ageing/WorldPopulationAgeing2019-Highlights.pdf.

207 An update of the study: "The Longevity Economy® Outlook," AARP, https://www.aarp.org/content/dam/aarp/research/surveys_statistics/econ /2019/longevity-economy-outlook.doi.10.26419-2Fint.00042.001.pdf.

208 Euromonitor International: Matthew Boyle, "Aging Boomers Befuddle Marketers Aching for $15 Trillion Prize," *Bloomberg News*, September 17, 2013, http://www.agewave.com/media_files/09%2017%2013%20Bloomberg%20 Business_AgingBoomersBefuddle%20Marketers.pdf.

209 The most progressive: Emma Charlton, "New Zealand Has Unveiled Its First 'Well-Being' Budget," World Economic Forum, May 30, 2019, https:// www.weforum.org/agenda/2019/05/new-zealand-is-publishing-its-first-well -being-budget/.

209 Near the end of my tenure: "Inaugural Report: The Aging Readiness & Competitiveness Report (ARC)," AARP and FP Analytics, AARP International, 2017, https://aarpinternational.cloud.prod.iapps.com/arc/home/the-aging -readiness-competitiveness-report.

Index

About the Author

Bradley Schurman is a demographic futurist and opinion maker on all things dealing with the business of longevity. You might know him as the founder of The Super Age - a global collective of change--makers that offers information and professional business consulting services geared to help organizations respond to demographic change, as well as harness the opportunities of an increasingly older and generationally diverse population, or for the groundbreaking AARP Aging Readiness and Competitiveness Report. Bradley is a social connector who has built his reputation by helping leading organizations understand our increasingly older and generational diverse world. He explains how shifting demographics and the collision of the megatrends of decreased birthrates and increased longevity are remaking social and economic norms in the United States and around the world.

Prior to launching The Super Age, Schurman was a cofounder and managing partner of EconomyFour, where he led business development in Asia and Europe. He also served AARP (formerly the American Association of Retired Persons)—the world's largest organization dedicated to improving the lives of older people—where he was the director of global partnerships and engagements. Schurman got his start at LeadingAge (formerly the American Association of Homes and Services for the Aging)—the nonprofit trade association representing nonprofit providers of long-term care, housing, and support services.

Schurman was instrumental in securing the topics of aging and longevity as focus areas at both the Organisation for Economic Co-operation and Development (OECD) and the World Economic Forum (WEF). He was also responsible for visioning and executing "The Aging Readiness and Competitiveness Report"—a groundbreaking collaborative research project between AARP and Foreign Policy Group.

Schurman has been featured on NBC's *Today* show and Cheddar, and has been quoted in the *New York Times*, *HuffingtonPost*, and *USA Today*, as well as in local and national media outlets around the world. He speaks regularly at thought leader forums, and corporate retreats, and has advised national leaders and corporate executives on their longevity strategies.